PRIMER ON
WAGE & HOUR LAWS

PRIMER ON WAGE & HOUR LAWS

Joseph E. Kalet

The Bureau of National Affairs, Inc., Washington, D.C.

Library of Congress Cataloging-in-Publication Data

Kalet, Joseph E., 1951–
    Primer on wage and hour laws/Joseph E. Kalet.
        p.   cm.

    Includes index.
    ISBN 0-87179-564-7
    1. Wages—Law and legislation—United States. 2. Hours of labor—
Law and legislation—United States.   I. Title.
KF3489.K35   1987
344.73′0121—dc19   87-18812
[347.304121]

Printed in the United States of America
International Standard Book Number: 0-87179-564-7

PREFACE

Legal developments in the field of wages and hours have accelerated in the past few years, making this area of the law turbulent where it once was quiescent. The change was abrupt rather than gradual: early in 1985, the U.S. Supreme Court in *Garcia v. San Antonio Metropolitan Transit Authority* decided that there was no constitutional bar to applying the Fair Labor Standards Act (FLSA) to state and local governments. This decision had the explosive impact of another Supreme Court decision from 1946, *Anderson v. Mt. Clemens Pottery Co.*, wherein the Court held that employers must compensate their employees for time spent in pre- and postshift activities, if these activities are a "necessary prerequisite" to their principal work activity. The intricate network of federal laws and regulations governing wages and hours of work has grown increasingly complex in recent years. This book represents a broad canvas on which the outlines of each of the major statutes have been drawn, with a general idea of the individual profiles of each law and how each law interacts with other laws within the network.

Other wage-hour laws existed prior to the FLSA, but Congress intended the FLSA to be the most comprehensive and pervasive federal statute in this area. The Act has been amended several times, most recently in December 1985, in the aftermath of *Garcia v. San Antonio Metropolitan Transit Authority*. In January 1987, the U.S. Department of Labor's Employment Standards Administration issued comprehensive regulations on the application of the FLSA to state and local government employees, with particular emphasis on police and firefighter personnel. The dust kicked up by these legislative, judicial, and regulatory actions may not settle for years.

v

Regulations interpreting and applying the wage-hour laws are the responsibility of the U.S. Department of Labor. The Wage-Hour Division and the Equal Employment Opportunity Commission (EEOC) are the two main enforcement agencies within the Labor Department's wage-hour mandate. The Division has historically had responsibility for ensuring compliance with these statutes. The EEOC was delegated authority to enforce the Equal Pay Act under the 1977 Reorganization Act. Together, these agencies constitute a comprehensive adjudicatory process that will enable the wage and hour laws to develop along consistent and predictable lines.

Employees are granted the right to bring a private lawsuit under several, but not all, wage-hour laws. Congress has determined that, in many instances, allowing employees to operate as "private attorneys-general" would enhance the policies underlying a particular statute, and to that end have granted employees the right to sue. Generally, where an act grants such a right, it also subordinates that right to the federal government's right to sue, on the theory of the greater good. That is, a lawsuit by the Secretary of Labor will create a greater benefit to the public as a whole than will an action by a private individual. Different remedies are available to the party instituting the action, depending on whether it is a private individual or a government official.

The Fair Labor Standards Act, the Walsh-Healey Act, the Davis-Bacon Act, and the McNamara-O'Hara Service Contract Act comprise the bulk of the wage-hour statutes discussed in this *Primer*. They are the primary statutes which govern wages and hours in the United States today. These laws were created during specific historic periods, with specific goals. They have withstood the test of time and continue to play a very important part in the federal statutory appartus, despite amendments and putative changes. Conflicts in the area of wages and hours appear to be proliferating beyond traditional battlegrounds and into new arenas of combat. For this reason, these laws must be clearly understood to ensure faithful compliance and fair enforcement.

Throughout the *Primer*, abbreviations have been used to designate various sources. In addition to abbreviations in the text, several abbreviations appear without explanation. These abbreviations include references to such publications of The Bureau of National Affairs, Inc. (BNA) as: "LRX" (Labor Relations Expediter); "WHM" (Wages and Hours Manual); "WH Cases" (Wage and Hour Cases); "LRRM" (Labor Relations Reference Manual); and "FEP Cases" (Fair Employment Practice Cases). BNA is the exclusive publisher of the source material that is cited in the *Primer*, unless otherwise noted. Where no source for a particular document or decision is provided, none was available.

Although many people contributed indirectly to the book, Mary Green Miner, Tim Darby, and Anne Scott of BNA Books must be singled out for their concern for quality, attention to detail, and patience as this book went through several drafts.

I wish finally to thank my wife, Margaret, and my son, Jude, for their advice, patience, and assistance throughout the course of writing the *Primer*.

Joseph E. Kalet

Washington, D.C.
July 1987

CONTENTS

1
THE FEDERAL SCHEME OF WAGE AND HOUR LEGISLATION

The federal law governing the payment of wages and the regulation of hours worked had its roots in the Hours of Work Laws enacted between 1892 and 1913. The most important piece of legislation enacted, however, is the Fair Labor Standards Act of 1938 (FLSA), because of its broad sweep. Currently, the federal statutory scheme for regulating wages and hours in the United States consists of the FLSA, the Portal-to-Portal Pay Act (Portal Act), five narrower statutes (Equal Pay Act, Walsh-Healey Public Contracts Act, McNamara-O'Hara Service Contract Act, Davis-Bacon Act, and Contract Work Hours and Safety Standards Act), and two laws directed at protecting specific classes of individuals through employer practices involving payroll deductions (Consumer Credit Protection Act and Child Support Enforcement Act).

These laws can be categorized under three classes of federal wage-hour statutes: the first class consists of the FLSA, the Portal Act, and the Equal Pay Act. These statutes are designed to reach most employees in the nation and to ensure fair compensation in terms of minimum wages, overtime pay, and equal pay for equal work.

The second class of federal laws consists of the Walsh-Healey Public Contracts Act (WHA), the McNamara-O'Hara Service Contract Act (SCA), the Davis-Bacon Act (DBA), and the Contract Work Hours and Safety Standards Act (CWHSSA). These statutes establish "prevailing" wage rates for certain classes of employees performing work for a contractor which has a contract to provide material or services to the federal government.

The third class of statutes consists of, among others, the Consumer Credit Protection Act (CCPA) and the Child Support Enforcement Act (CSEA). These laws are designed to protect specific classes of individuals. The CCPA limits the amount of wages that can be garnisheed from an employee's paycheck and establishes the conditions under which an employee may be discharged for having his wages garnisheed excessively. The CSEA requires employers to withhold from employees' wages any amounts determined to be due under support orders issued by a court or an administrative body. This law also protects employees from employer retaliation as a result of having wages withheld pursuant to the CSEA.

This *Primer* discusses the federal statutory scheme governing wages and hours according to the three classes previously mentioned, and in that sequence.

In addition to the federal laws, it should be pointed out that most states have adopted their own versions of some of the federal laws. Under principles established in the U.S. Constitution, states may pass laws that are stricter, but not less stringent, than the federal apparatus. As a consequence, many states have enacted "little" Davis-Bacon laws, and "little" Walsh-Healey acts, and so on. These state statutes coexist with the federal apparatus, and employers and contractors may be liable for wage violations under either or both statutes simultaneously. For further information, contact the U.S. Department of Labor (see Appendix A), or the appropriate state agency.

FAIR LABOR STANDARDS ACT

Prior to passing the Fair Labor Standards Act (FLSA) in 1938 (WHM 90:51), Congress attempted to establish fair minimum and overtime wage standards with limited success. These efforts to regulate wages and hours had been limited to workers employed either by the federal government or by specific industries in the private sector. Between 1892 and 1913, for example, Congress passed a series of statutes governing public works employees that became known collectively as the Eight-Hour Law, since the legislative purpose of these enactments was to establish a standard eight-hour work day for these workers. Once this limit had been exceeded, overtime pay was mandatory, to be calculated at the rate of one-and-one-half times (or time-and-one-half) the employee's basic rate of pay. This overtime rate was payable for all overtime hours worked.

When the onset of the Great Depression led to widespread unemployment, the scarcity of jobs was perceived as an invitation to wage abuses by employers who knew that it was a "buyer's market" for labor, particularly since many industries were not covered by either state or federal wage-hour laws. In 1937, for example, the employer in *West Coast Hotel v. Parrish*, contended that the state's Minimum Wage Law violated the Due Process Clause of the Fifth Amendment to the U.S. Constitution. But the Supreme Court affirmed the validity of a Washington State law setting minimum wages for women, reasoning that the statute was a legitimate and reasonable exercise of the state's police power to protect the health of women, to guard them against unscrupulous employers, and to correct the abuse of casting a direct burden upon the community for the support of women who are denied a living wage. This decision created the impetus for the federal government to establish wage and hours of work standards for industries not covered by state law.

The FLSA regulates employment practices in the areas of minimum wage, overtime pay, equal pay, recordkeeping, and child labor. The Act specifically requires employers to maintain adequate records reflecting employees' hours of work and pay for all hours worked. It covers employees who are "engaged in interstate commerce," or in the "production"of goods for travel in interstate commerce, or employed in "an enterprise engaged in commerce or the production of goods for commerce."

Coverage was extended to certain federal government employees and to state and local hospitals and educational institutions by the 1966 amendments to the Act. The 1974 amendments extended coverage to household domestic service workers and to most federal employees and to employees of any "state, political subdivision of a state" and interstate government agencies. However, this latter aspect of the 1974 amendments was overturned by the Supreme Court in 1976 when it decided in *National League of Cities v. Usery* that the amendments "operated to directly displace the States' freedom to structure integral operations in areas of traditional governmental functions."

In February 1985, however, the Supreme Court decided that the FLSA applies to state and local government employees, notwithstanding the principle of state sovereignty under the Tenth Amendment to the U.S. Constitution. *(Garcia v. San Antonio Metropolitan Transit Auth.* overruling *National League of Cities v. Usery)* The extension of the FLSA to cover these governmental entities created a chaotic situation, and soon Congress was forced to act. In November 1985, Congress passed and President Ronald W. Reagan signed into law the Fair Labor Standards Amendments of 1985, effective April 15, 1986.

The 1985 amendments govern the wage and hour practices of state and local government employers. They provide for the payment of compensatory (comp) time in lieu of cash payments for overtime work; the comp time is calculated at the rate of time-and-one-half of the employee's regular rate of pay for each hour of overtime worked. The amendments provide limits on the amount of comp time that may be accrued, a higher ceiling being allowed for safety, emergency, and seasonal personnel than is allowed for other public employees. They also provide special rules for firefighters and police personnel concerning tour-of-duty practices. (The FLSA is discussed in greater detail in Chapter 2.)

Employers are covered under the Act if they meet a minimum threshold dollar-volume-of-business test of $362,500 per annum. If the employer takes in this much money per year, then the next step is to determine whether the employer is an "employer" within the meaning of the Act. For this determination, the courts apply the "economic realities" test to the employer's relationship with the employee: Do the *economic realities* of the relationship indicate that the employer in fact controls the employee in the payment of wages and performance of work? The test is complex and is addressed in greater detail in

Chapter 2. An employer may also be covered under the Act by virtue of the "enterprise" concept, which means that the employer's total business operations, taken as a single enterprise, may bring the employer within the Act's coverage under the dollar-volume test. FLSA case law also indicates that an employer may be covered if it is a "joint employer" with another entity; in such situations all individual businesses that make up the "joint employer" can be liable for wage violations.

The Act provides numerous exemptions from coverage for certain classes of employees, along with "tests" to determine whether individuals fall within these classes. Executive, administrative, and professional employees fall within the so-called "white-collar" exemptions. An individual may qualify for more than one exemption, but the effect is not cumulative. Finally, the Act provides a list of employees involved in certain industries who are exempt from FLSA coverage.

The Act states that an employer who *willfully* violates the minimum wage or overtime requirements is liable for liquidated damages in an amount equal to the back pay due the employee. A two-year statute of limitations is established for filing a timely action under the Act. (The FLSA is discussed in greater detail in Chapter 2.)

PORTAL-TO-PORTAL PAY ACT

The 1947 Portal-to-Portal Pay Act (Portal Act; WHM 90:121) was enacted to rectify a situation that arose after the U.S. Supreme Court decided in *Anderson v. Mt. Clemens Pottery Co.* that employees were entitled to compensation for time spent in preliminary and postliminary activities ("from portal to portal"). The Portal Act also amends the Davis-Bacon and Walsh-Healey Public Contracts acts, which govern the construction of public buildings for the federal government and the manufacture or supply of goods for the government, in the same way it affects the FLSA.

The Portal Act, which is discussed in Chapter 3, provides a "good-faith" defense to the otherwise mandatory provision of the FLSA which imposes liquidated damages liability on employers who *willfully* violate the wage provisions of the FLSA. If an employer can demonstrate that it acted in good faith with a reasonable belief that its actions did not violate the Act, then the Portal Act gives the court discretion to reduce or deny any liquidated damages award. The U.S. Department of Labor's Wage-Hour Division has participated in the development of regulations applying this difficult aspect of the Portal Act; a more detailed discussion of this area of the law is provided in Chapter 3.

The Portal Act also provides a two-year limitations period for actions brought under the FLSA and the Walsh-Healey and Davis Bacon acts; this period will be extended to three years upon a finding that the employer's violations were willful. Under established case law, the courts have applied an "in the picture" standard to determine whether the employer's violations were willful. That is, if the employer knew or had reason to know that the FLSA was "in the picture" in the employment situation with its employees, then the employer is presumed to have acted willfully (*Coleman v. Jiffy June Farms, Inc.*)

Recently, the Court of Appeals for the Third Circuit expanded on the meaning of "willfulness" in the context of an alleged violation of the FLSA. The court reversed the "in the picture" standard, even though the meaning of "willful" is not fixed and determinate, where a willful act requires a *deliberate effort beyond mere negligence.* The *Jiffy June Farms* standard imposes liability when the employer is merely negligent, according to the court, and the in the picture standard is therefore contrary to the plain meaning of the FLSA. (*Brock v. Richland Shoe Co.*) (See Chapter 3 for a more detailed discussion of this area of the law.)

The Portal Act also banned actions brought by unions or other representatives of employees, but allowed employees to sue on behalf of themselves and similarly situated employees. In these actions, each participant is required to give his or her consent in writing, that is, affirmatively to "opt in" to the action.

EQUAL PAY ACT

In June 1963, President John F. Kennedy signed into law the Equal Pay Act of 1963 (EPA; WHM 90:131). The EPA requires employers to pay equal pay to men and women performing work requiring equal skill, effort, and responsibility and performed under similar working conditions. The Act amended the FLSA and was incorporated into Title VII of the Civil Rights Act of 1964; it may be enforced in an action initiated under either amended statute.

Congress specified that the EPA would cover employers who are covered under the FLSA. However, Congress removed the "enterprise" concept from EPA coverage, thus restricting the number of employers (and hence, employees) who were covered under the EPA. Although the FLSA provides for enterprise coverage, any EPA action is limited to the employer's individual "establishment" and may not extend to the employer's enterprise.

While the EPA requires equal pay for work of equal skill, effort, and responsibility, it provides an exception where such payment is made pursuant to a seniority system, a merit system, a system that measures earnings by quantity or quality of production, or a differential based on any factor other than sex. (The EPA was inadvertently drafted with the phrase "any *other* factor other than sex.") The EPA, perhaps anticipating employer intransigence in complying, precludes employers from reducing the wage rate of any employee to comply with the requirement to pay equal wages for equal work.

The EPA is essentially enforced, as is the FLSA , by private actions, class actions, or actions by the Secretary of Labor. However, the EPA also provides an administrative route to enforcement under Title VII through the Equal Employment Opportunity Commission, which is specifically authorized to enforce the EPA. Any amounts owing under the EPA are treated as if they were owed under the FLSA, including the imposition of liquidated damages and attorneys' fees liability, where appropriate. (The EPA is discussed in greater detail in Chapter 4.)

WALSH-HEALEY ACT

The Walsh-Healey Public Contracts Act (WHA; WHM 90:201) was enacted in June 1936 to regulate employment conditions under government contracts. In addition to regulating hours of work and wages, the Act deals with the problems of child labor, convict labor, and hazardous working conditions. It covers all government contracts for the manufacture or furnishing of materials, supplies, articles, and equipment in any amount exceeding $10,000. Any contract covered by the WHA must provide that all workers will be paid not less than the prevailing minimum wage rate determined by the Secretary of Labor for similar work in the locality. Employees are entitled to overtime pay for any work in excess of 40 hours per week. Prior to the passage of the Department of Defense Authorization Act of 1986 (DOD Act), which amended the WHA, employees who worked on a contract that was covered by the WHA were entitled to overtime for any work in excess of 8 hours per day, but the DOD Act removed the 8-hour limit, while maintaining the 40-hour per week overtime limit. As with most other wage-hour laws, overtime under the WHA is calculated on the basis of time-and-one-half the employee's regular rate of pay.

The Secretary of Labor is authorized to investigate and decide cases involving alleged violations of the WHA. Liquidated damages found due in such proceedings may be obtained by the government through a lawsuit, or may be deducted by the government from amounts due the contractor under another contract.

The most significant sanction for violating the WHA is the rarely used debarment ("blacklist") penalty, under which contractors who are serious and willful violators of the Act are barred from receipt of government contracts for a period of three years. (The WHA is discussed in greater detail in Chapter 5.)

McNAMARA-O'HARA SERVICE CONTRACT ACT

The McNamara-O'Hara Service Contract Act (SCA; WHM 90:225), commonly known as the Service Contract Act, was enacted in 1965 to complement the WHA in regulating labor standards for employees who work under contracts let by the federal government.

Whereas the WHA covers the manufacture or furnishing of materials and supplies which exceed $10,000, the SCA covers contracts for the performance of services for the federal government which exceed $2,500. (Attempts were made in 1986 to raise the minimum dollar amount, but they were unsuccessful. In light of government efforts to reduce federal spending, additional attempts to raise the threshold may be expected.)

The SCA requires the payment of wages and fringe benefits found to be prevailing locally or as found in a previous existing contract, but in no event less than the federal minimum wages under the FLSA. The same enforcement provisions as apply in the WHA—the withholding of payments to a contractor to correct underpayments to its employees—applies in the SCA, including the three-year debarment penalty. (The SCA is discussed in greater detail in Chapter 6.)

DAVIS-BACON ACT

The Davis-Bacon Act of 1931 (DBA; WHM 90:251) regulates the rate of wages for laborers and mechanics employed in the construction of public buildings for the federal government by contractors and subcontractors, where the contract calls for an expenditure of more than $2,000. (Attempts were made to raise the minimum amount in Congress in 1986, but they were unsuccessful.) The Act also applies to work performed under certain other laws, such as the Federal Aid Highway Act and the Area Redevelopment Act of 1961. Under the DBA, the Secretary of Labor is required to establish prevailing minimum wage rates to be incorporated into contracts covered by the Act. The Comptroller General, however, is the official authorized to withhold payments to the contractor if necessary to make good any underpayments to employees; employees may sue the contractor for back pay owing to them if the amount withheld by the Comptroller General is insufficient to reimburse them.

The DBA provides a three-year debarment or blacklist penalty which bars *willful* violators of the Act from obtaining a contract under the DBA. (The DBA is discussed in greater detail in Chapter 7.)

CONTRACT WORK HOURS AND
SAFETY STANDARDS ACT

The Contract Work Hours and Safety Standards Act (CWHSSA; WHM 90:271) was enacted in 1962 to regulate employer practices in the area of contracts calling for the performance of services for the federal government. The Work Hours Act, as it is commonly called, covers mechanics and laborers employed on any public work for the federal government and employees performing services similar to those of mechanics and laborers in connection with dredging or rock excavation in any river or harbor of the United States or the District of Columbia. The CWHSSA also requires the payment of overtime at the rate of time-and-one-half the employee's regular rate of pay for all hours worked in excess of 40 per week. Prior to the enactment of the Department of Defense Authorization Act of 1986 (DOD Act), the Work Hours Act required overtime pay when an employee exceeded 8 hours per day or 40 hours per week. The DOD Act eliminated the 8-hour day limit for overtime so that only the 40-hour per week limit now applies.

The enforcement mechanism for the CWHSSA is different from most of the federal labor standards acts in that inspectors must report to the contracting officer any violations of the Act they find. The officer may then withhold from the contractor any amounts due the employees, including penalties, as a result of such violation. Decisions made by the contracting officer can be appealed to the head of the contracting agency and then to the U.S. Court of Claims. Willful violations of the Act are punishable by a fine of up to $1,000 and/or imprisonment of up to six months. (The CWHSSA is discussed in greater detail in Chapter 8.)

CONSUMER CREDIT PROTECTION ACT

The Consumer Credit Protection Act (CCPA; WHM 90:141), enacted in 1968, limits the amount of an employee's wages that can be subjected to garnishment to not more than 25 percent of the employee's "disposable earnings" for any workweek; or to the amount by which his disposable earnings are greater than 30 times the federal minimum hourly wage, whichever is greater. It covers all employees, regardless of the size of the employer's business. Under the Act, the Secretary of Labor is authorized to bring enforcement proceedings, however, proceedings are carried out by the Wage-Hour Division which is the Department of Labor's enforcement arm. The Act's restrictions on the amount of an employee's wages that are subject to garnishment do not apply in cases of wage deductions based on a court order for the payment of support, or on an order from a bankruptcy court, or to a wage deduction for any debt due on any state or federal tax.

Under the Act, employers are precluded from discharging employees solely because of a single wage garnishment. This relatively straightforward language has led to much litigation over whether the issuance of consecutive, but not concurrent, garnishment orders constitutes a "single" order for purposes of the protection afforded the employee under the Act. Employers who violate this prohibition are subject to criminal penalties of a $1,000 fine and/or one year imprisonment.

One important aspect of the Act concerns state sovereignty under the Tenth Amendment to the U.S. Constitution. The CCPA purports to set standards in areas that have traditionally been controlled by the states. In view of the constitutional protections retained by the states, the Act does not prohibit states from applying their own garnishment laws where they prescribe stricter garnishment restrictions than federal law. The Act also does not affect or alter state laws which prohibit an employer from discharging an employee because the employee had more than one wage garnishment. Any state may have garnishments that are issued under its own laws exempted from the Act, where the state laws provide for restrictions that are substantially similar to the Act. The state must apply to the Secretary of Labor for this exemption. (The CCPA is discussed in greater detail in Chapter 9.)

CHILD SUPPORT ENFORCEMENT ACT

The Child Support Enforcement Act of 1984 (CSEA; WHM 90:143) requires employers to withhold from employees' wages any amounts determined to be due under support orders issued by a court or administrative body.

Employers are prohibited from disciplining, discharging, or refusing to hire an individual because of a withholding order for support. Employees are entitled to advance notice and a hearing before the order becomes effective. Employers who fail to comply with the Act may be subject to penalties. (The CSEA is discussed in greater detail in Chapter 9.)

2
FAIR LABOR STANDARDS ACT

The Fair Labor Standards Act of 1938 (FLSA; WHM 90:51) was enacted to meet the economic and social problems existing during the Great Depression. Low wages, long working hours, and high unemployment were rampant during this time, and Congress sought a way to establish minimum wage standards while encouraging the spread of employment. The policy of the FLSA was to correct and, as rapidly as practicable, to eliminate labor conditions detrimental to the Act's goals of establishing minimum wage standards.

The Act, as amended, sets general standards for minimum wages, overtime compensation, equal pay, and child labor for all employees who are not specifically exempted under the Act. All covered employees include those who are:

- engaged in interstate commerce. "Commerce" under the Act and case law developed under it, includes both incoming and outgoing foreign transportation of goods, as well as such trade between the states; or
- Engaged in the production of goods for commerce. This production of goods includes not only the actual production operations, but also "any closely related process or occupation directly essential" to the production; or
- Employed in an "enterprise engaged in commerce or in the production of goods for commerce." This standard relates directly to the "enterprise" coverage for employers, all of whose employees in a particular business unit may be covered, regardless of how their individual duties relate to commerce or the production of goods

for commerce. In 1966, the Act was amended to bring state and local hospitals and educational institutions within the definition of an "enterprise engaged in commerce."

AMENDMENTS

In 1963, Congress passed the Equal Pay Act (EPA; WHM 90:131) which amended the FLSA in several important respects. The EPA requires that male and female workers receive equal pay for work requiring equal skill, effort, and responsibility, where the work is performed under similar working conditions. Since EPA coverage is the same as that for the minimum wage provisions of the FLSA, an employer covered by the minimum wage provisions of the FLSA is therefore also covered by the EPA.

The EPA does not exempt from coverage those categories of executive, administrative, and professional employees and outside salesmen who are exempt from FLSA minimum wage and overtime provisions. The EPA provides specific exemptions from liability when wage differentials are:

- Based on any factor other than sex;
- Paid pursuant to a bona fide seniority system;
- Paid pursuant to a bona fide merit system; and
- Paid pursuant to a system which measures earnings by quantity or quality of production.

In equalizing past wage disparity based on sex, an employer may not lower the wages of the higher-paid worker to those of the lower-paid worker.

As with the FLSA, unpaid wages may expose an employer to liquidated damages liability for willful violations, and to attorney's fees and costs. The EPA is enforced by private actions and by the Equal Employment Opportunity Commission for agency actions, unlike the FLSA which is enforced by private actions and by the Secretary of Labor through the U.S. Department of Labor's Wage-Hour Division. (For further information on the EPA, see Chapter 4.)

In 1966, the Act was amended to bring state and local hospitals and educational institutions within the definition of enterprises engaged in commerce, the third prong of the coverage test discussed earlier in this chapter. At that time, Congress also extended coverage of the FLSA to certain federal employees, without regard to the three prongs of the coverage test.

In 1974, Congress amended the Act to cover most federal employees; to employees of states, political subdivisions of states, and interstate agencies; and to private household domestic service workers.

In 1976, the U.S. Supreme Court ruled in *National League of Cities v. Usery* that the 1974 FLSA amendments extending the Act's coverage to state and local government employees were unconstitutional, insofar as the amendments operate "directly to displace the States' freedom to structure integral operations in areas of traditional governmental functions." The Court said that the Commerce Clause of the U.S. Constitution, which authorizes Congress to regulate in areas involving interstate commerce, did not provide a sufficient basis for Congress to interfere with states' relationship with their employees in such areas as fire prevention, police protection, sanitation, and public health.

In 1985, the Supreme Court overruled the *National League of Cities* decision, stating that the extension of the FLSA to state and local government employees did not violate any affirmative limit placed on Congress under the Commerce Clause. (*Garcia v. San Antonio Metropolitan Transit Auth.*) The effect of this decision was to impose FLSA overtime requirements and the Act's general ban against using compensatory time to most state and local government employees.

Following a storm of criticism from public sector employers, who said the decision would wreak havoc on state and local budgets and services, Congress passed the Fair Labor Standards Amendments of 1985, (WHM 90:89), which became effective on April 15, 1986.

The 1985 amendments allow for the payment of compensatory (comp) time in lieu of cash payments to certain employees, establish limits on how much comp time an employee may accrue before cash overtime payments become mandatory, and set standards for determining payment for comp time upon termination of employment. They also establish methods for the treatment of "volunteers," and those employees involved in sporadic and substitute employment in a public agency. The amendments also provide protection against discrimination or adverse action by an employer in retaliation for an employee's assertion of coverage under the FLSA overtime provisions.

Finally, the amendments treat the accrual of comp time by public safety, emergency, and seasonal personnel different from accrual by all other public employees, by allowing a higher ceiling for the former group to accrue comp time than is available for the latter group. The amendments also provide special rules for firefighters and police personnel concerning tour-of-duty practices. (These issues are discussed in greater detail later in this chapter under State and Local Government Employees.)

INTERSTATE COMMERCE REQUIREMENT

The Act extends coverage over employers based on the nature of the employer's business. The interstate commerce aspect of the employer's business allows the courts to extend the Act's coverage to the "farthest reaches of interstate commerce." (*Overstreet v. North Shore Corp.*)

The courts have established the following principles for determining the appropriateness of extending coverage based on the interstate character of the employer's business:

- If goods are produced in an establishment for sale in interstate commerce, there is a presumption that all employees who worked in the establishment contributed to the production of the goods. To overcome this presumption, the employer must establish that the functions of certain employees were segregated from the production of the goods for interstate commerce. (*Guess v. Montague*) However, such segregation will not assist employers in avoiding coverage if their employees qualify under the "enterprise" concept.
- Employers are deemed within the Act's coverage as producing goods for commerce where the employer intends, hopes, or has reason to believe that the goods or any unsegregated part of them will move in interstate commerce. (*United States v. F.W. Darby Lumber Co.; Walling v. Burch*)

- If only a minor part of the employer's business is shipped in interstate commerce or is involved in the production of goods for interstate commerce, the employer may still be covered under the Act where the interstate shipments are "regular and recurrent." (*Mabee v. White Plains Publishing Co.*)

EMPLOYER COVERAGE

The FLSA was intended, as remedial legislation, to cover the broadest possible scope of employment situations. To that end, the Act does not define covered employers, but describes them in terms of the amount of business transacted per year. On the other hand, the Act emphasizes who is an employee, and whether individuals are in fact involved in an employer-employee relationship under the so-called "economic realities" test, which is discussed later in this chapter under Employee Coverage.

Dollar-Volume Test

The basic determining factor for employer coverage involves the size of the employer's business. Congress found that the larger the business, the greater its harm to the public by its FLSA violations and the easier it would be to identify and regulate because of its size. Congress therefore established a minimum gross receipts amount—the dollar-volume test—that would serve as the cutoff between covered and noncovered employers. For nonretail and nonservice businesses, the dollar-volume amount per year is $250,000; for retail and service establishments not covered by the FLSA prior to December 31, 1981, the dollar-volume amount currently is $362,500 per year. Excise taxes at the retail level which are separately stated and identified in the customer's bill need not be included in the calculation of gross dollar-volume of sales.

Businesses whose dollar-volume is less than the established minimum are not covered under the Act. However, the dollar-volume test has been "grandfathered" with each revision in the minimum amount, so that companies covered under a lower limit will not be deemed exempt under a more recent, higher limit.

In addition, there is no dollar-volume test for businesses engaged in laundry or dry cleaning; construction or reconstruction; operation of hospitals, institutions, or schools; or public agencies.

"ENTERPRISE" COVERAGE

Under the 1961 amendments to the FLSA, Congress specifically acknowledged the necessity of the enterprise concept for FLSA coverage, to reach subsidiary branches of an employer's operations. The Act defines enterprise as:

> The related activities performed (either through unified operation or common control) by any person or persons for a common business purpose, and includes all such activities whether performed in one or more establishments or by one or more corporate or other organizational units including departments of an establishment operated through leasing arrangements, but shall not include the related activities performed for such enterprise by an independent contractor.

In the absence of the enterprise concept, an employer's subsidiary branches might otherwise be exempt from FLSA coverage, based on the dollar-volume standard. The Act extends coverage to employees, not specifically exempted otherwise, who are employed by certain enterprises engaged in interstate commerce or in the production of goods for commerce.

Where an employer operates several small entities, none of which individually may meet the minimum dollar-volume tests discussed above, the employer may still be covered under the Act by virtue of the enterprise concept of coverage.

The enterprise concept is not independent of the other bases of coverage, because it is still necessary to determine whether the enterprise or two or more of its employees are engaged in interstate commerce or the production of goods for interstate commerce.

However, unlike other bases of coverage, the enterprise concept does not base coverage on the activities of the individual employees: all of the employees in a particular enterprise or establishment may be covered, provided the enterprise and two or more of its employees are sufficiently engaged in interstate commerce or the production of goods for interstate commerce.

An employer that operates an investigative agency specializing in background and surveillance checks on individuals claiming workmens' compensation benefits for clients in more than one state and that has an annual dollar-volume of over $250,000 is an enterprise within the meaning of the Act, a federal court in Maryland has ruled. Under the current FLSA definition of the word "commerce," the court reasoned, the employer was clearly engaged in commerce. (*Brock v. Commercial Index Bureau*)

The interstate character of the goods as a product that has been moved in interstate commerce is not destroyed by the fact that the product is used to make a different product, which is then sold to intrastate purchasers. And the mingling of the intrastate goods with this product does not negate the product's origin in interstate commerce. (*Wirtz v. Melos Constr. Corp.*)

Although the courts have held that the coverage of the law must be liberally interpreted, they consistently have placed the burden of proving coverage on the employee in an employee-initiated wage suit, and on the Secretary of Labor in a wage-recovery suit or in a suit to restrain violations of the Act. The Act is set up in a way that employees may only sue on their own behalf, and only for the recovery of wages due, while the Labor Secretary may sue on behalf of a class of employees and may obtain injunctive relief in addition to obtaining wages due the employees.

In determining whether a particular business is covered under the enterprise concept, the courts have examined such factors as:

- Related activities of separate business entities; (*Wirtz v. Savannah Bank & Trust Co. of Savannah*)
- The relationship between a "house" agency and the parent organization (WH AdmOp, Feb. 7, 1962);
- Related activities of conglomerates (FLSA, Sec. 13(g));
- Work performed by an "independent contractor"; (*Rutherfood Food Corp. v. McComb*)
- Work performed for an independently owned retail or service establishment (*Wirtz v. Charleston Coca-Cola Bottling Co.*);

- Whether there was a common business purpose, common control, and unified operations. (*Wirtz v. Mack Farland & Sons Roofing Co.; Wirtz v. Hardin & Co.; Donovan v. Janitorial Servs.;* and *Donovan v. Sideris*)

EMPLOYEE COVERAGE

Employees Engaged in Commerce

In view of the congressional intent to extend the FLSA, as remedial legislation, to the farthest reaches of interstate commerce, Congress and the courts have delineated categories of employees whose employers are involved in interstate commerce. The employees are categorized according to the functions they perform under the "employees engaged in commerce" doctrine:

- Employees in the telecommunications and interstate transportation industries;
- Employees who participate in the distribution of goods that move through channels of commerce; and
- Employees who directly aid or facilitate the operation of instrumentalities of commerce by providing materials or power used by the instrumentalities or by maintaining or reconstructing or repairing them.

Since employees engaged in interstate transportation and telecommunications generally are conceded to be covered by the Act, most litigation under the commerce test of coverage involves the "distribution of goods" and "operation of instrumentalities of commerce" prongs of the test.

Cutting against the congressional intent of broad coverage of the FLSA is the complex statutory scheme that exempts many employees covered under other laws such as railway labor, motor carriers, airlines, small telephone exchanges, and water transportation acts, which preempt FLSA coverage in those areas.

"Production for Commerce" Test. Under the "production for commerce" test of coverage, the Act defines "produced" as:

- Employees producing, manufacturing, mining, handling, transporting, or in any other manner working on goods shipped in commerce; or

• Employees engaged in any "closely related process or occupation directly essential" to the production of such goods.

Under these criteria, courts have attempted to define the parameters of "actual production operations" (*Western Union Tel. Co. v. Lenroot*), and to define the meaning of "goods" (*Powell v. U.S. Cartridge Co.*). Section 3(i) of the Act excludes goods "after their delivery into the actual physical possession of the ultimate consumer thereof." Consequently, the courts have also had to address what was intended by the phrase "ultimate consumer." (*Marshall v. Brunner*)

"Fringe" Production Employees

Section 3(j) of the Act provides for coverage of any employee engaged in "any closely related process or occupation directly essential" to production. These fringe production employees were specifically described in the Statement of the House Managers in the 1949 amendments to the Act, which listed some fringe employees who still would be covered under the "closely-related and directly-essential" test. Applying these provisions, the Court of Appeals for the Ninth Circuit ruled that employees of a liquid waste disposal company who regularly remove liquid waste from customers' plants producing goods for interstate commerce, and who perform services for airlines directly related to interstate commerce, are engaged in the production of goods for such commerce under the Act. (*Brennan v. Carrasco*)

Congress intended by these amendments to exclude from FLSA coverage those employees whose work is several degrees or stages removed from the production of goods for interstate commerce. These provisions were interpreted in *Allstate Construction Co. v. Durkin*, where "off-the-road" employees employed by a road contractor in the production of material to repair interstate roads were found to be covered by the Act, even though the material was produced in a state for use on the roads within that state. The U.S. Supreme Court reasoned that these employees were engaged in the production of goods for interstate commerce because "he who serves interstate highways and railroads serves commerce. By the same token, he who produces goods for these indispensable and inseparable parts of commerce produces goods for commerce."

Construction workers on a dam, however, were found not to be involved in an activity that was closely related or directly essential to the production of goods for interstate commerce, according to the Supreme Court, in view of the remoteness of construction from the production of the goods, and the absence of the dedication of completed facilities either exclusively or primarily to such production. The Court also observed that the purpose of the dam—to provide water to a locality—could not be regarded as the production of goods for commerce. (*Mitchell v. H.B. Zachry*) This case illustrates the fact that the employer may meet the dollar-volume test and be engaged in interstate commerce, only to be excluded from coverage because its employees do not produce the type of goods that the Act was intended to cover.

EMPLOYEE EXEMPTIONS

The Act contains a complex scheme of exemptions for employees and employers in certain specified industries. In addition, the Act also carves out specific exemptions for employees having certain responsibilities, where coverage of the employee is thought to be inconsistent with the Act's purpose. These employees fall under one or several of the exemptions for executive, administrative, or professional employees, depending on job duties. These three classes of exemptions are collectively referred to as the "white collar exemptions." Each exemption carries with it a specific set of criteria, or test, that must be met for the employee to fall within the exemption. (See Appendix B for a summary of white-collar exemptions.)

Some employee exemptions suspend only the overtime requirements, while others suspend only the minimum-wage and equal pay requirements. Still others suspend two or all four standards—minimum wage, overtime, equal pay, or child labor. Exemptions may apply to all the employees in an establishment, or only to certain individuals. As an added complication, the exemptions frequently overlap. (See Appendix C for a summary of FLSA exemptions from minimum wage and overtime requirements.)

All of the exemptions under the Act are subject to a rule of "strict construction," that is, any doubt must be resolved in favor of the employee's coverage. *(Calaf v. Gonzalez)* The burden of proving that a particular exemption applies lies with the employer who asserts it. *(Coast Van Lines, Inc. v. Armstrong)*

White-Collar Exemptions

The Act expressly exempts "executive, administrative, and professional" employees from its minimum wage and overtime provisions. The Act charges the Secretary of Labor with responsibility to define and limit these exempt categories.

An executive employee is limited to one whose duties "include some form of management authority—to persons who actually direct the work of other persons." To qualify as an "exempt executive" employee under the Department of Labor regulations, the employee must:

- Have as his primary duty the management of (a) the enterprise in which he is employed or (b) a customarily recognized department or subdivision of the enterprise;
- Regularly supervise the work of two or more full-time employees;
- Have the authority to hire, discharge, and promote, or effectively to recommend such action;
- Regularly exercise discretion in the course of his primary duty;
- Spend at least 80 percent of the workday engaged in the primary duty and receive a stipulated amount of pay per week. This stipulated amount per week is either $155 (under the "long test") or $250 (under the "short test"). The regulations were drafted with an eye to expeditious determinations. To that end, individuals who are proffered as executives will be examined under a more detailed set of factors if they are paid less than $250 per week, and under a more streamlined test if

they earn more than $250 per week. (The tests have not been revised for many years, and for all practical purposes, no executive earns less than $250 per week. Therefore, the long test has very little applicability. However, the Labor Department is considering changes in these dollar amounts.)

The courts have held that an employee must meet *all* the applicable tests to qualify for the exemption. *(Wirtz v. C.&P. Shoe Corp.; Wirtz v. Williams)* The employee's job title is not controlling, but the duties involved determine whether the executive exemption should apply. *(Associated Builders v. Brennan)* In addition to receiving the minimum-dollar amount specified in the regulations, the employee must be paid on a "salary basis." The Wage-House Administrator has stated that this means the employee must receive his full salary for any week in which he performs any work, regardless of the number of hours or days worked.

The salary aspect of the executive employee exemption is complicated and may involve such factors as offsets for jury duty or military leave, salary plus bonus calculations, bona fide reductions not intended to circumvent the salary basis requirements, offsets as credit for board and lodging, and other issues. Specific problems should be addressed to the local office of the U.S. Department of Labor, Employment Standards Administration, Wage-Hour Division. (See Appendix D)

Finally, the regulations provide that an employee who is in "sole charge" of a particular operation is to be deemed an "executive" employee. In addition, an employee may fall under an executive, administrative, and professional exemption simultaneously. *(Legg v. Rock Prods. Mfg. Corp.*, WH-463, WH AdminOp, Aug. 21, 1978)

The second white-collar exemption removes the administrative employee from protection of the minimum wage and overtime provisions of the FLSA. The salary tests are similar to those that apply to the executive employee. The administrative employee must:

- Perform office or nonmanual work directly related to management operations;

- Regularly exercise discretion beyond clerical duties;
- Perform specialized or technical work, or perform special assignments with only general supervision; and
- Spend at least 80 percent of work time on exempt work. Retail-service employees must spend at least 60 percent of work time on exempt work.

The phrase "directly related to management policies or general business operations" contained in the regulations may cover the responsibilities of a wide variety of employees who carry out major assignments in conducting the business or whose work affects business operations to a substantial degree. The Wage-Hour Division warns that job titles will not control.

Highly paid administrative employees (those earning over $250 per week on a salary basis) are exempt if they meet all the criteria of the short test:

- The employee's position must include work requiring the exercise of independent judgment and discretion; and
- The employee's primary duty is office work or work that is not of a manual nature, and is directly related to management policies or to general business operations of the company or its customers. The Wage-Hour Administrator has issued an Explanatory Statement concerning the meaning of "administrative employee" under the regulations (WHM 92:561-92:572).

The last white-collar exemption is the professional employee category, which covers a wide variety of occupations from law and medicine to writing, acting, and other artistic professions. Elementary and secondary school teachers are covered under this exemption by virtue of the 1966 amendments to the Act. As with other white-collar employees, the professional employee is exempt from both the minimum wage and overtime provisions of the Act.

A former senior research associate in a chemical development department who earned more than $250 per week brought suit against his employer claiming he should have been paid overtime during the two years preceding his dismissal because he did not consider his status as that of a professional employee.

A federal district court in Pennsylvania found to the contrary because the associate was engaged in a learned profession and had as his primary duty the "performance of work . . . requiring knowledge of an advanced type in a field of science or learning" under the regulations. In addition, he was part of a research team that investigated and evaluated new syntheses for pharmaceutical products, he had discretion to exercise professional judgment, and he did not contest the employer's evidence which proved that he was fully qualified to perform professional work. *(Molinari v. McNeil Pharmaceutical)*

As with administrative employees, the professional employee exemption is available if the employee is paid on a salary basis and the salary meets the minimum-dollar amount specified in the regulations for 40 hours of work per week. Lawyers and doctors actually practicing in their fields need not meet the minimum-dollar amount.

"Long Test." The Wage-Hour Division has devised an elaborate test ("long test") for determining whether low-paid (between $155 and $250 per week) white-collar employees qualify for exempt status. It has also devised a streamlined test ("short test") for these employees who are higher-paid (more than $250 per week) workers. For each category of exempt employee (executive, administrative, professional), there is a separate long test and short test. (Ed. note: These tests share some common criteria, but differ in significant ways. Consult Appendix B in this Primer for more information.)

Because the minimum-dollar amounts under both the long and short tests were devised many years ago, the long test is not in use for any practical purpose. Nevertheless, it has historical significance. Under the long test, a low-paid white-collar employee is required to have as his primary duty work that either:

- Requires advanced knowledge in a field of science or learning, of a type customarily acquired by a prolonged course of specialized study; or
- Is original and creative in character in a recognized field of artistic endeavor, so that the result depends primarily on the employee's invention, imagination or talent.

Since this description is fraught with subjective, ill-defined phrases, the Wage-Hour Division has attempted to provide guidance by issuing a plethora of Administrative Opinions.

"Short Test." For white-collar employees earning more than $250 per week on a salary basis, the short test requires that an exempt employee must:

- Have as his primary duty the performance of work requiring advanced knowledge in a field of science or learning, including work that requires the consistent exercise of discretion and independent judgment; or
- Have as his primary duty the performance of work requiring invention, imagination, or talent in a recognized field of artistic endeavor.

The short test is truly shorter than the cumbersome and ambiguous long test. To facilitate matters, the Wage-Hour Division has issued a chart of professions whose employees fall within the exemption. Such professional employees include registered or certified medical technologists, registered nurses, computer systems analysts, and supervisory programmers.

Nonemployees

In addition to employees and exempt employees, the Act recognizes "nonemployees" as individuals who do not qualify for employee status. For example, apprentices are regarded by the Wage-Hour Division as nonemployees, because apprentices are not what Congress intended to cover by the word employee. According to the Division, an apprentice is a person at least 16 years old (or older, if required by state or federal law) who is employed to learn a skilled trade pursuant to the terms of a *written* apprenticeship agreement with the employer. (Regulations covering employment of apprentices appear at 29 C.F.R. 521, WHM 92:25.) Trainees for work on railroads are not employees, according to the U.S. Supreme Court, since two important qualifications are lacking: *(a)* any benefit to the employer and *(b)* compensation or an intent that the services rendered be paid for. *(Walling v. Portland Terminal Co.)*

A major category of nonemployee is the independent contractor. Certain jobs may be performed with an independence in judgment that is contrary to an employer-employee relationship which is characterized by the employer's direction of the employee on the job. This is one of the wide range of factors the courts examine to determine whether a particular individual is an employee or an independent contractor. The determining factors include:

- The extent to which the services rendered are an integral part of the employer's business;
- The permanency of the relationship;
- The amount of the individual's investment in facilities and equipment;
- The individual's opportunity for profit or loss;
- The degree of independent business organization and operation;
- The nature and degree of control exercised over the individual by the employer; and
- The degree of independent initiative, judgment, or foresight used by the individual providing the service. (*Real v. Driscoll Strawberry Assocs., Inc.*)

This set of criteria for independent contractor status has come to be known as the economic realities test. The courts have applied these factors in a way that no one factor will be regarded as determinative; rather, all must be weighed in order to decide the economic realities of the situation. (*Brock v. Lauritzen Farms*) Central to a court's decision is whether the worker is *economically dependent* upon the business to whom he or she renders services. (*Usery v. Pilgrim Equip. Co., Inc.*) The difficulty with independent contractors is that they receive, and expect to receive some compensation for their efforts. The *dependency* on the employer is the litmus test for determining whether a particular individual is an independent contractor or an employee. The language of the Act defines "employ" as "to suffer or permit to work," and the courts have adopted a common sense understanding of the term, with respect to a claimed independent contractor, in the context of the relationship that existed at the time. (*Walling v. Jacksonville Terminal Co.*)

Migrant farm workers have occasionally been the subject of independent contractor disputes. An additional complexity in such cases is the presence of the farm labor contractor, who stands between the farm worker and the farm owner. The courts have had no difficulty finding an employer-employee relationship involving the farm worker and both the contractor and the farm owner. *(Hodgson v. Griffin & Brand of McAllen, Inc.)*

Trainees are another category of nonemployee. The U.S. Wage-Hour Administrator applies a six-part test to determine whether a particular individual falls into this category. The individual must meet *all six* factors:

- The training, even though it includes actual operation of the employer's facilities, is similar to that which would be provided in a vocational school;
- The training is for the benefit of the trainee;
- The trainee does not displace regular employees, but works under closer supervision;
- The employer providing the training gains no immediate advantage from the trainee's activities—on occasion, the employer's operation may in fact be hindered;
- The trainee is not guaranteed a job at the completion of his training; and
- The employer and the trainee understand that the employer is not obligated to pay wages during the training period.

Typically, a graduate research assistant and a senior in college who is required to do on-the-job training as part of his course work are regarded as "trainees." (WH AdminOp, June 7, 1967 and WH-20, Mar. 31, 1970 (WHM 91:417))

Airline trainees for the position of flight attendants have given rise to much litigation, with the courts holding that these trainees are not employees under the FLSA. *(Donovan v. American Airlines)*

Other categories of individuals who may perform work for an employer but who are exempt from FLSA coverage include volunteers, apprentices, handicapped workers, outside salespersons, mental patients or patient workers at rehabilitation facilities, and certain agricultural and prison laborers.

MINIMUM WAGES

The current minimum hourly wage under the FLSA is $3.35 per hour. The Act sets standards for offsetting tips against the minimum wage and rules for averaging wages over a given period of time to comply with the minimum wage requirement. Exceptions to the minimum wage are made for learners, apprentices, messengers, and superannuated workers. However, an employer should obtain a certificate of exemption from the Wage-Hour Division before paying the reduced rate. In addition, certain industries and occupations are exempt from the minimum wage requirement; the Wage-Hour Division should be consulted for such information.

In 1986, Congress passed and President Ronald W. Reagan signed legislation amending the FLSA (S. 2884) which is designed to simplify the administration of sheltered workshops. Prior to the legislation, handicapped workers were exempt from the minimum wage provisions and sheltered workshop employers were required only to pay their handicapped workers at least 50 percent of the minimum wage. The new legislation eliminates separate certification requirements for various categories of handicapped workers and bases all wages on individual productivity.

The Wage-Hour Administrator has established rules for computing and paying the minimum wage, the unit of time over which the minimum wage may be averaged, the types of deductions permitted, the effect of piece rates or bonuses, and other matters. Although the Act requires employers to maintain adequate and accurate records, the employer may decide for himself *how* to maintain his records if he is able to provide the Administrator with basic data on the subjects specified above concerning minimum wages.

The two main sources of difficulty in administering this part of the Act concern the length of time over which wages may be averaged to comply with the minimum wage and which deductions may be legally made from employees' wages.

Employees receive pay in various forms: hourly, fixed weekly, fixed monthly, fluctuating workweek, piece rates, bonuses, and commissions. Since the Act sets $3.35 as the minimum for each hour, an hourly paid employee must receive this rate for all hours worked. An employer may not "juggle" the books to pay the employee less than this rate for some hours and more than this rate for other hours in the workweek, even if the average hourly rate meets the minimum wage rate.

A fixed weekly salary is determined by the number of hours worked during a week divided by the actual compensation received. This amount must equal or exceed the minimum hourly wage rate. For a fixed monthly rate, or for any fixed rate that exceeds one week, the employer must translate the salary into a weekly wage rate and satisfy the fixed weekly salary standard set forth above. Under this formula, the fixed monthly salary is multiplied by 12 (months) and divided by 52 (weeks per year) to ascertain the weekly rate; the bimonthly salary is multiplied by 24 (bimonthly periods) and divided by 52 (weeks per year) to determine the weekly rate under that payment schedule.

For employees who are paid on a piece-rate basis, or for those paid under an incentive plan, the salary must meet the average hourly minimum wage rate for all hours worked in the week, although the employee may not earn the minimum wage for every hour worked.

Where there is a mixed rate, such as where an employee receives an hourly rate for some hours worked and a piece rate for other hours in the same week, the hourly rate must be at least the minimum and the piece-rate wages must average at least the minimum for the piece-rate hours.

With regard to a "tipped employee," the employer may credit the tips received up to 40 percent of the applicable minimum wage, but the employer's credit (in the form of an offset against wages) may not exceed the value of the tips actually received by the employee.

The minimum wage required by the FLSA must be paid in cash or "facilities furnished" and not in scrip, tokens, or anything else that is not readily convertible into money, at face value. The Wage-Hour Administrator treats any kickbacks that reduce the employee's wages below the hourly minimum as illegal.

Under the Act, employer's are entitled to deduct from an employee's wages the "reasonable cost of fair value (not retail value) of meals, lodgings, and other facilities" provided to employees, provided the employer satisfies the conditions listed below. The Wage-Hour Division has defined "other facilities" used in Section 3(m) of the Act as being "like board or lodging," such as:

- Meals furnished at company restaurants or cafeterias;
- Housing furnished for dwelling purposes;
- General merchandise furnished by company stores and commissaries;
- Fuel;
- Electricity and other utilities for the employee's noncommercial use; and
- Transportation for the employee between home and work, where the travel time is noncompensable under the Act, and the transportation is not an incident of and necessary to the employment.

Such facilities may be considered wages paid to the employee only if they are customarily furnished by the employer. Employee discounts at retail establishments may not be considered part of the wage, since these discounts simply accommodate employees by reducing the prices of purchases they make. (WH AdminOp, Oct. 5, 1961)

In order for the employer to deduct the reasonable cost or fair value of meals, lodging, and other facilities from employees' minimum wages, the employer has the burden of establishing that:

- The facilities were furnished for the employee's benefit;
- The employees were told that the value was being deducted from their wages;
- The facilities were of a kind customarily furnished by the employer; and
- The employees accepted the facilities voluntarily.

Reasonable cost to the employer may not include any profit to any other "affiliated persons" such as:

- Spouse, child, parent or other close relative of the employer;
- Partner, officer, or employee in the employer's organization;

- Parent, subsidiary, or other closely connected operation of the organization; and
- An agent of the employer's organization.

An employer may make other deductions from minimum wages, such as taxes, uniform cleaning, credit union loans, payroll savings plans, insurance premiums, and voluntary contributions to church, charitable, or other institutions. Illegal deductions include those for meal periods, breakage of merchandise, cash register shortages, and theft losses. However, where there is a debt that the employee owes the employer, a deduction to remove this indebtedness will be allowed, but only if the deduction does not reduce the employee's wages below the minimum wage rate. (*Brennan v. Veterans Cleaning Service, Inc.*) (State minimum wage requirements appear in Appendix E.)

OVERTIME

The FLSA requires the payment of overtime at a rate of one-and-one-half times (or time-and-a-half) the employee's regular rate of pay for all hours worked in excess of 40 per week. The Act does not establish a daily maximum hours limit, after which overtime would be required. Overtime need be paid over to the employee only on the regular payday for the workweeks in question. (Appendix F sets forth the Wage-Hour Division's explanation of how to calculate overtime via its coefficient table.)

The question occasionally arises whether the employer authorized the employee to work the overtime for which he seeks compensation. The Act authorizes overtime if the employer "suffered or permitted" the employee to work the overtime hours. If the employer knew the employee was working the additional hours or if the overtime appeared on the payroll records, the employer will be presumed to have suffered or permitted the employee to perform the overtime work. If the circumstances indicate that the employer knew or should have known that the employee was working overtime for the employer's benefit, then the employer may be liable for those hours.

Since overtime is calculated based on the employee's regular rate of pay, it often becomes crucial to determine that regular rate. Items usually included in this rate are:

- Wages, salary, commission, or piece rate;
- Incentive bonuses;
- Shift premiums;
- Cost-of-living allowances;
- Premiums for hazardous duty or "dirty" work; and
- Other payments that are regarded by the employee as part of his regular compensation.

Types of compensation usually excluded from overtime, as not being part of the regular rate of pay, include:

- Premium pay under union contracts for work on Saturdays, Sundays, and holidays;
- Pay for time not worked, for example, vacations, sick leave, and holidays;
- Contributions to a pension or insurance plan;
- Outright gifts;
- Bonuses that are completely discretionary with the employer;
- Distributions from a profit-sharing plan that meets the Wage-Hour Administrator's regulations; and
- Contributions to a bona fide thrift or savings plan that meet the Wage-Hour Administrator's regulations.

As mentioned earlier, the method of payment determines the overtime calculation. Where an employee performs more than one job for the employer, or is paid partially on an hourly rate and partially on a piece rate, or on a commission basis, the overtime rate will vary according to what the employee's regular rate is determined to be. (State maximum hours and overtime requirements appear in Appendix G.)

Fluctuating Workweek

An important variation on the standard overtime situation involves the employee whose workweek fluctuates. In order for the employer to comply with the Act's overtime provisions where the employee works irregular hours that fluctuate from week to week, there must exist an agreement—preferably written—that provides at least for the FLSA minimum wage, for overtime at the statutory rate for all hours worked per week, and for a weekly wage guarantee for not more than 60 hours calculated according to the rate specified in the agreement.

These agreements, called Belo agreements, are named after the 1942 U.S. Supreme Court decision in *Walling v. A.H. Belo Corp*. Belo agreements require two essential elements:

- Neither the employer nor the employee can anticipate or control with any certainty the number of hours worked from one week to the next; *and*
- the employee's workweek must fluctuate both *above and below* the FLSA overtime limit of 40 hours per week.

The failure of an employee's workweek to dip below the 40-hour mark will constitute a failure to meet the "irregular hours" requirement of the Belo plan. *(Donovan v. Tierra Vista, Inc.)*

The Belo agreements allow employers to control labor costs and limit overtime expenses, while guaranteeing the employee a fixed weekly pay regardless of the irregular hours worked. Where the agreement fails to meet the Belo requirements, the employer will be required to pay overtime based on fixed pay for fluctuating hours.

STATE AND LOCAL GOVERNMENT EMPLOYEES

Congress amended the FLSA to allow a proper "fit" of the Act over previously noncovered employees of state and local governments, following the U.S. Supreme Court's decision in *Garcia v. San Antonio Metropolitan Transit Authority*.

The Fair Labor Standards Amendments of 1985, effective April 15, 1986, allow for the payment of compensatory (comp) time off in lieu of cash payments for overtime work, and provide standards for determining payment of comp time upon termination of employment for state and local government employees. The amendments also provide for the treatment of volunteers and sporadic employment and substitute employment in a public agency, compensatory time limits, and protection against discrimination or adverse treatment in retaliation for an assertion that an employee is covered by the FLSA overtime provisions.

The amendments treat differently accrual of comp time by public safety, emergency, and seasonal personnel, and accrual by all other public employees. They also provide special rules for firefighters and police personnel concerning tour-of-duty regulations.

Comp Time Limits

Comp time may be paid in lieu of overtime, but it must be computed on the basis of time-and-one-half for each overtime hour worked.

Public safety, emergency, and seasonal employees may earn up to 480 hours of comp time before cash payments are required; under the time-and-one-half measure, this means that these employees can only work 320 actual overtime hours before becoming eligible for cash payments. All other state and local workers may accrue up to 240 comp time hours, or 160 overtime hours actually worked. Volunteers to state and local governments who receive no compensation or varying forms of compensation (e.g., expense reimbursements or a "nominal fee") are not considered employees under the Act. The hours in which public employees perform occasional or sporadic part-time work that is different from their regular assignments will not count toward overtime calculations.

Tour of Duty for Fire and Police Personnel

The rules allow state and local employers to establish a longer work period than the normal seven-day week for purposes of computing overtime pay for firefighters and police officers. (The FLSA exempts from overtime pay firefighters or law enforcement personnel employed by public agencies with fewer than five employees; this exemption was unchanged in the 1985 amendments.)

Under the special overtime rules, a public employer may establish a work period or "tour of duty" for its firefighters or police officers of up to 28 consecutive days. Overtime eligibility for firefighters begins once they work more than 212 hours during a 28-day work period (based on a 7.57-hour workday). Public employers may use a shorter tour of duty for firefighters and police officers, provided that the maximum hours are reduced proportionally. For example, firefighters on a 14-day tour would be eligible for overtime after 106 hours. Under these rules, the shortest permissible work period is seven days, during which a firefighter may work 53 hours and a police officer may work 43 hours (based on a 6.11-hour workday). (Appendix H reproduces the Overtime Compensation Rules for police officers and firefighters of state and local governments.)

RECORDKEEPING

The Act requires employers to maintain adequate records of all hours worked, all employees, the wages received, and other terms and conditions of employment. Where records were inadequate or nonexistent, courts have ruled that:

- Employers must "disprove" the evidence of hours worked by the employee; *(Skipper v. Superior Dairies, Inc.)*
- Employers may not claim that there is no evidence of the precise amount of time worked; *(Wirtz v. First State Abstract & Ins. Co.)*
- An employer's failure to rebut the employee's evidence based on employee testimony allows a court to establish the hours actually worked; *(Wirtz v. Durham Sandwich Co.)*
- An employee may establish by "just and reasonable inference" the amount of hours worked in the absence of employer records. *(Anderson v. Mt. Clemens Pottery Co.; Duchon v. Cajon Co.)*

An employer did not violate the overtime provisions when it refused to compensate an employee for five minutes of overtime work, according to a federal appeals court, since the employer had a policy of compensating overtime work only if it constituted at least six minutes per week. The appeals court held that nonpayment for the five-minute segment was a *de minimis* (i.e., trifling) violation. The amount of overtime for which the employee would not be paid accrued over a period of one year, the court noted, but did not constitute a substantial measure of his time and effort. *(Brandon v. United States)*

There is no required format for maintaining records, so long as the information is accurate and complete. Employers are advised to retain these records for six years, which is the general statute of limitations adopted by Congress in Title 28 of the U.S. Code (28 U.S.C. Sec. 241(a)). Although the Portal-to-Portal Pay Act establishes a three-year limitations period for willful violations, an administrative proceeding may reach back six years to the employer's records.

Finally, the Act requires the display in a prominent place of the FLSA poster which states the minimum wage, overtime, and equal pay requirements of the Act, and how an employee may pursue wages due and the exercise of other statutory rights. The Wage-Hour Division provides copies without charge.

ENFORCEMENT

Congress provided that the Act would be enforced only through lawsuits, initiated either by the Secretary of Labor or by private individuals. The Act provides for the following actions:

- Suits by the Secretary of Labor to collect unpaid minimum wages and overtime pay due employees and an equal amount in liquidated damages;
- Suits by the Secretary for injunctions to restrain employers from violating the law. The 1961 amendments to the Act grant jurisdiction to the federal courts to order payment of back wages in such an injunction action, and as part of such an order, a federal court may enjoin the interstate shipment of goods produced by employees not paid in accordance with the Act's wage requirements (hot goods injunction);
- Suits by employees themselves to recover any back wages due them under the Act, an equal additional amount as liquidated damages, and attorney's fees and court costs;
- Criminal actions by the U.S. Department of Justice against "willful" violators of the Act. Conviction in such an action may lead to a fine or, in the case of a second offense, imprisonment.

The primary responsibility for enforcing and administering the FLSA rests with the Wage and Hour Division of the Labor Department. The Division makes inspections and investigations to determine compliance with the Act, issues rules, regulations, and interpretations, and makes determinations on requests for exemptions.

In addition, the FLSA requires the Secretary of Labor to conduct certain studies and reports and to present the results to Congress. These provisions require the Secretary to:

- Investigate whenever he has reason to believe that, in an industry subject to the Act, foreign competition has resulted or is likely to result in increased unemployment in the United States. Should the Secretary determine that increased unemployment has resulted or is likely to result, he then must make a full report of his findings and determinations to the President and to Congress;
- Conduct studies on the justifications or the lack thereof for each of the exemptions provided by Section 13(a) and (b) of the Act. The studies are to include an examination of the extent to which employees of "conglomerates" are subject to these exemptions and the economic effect of their inclusion in such exemptions;
- Study and report back to Congress biennially on ways to prevent curtailment of employment opportunities for disadvantaged minorities, youth, and the elderly;
- Report to Congress annually on the economic impact of the FLSA—the so-called (Section) "4(d)" reports.

Finally, employers may be liable for amounts found due as underpayments, plus an equal amount as liquidated damages, plus attorney's fees and court costs. Employers who are found to have "willfully" violated the Act (with the knowledge that the Act was "in the picture") (*Coleman v. Jiffy June Farms, Inc.*) may be fined up to $10,000, imprisoned up to six months, or both.

STATUTE OF LIMITATIONS

Under the FLSA, an aggrieved employee has two years from the date of the alleged violation to file an action. In civil rights and other litigation, a body of case law has developed as to when the right to file accrues. The courts have had to choose between the time when the employee receives notice of the adverse decision, or when the decision is implemented. Generally, the courts have held that the time when the employee receives notice is the time when his right to file an action accrues. *(Delaware State College v. Ricks)*

In the context of FLSA litigation this conflict of when the right to bring an action accrues has not been an area of contest. However, the prudent employee will file an action as soon as he learns of the alleged violation in order to preserve his rights.

Under the Portal-to-Portal Pay Act, the limitations period for filing an FLSA action is extended to three years if the employee can show that the employer engaged in a "willful" violation of the FLSA. It should be noted that such a finding will be persuasive, if not conclusive, as to any good-faith belief defense to the imposition of liquidated damages liability on the employer. (See Chapter 3 for further information on this subject.)

Finally, there is a general six-year limitations period enacted by Congress in 1966 under Title 28 of the U.S. Code (28 U.S.C. Sec. 241(a)) to an administrative action before a federal agency. In those cases where the Portal Act does not apply, the six-year period controls. *(Glenn Elec. Co. v. Donovan)*

LIQUIDATED DAMAGES

The Act provides that employers who violate the minimum wage and/or overtime provisions of the FLSA are liable for these wages, plus liquidated damages equal to the unpaid wages. Under the Act, the liquidated damages are mandatory; once the employer is found to have violated the Act's wage provisions, the employee stands to collect twice the amount of the unpaid wages. The employee may also collect costs and reasonable attorney's fees. The employer's liability can therefore be quite extensive.

The Portal Act provides that court's may use discretion in awarding liquidated damages, if the employer can show that he had a good-faith belief based on reasonable grounds that his conduct did not violate the Act. Under this good-faith belief defense, the court may reduce or deny entirely an award of liquidated damages that is otherwise mandatory under the FLSA. (For further discussion of this issue, see Chapter 3.)

3
PORTAL-TO-PORTAL PAY ACT

Congress passed the Portal-to-Portal Act (Portal Act; WHM 90:121) in May 1947 as an amendment to several statutes. The Portal Act was created as a result of the U.S. Supreme Court's decision in *Anderson v. Mt. Clemens Pottery Co.* in which the Court examined a situation involving nonpayment for time employees spent walking to and from their workplaces within the employer's compound. Studies indicated that it took approximately 14 minutes for employees to enter the premises, punch in, walk to their respective worksites, put on uniforms, and begin working. The employer credited the employees for time worked in a manner that resulted in their being compensated for 56 minutes less *per day* than the time recorded by the time clocks.

The Supreme Court held that the time necessarily spent by the employees walking to work on the employer's premises, following the punching of the time clocks, was working time within the scope of the FLSA overtime provisions. The time employees spent pursuing "preliminary" activities after arriving at their places of work, such as putting on aprons and overalls, removing shirts, taping or greasing arms, putting on finger cots, preparing equipment for productive work, turning on switches for lights and machinery, opening windows, and assembling and sharpening tools, was also working time within the scope of the Act's overtime provisions.

The Court ruled that time spent by employees must be counted as work time under the FLSA whenever all of the following conditions are present:

41

- Physical or mental exertion by the employee (whether burdensome or not);
- Exertion controlled or required by the employer; and
- Exertion pursued necessarily and primarily for the benefit of the employer and his business.

These standards were first applied by the Court in cases involving underground travel time of iron and coal miners. (*Tennessee Coal, Iron & R.R. v. Muscoda Local 123; Jewell Ridge Coal Corp. v. Mine Workers Local 6167*) However, *Mt. Clemens Pottery* represented the first application of these criteria in a manufacturing environment. This prework activity, literally from the entry "portal" of the workplace, to the exit "portal" off the employer's premises at the end of the shift, became known as preliminary activity (and the courts now recognize its counterpart—postliminary activity) in issues involving compensable time under the FLSA.

In *Mt. Clemens*, the Court also held that these preliminary activities must be included in overtime computations under these rules, unless such time is so inconsequential as to fall within the rule on trifles. Today this rule is known as the *de minimis* rule.

The effect of the *Mt. Clemens* decision was explosive. In the months following the decision, the courts were flooded with what were called portal-pay suits, involving an estimated five billion dollars in back pay and liquidated damages. The impact was nationwide.

BASIC PURPOSE

Congress responded to *Mt. Clemens* by passing the Portal-to-Portal Pay Act, which affected not only the FLSA, but also the Walsh-Healey Act and the Davis-Bacon Act. The basic objective of the Portal Act was to relieve employers from the unforeseen liabilities of the *Mt. Clemens* decision. The most significant aspects of the Portal Act's changes are:

- The Act banned future suits by employees to recover back pay for activities that take place before the start or after the completion of an employee's "principal activities," unless these preliminary or postliminary activities must be paid for under a contract, custom, or practice in the plant;

- Actions brought by unions or other representatives of employees on their behalf were prohibited. However, actions by employees on behalf of additional employees similarly situated were still permitted, provided each participant gave his consent in writing; and
- A two-year statute of limitations was established on all claims under the FLSA and the Walsh-Healey and Davis-Bacon acts. The limitations period is calculated back from the date the action is filed in court. This means that only violations occurring within two years (three years if the court finds willful violations) of the date the action is filed will be heard.

An action *accrues*, for purposes of the two-year limitations period, when the employee becomes or should become aware of the violation. Accrual of an action is determined so that a prospective calculation can be made, from the date the employee learns of the violation to two years forward from that time. For example, if a violation occurred in December 1984, then the employee must bring the action by December 1986 or he is "time-barred" by the two-year statute of limitations.

The limitations period theoretically protects the employer from having to defend against "stale" claims where the evidence and/or witnesses are no longer available for the employer's best defense. On the other hand, the accrual rule is intended to encourage aggrieved employees to bring timely claims.

Courts have readily accepted the theory of the "continuing violation" which consists of an employer's repeated violation of the Act for a period of time. Each new violation renews the accrual date, so that the two-year period begins to run from the date of the most recent violation.

WILLFUL VIOLATIONS

The Portal Act was amended in 1966 to provide that where a cause of action arises out of a willful violation of the FLSA, the action may be commenced within three years after the *accrual* of the cause, when the employee knew or should have known of the violation. This extension of the limitations period from two to three years also extends any back pay due by a significant degree (an additional year of unlawfully withheld wages), and also exposes the employer to substantially greater liquidated damages liability. An employer who has not engaged in any willful violation of the FLSA may face up to two years of back-pay liability. If the employer is found to have committed willful violations, the monetary liability is potentially three times the amount facing the nonwillful violator (three years of back pay plus an equal amount as liquidated damages equals six years of back pay).

Consequently, the determination of what is a willful violation has taken on additional importance to contesting parties, and to the courts which must attempt to formulate clear, predictable, and fair standards for determining when a willful violation has occurred.

The first important pronouncement of what was meant by the term willful in the context of the FLSA arose in the case of *Coleman v. Jiffy June Farms, Inc.* In this case, the Court of Appeals for the Fifth Circuit said that an employer willfully violates the FLSA where the employer "knew or suspected that his actions might violate the FLSA. Stated most simply . . . Did the employer know the FLSA was *in the picture?*" (Emphasis supplied.) This came to be known as the "in the picture" standard for determining willfulness.

Recently, the Third Circuit rejected the in the picture test, even though it conceded that the meaning of willful is not fixed and determinate. The court adopted a more rigorous standard: a "willful violation requires a *deliberate effort beyond mere negligence.*" (Emphasis supplied.) The court reasoned that the in the picture standard imposes liability even if the employer is merely negligent. It noted, however, that the Portal Act's imposition of liquidated damages liability was intended to be punitive, based on the congressional perception that willful violations are more culpable than negligent ones. Therefore, it held, the in the picture standard, which imposes liability for mere negligence, is contrary to congressional intent, and a requirement for some deliberate effort beyond mere negligence satisfied that congressional intent. *(Brock v. Richland Shoe Co.)*

The U.S. Court of Claims, which hears all actions by federal employees against the U.S. government, also addressed the propriety of the in the picture standard for determining willfulness in the context of an FLSA violation. The Court of Claims first rejected the *Jiffy June Farms* in the picture standard, since the federal Office of Personnel Management is both part of the employer and an adjudicator of the employees' claims in this case. This means, according to the court, that the federal government as the employer, *always knows* that the FLSA is in the picture.

The Claims Court provided a new interpretation of what constitutes a willful violation of the FLSA by the federal government: whether there was an "absence of significant uncertainty" by the employer as to whether the FLSA applies to the employees. It stated that Congress legislated that some threshold showing would be made of willful conduct by some standard appropriate to remedial legislation. In this case, the court applied the two-year, rather than the three-year limitations period, on the ground that the government had a "significant uncertainty" whether the employees in question were exempt from the FLSA's overtime provisions. *(Hickman v. United States)*

The willfulness standard is currently in a state of flux, with courts struggling to formulate a workable plan that satisfies the congressional intent and protects the interests of employers and employees. Further developments in this area are expected.

The 1966 amendments also removed the two-year time limit from injunction actions brought by the Secretary of Labor, unless the Secretary also seeks an order requiring payment of back wages. And there is no time limit on contempt proceedings for violation of an injunction issued in an earlier proceeding.

Finally, there are two generally applied limitations periods that also affect actions under the FLSA. There is a five-year limitations period on criminal actions brought by the federal government, and this period applies to criminal actions brought by the government under the FLSA.

There is also a general six-year limitations period for administrative proceedings (WHM 98:206) and a general six-year period for lawsuits that were not affected by the Portal Act. *(Glenn Elec. Co. v. Donovan)*

OTHER PROVISIONS

The Portal Act amended the FLSA, and the Walsh-Healey and Davis-Bacon acts in other significant ways. In addition to the limitations-period changes discussed above, which controls all three statutes, the Portal Act also amended these laws in the areas of:

- Barring future suits for back pay for preliminary or post-liminary activities, unless these activities are otherwise to be compensated at the worksite;
- Barring representative suits, except where the employees sue on behalf of themselves and other employees similarly situated. However, joining in such a suit requires the employee affirmatively to "opt-in" to the lawsuit, in writing;
- Establishing a good-faith defense to any liability under the Act, as to back pay and liquidated damages. The employer must plead and prove that he acted in good-faith reliance on and in conformity with a written administrative regulation, order, ruling, approval, interpretation, practice, or enforcement policy issued under the respective statute. Under an FLSA claim, the employer must point to a ruling of the Wage-Hour Administrator; under Davis-Bacon Act claims, the employer must refer to a ruling or order of the Secretary of Labor; and under Walsh-Healey Act claims the Labor Secretary or any federal official designated by him in administering the Act may be the source of an order or ruling on which the good-faith defense may be based;
- Granting courts hearing FLSA actions discretion to deny or reduce liquidated damages if the employer acted in "good faith" and had "reasonable grounds" for believing that no violation of the Act was being committed; and
- Relieving employers of all retroactive liability that arose as a result of the Wage-Hour Division's definition of the term "area of production" within the meaning of the FLSA's agricultural processing exemptions.

Shortly after the Portal-to-Portal Pay Act was passed, the Wage-Hour Division issued a detailed Interpretative Bulletin

(WHM 90:731) setting out its interpretation of the Act. According to the Division, the Act's legislative history indicates that a strict construction of the statutory terms is warranted, and that the Act was not intended to modify the general policy of the FLSA as remedial legislation. The Portal Act in fact was intended to relieve employers in certain situations where liability was both unforeseen and catastrophic. The Bulletin counsels that the FLSA is to be liberally interpreted to foster the congressional policy of establishing fair labor standards, and that the FLSA exemptions are to be narrowly construed for the same reason.

GOOD-FAITH DEFENSE

Perhaps the most heavily litigated aspect of the Portal Act involves the good-faith defense contained in Sections 9 and 10 of the Act because a finding that the employer acted in good faith when it violated the FLSA precludes any determination that the violation was willful. A willful violation, as we have seen, entitles the prevailing plaintiff to an award of liquidated damages equal to the amount of the unpaid wages, and exposes the employer to an extended limitations period from two to three years. Of course, this exacerbates the employer's monetary liability for back wages from two years to potentially six years.

The good-faith defense provides the employer with a shorter limitations period for back-pay liability, and it grants to the courts *discretion* to deny or reduce any liability for liquidated damages. However, the court must find that the employer's violation occurred in good faith, that it had reasonable grounds for believing that no violation was being committed.

The Act defines "good faith" as compliance with a written administrative regulation, order, ruling, approval, or interpretation, or any administrative practice or enforcement policy issued by the specified official administering the FLSA, the Walsh-Healey Act, or the Davis-Bacon Act. Such writing or practice will provide a complete defense to any claim of willful conduct under the language of the Act.

It appears from a review of the case law decided under the Portal Act that the good-faith defense is most frequently contested when there is no written administrative regulation, order, ruling, or the like, and the employer has proffered some evidence that his actions were reasonably based. Such evidence could take the form of a written opinion from privately retained legal counsel in an unsettled area of law. The employer must show that it *received* such advice, and that it relied in good faith *on that advice*. A post hoc awareness of the existence of such a writing is insufficient to demonstrate that the employer in fact relied on that advice in selecting its course of action.

The Wage-Hour Division's Interpretative Bulletin (WHM 90:731) discusses the good-faith defense in detail, and is the most thorough and reliable discussion of this aspect of the Portal Act available.

In construing this defense, the Division emphasizes that the employer's action must have been *(a)* in conformity with the ruling, administrative opinion, order, and the like; *(b)* in reliance on the ruling; and *(c)* in good faith. An action may not be considered to have been "in conformity with" the administrative ruling or interpretation, unless it is in *strict* conformity with that determination, according to the Interpretative Bulletin. An erroneous belief by the employer that it acted in conformity with the ruling would not be sufficient to meet the good-faith defense prerequisites. Actual and substantial conformity is required.

Likewise, it is pointed out in the Bulletin, an employer's action may not be considered to have been "in reliance on" an interpretation or ruling unless the employer had actual knowledge of the ruling or interpretation at the time of the employment decision, and in fact, relied upon *that* ruling.

As to the final requirement, the Division's position is that good faith is not the actual state of mind of the employer, but an objective test as to whether the employer, in acting or omitting to act as it did, and in relying upon the regulation, order, ruling, and the like acted as a "reasonably prudent man would have acted under the same circumstances." Part II of the Bulletin also defines the terms "regulation and order," "interpretation," "ruling," "approval," and "practice or enforcement policy."

4
EQUAL PAY ACT

On June 10, 1963, President John F. Kennedy signed the Equal Pay Act (WHM 90:131), which was designed to eliminate wage differentials based on sex. The Equal Pay Act (EPA) amended Section 6 of the Fair Labor Standards Act (FLSA) and shares the FLSA's minimum-wage coverage standards, with certain exceptions.

In 1977, Congress passed the Reorganization Act of 1977, authorizing President Jimmy Carter to "reorganize" and streamline certain federal government agencies. Under Reorganization Plan No. 1 of 1978, the Equal Employment Opportunity Commission (EEOC) was given authority, previously vested in the Department of Labor, to enforce the EPA and the Age Discrimination in Employment Act (ADEA). Executive Order 12144 (1979) implemented the transfer of authority. (See Appendix I for Directory of EEOC offices.)

The EEOC adopted regulations established by its predecessor, the Labor Department's Wage-Hour Division, for recordkeeping under the EPA. While the Act was under the authority of the Wage-Hour Division, the Wage-Hour Administrator had issued numerous Administrative Opinions and an Interpretative Bulletin concerning agency policy toward enforcing the EPA.

Upon assuming responsibility for this new task, the EEOC stated that an employer who acted in good-faith reliance on and in conformity with any written interpretation by the Wage-Hour Administrator may establish a good-faith defense to liquidated damages liability under the EPA, in line with Section 10 of the Portal-to-Portal Pay Act (Portal Act), as it modifies the

49

FLSA. The Commission cautioned, however, that an employer may not establish a good-faith defense where it relied on any interpretation contained in the regulations promulgated under the EPA that had been rejected by the courts.

MAJOR PROVISIONS

The EPA, incorporated into the FLSA, requires that male and female workers receive equal pay for work requiring equal skill, effort, and responsibility, and performed under similar working conditions. The Act's coverage is essentially the same as that of the minimum-wage provisions of the FLSA. An employer covered by the FLSA's minimum-wage provisions is most likely to be covered by the EPA. However, the EPA does not share the FLSA's exemption from coverage for certain categories of employees, such as executive, administrative, and professional employees and outside salesmen. These categories are covered by the EPA. The EPA provides specific exemptions from liability where wage differentials are:

- Based on any factor other than sex;
- Paid pursuant to a bona fide seniority system;
- Paid pursuant to a bona fide merit system; and
- Paid pursuant to a system which measures earnings by quantity or quality of production.

In equalizing past wage disparity based on sex, an employer may not lower the wages of the higher-paid worker to that of the lower-paid worker. As with the FLSA, unpaid wages may expose an employer to liquidated damages for willful violations, and to attorney's fees and costs.

In applying the test of "equal pay for work requiring equal skill, effort, and responsibility, performed under similar working conditions," the courts have discerned a number of crucial questions that must be answered. The litigants must present the question of which jobs are properly to be compared ("comparators"), when equal salaries may not constitute equal "pay," and whether equal work is being performed under "similar" working conditions, among others. The plethora of variables makes this area of wage-hour law particularly fertile.

For example, a federal appeals court, affirming the district court, has ruled that a female former college professor was not assigned a heavier instructional workload than male professors. The female professor alleged that the heavier workload precluded her from coaching extramural activities, but the appeals court observed that she attempted to compare herself with five male "comparators" who were primarily assigned administrative duties. *(Berry v. Board of Supervisors, LSU)*

Wage comparisons are made only between wages paid to employees of the opposite sex within the same establishment, rather than between members of the same sex, or between employees within different establishments. The EPA meaning of establishment follows the FLSA definition: a "distinct physical place of business" and not "any entire business or enterprise" that might encompass separate places of business. (29 C.F.R. Sec. 1620.9) However, in determining an employer's obligations under the EPA, employer and establishment are not synonymous terms. An employer may have more than one establishment in which he employs workers within the meaning of the Act. In such cases, the legislative history makes clear that there shall be no comparison between wages paid to employees in different establishments. (29 C.F.R. Sec. 1620.7)

The courts and the EEOC have attempted to provide definitive answers to the meaning of equal "pay," (i.e., "wages"), equal "work," equal "skill," equal "effort and responsibility," and the effect of additional duties on this evaluation. The Wage-Hour Administrator had previously called for a "practical" approach to the interpretation and application of the "similar working conditions" criterion. The regulations currently control this element of the equal pay standard. (29 C.F.R. Sec. 1620.13, WHM 95:601-95:615; *Maguire v. Trans World Airlines*)

ENFORCEMENT

Prior to the 1978 transfer of enforcement authority to the EEOC, the Commission solely administered equal pay issues under Title VII of the Civil Rights Act of 1964. Under Title VII, the Commission is required to attempt informal methods of conciliation before resorting to litigation. Congress failed to specify in the Reorganization Act of 1977 whether the same philosophy of conciliation-before-litigation applied to EPA enforcement.

A federal district court decided in 1982 that the Commission was indeed required to engage in good-faith conciliation efforts before it could bring an action under the EPA. *(EEOC v. Home of Economy, Inc.)* Imposing the conciliation requirement fulfills the congressional intent embodied in the Reorganization Act of 1977 that the EEOC's enforcement functions "should not be limited" to the functions related to equal pay administration previously vested in the Secretary of Labor, the Wage-Hour Administrator, and the Civil Service Commission (currently the Office of Personnel Management). The court reasoned that the Commission should act as a conciliator before it acts as a litigator under the EPA, in conformity with its conduct under Title VII.

COVERAGE

Employees

As with the FLSA, the EPA covers employees engaged in interstate commerce, employees who participate in the distribution of goods which move through channels of commerce, and employees who directly aid or facilitate the operation of instrumentalities of commerce. This last group includes such instrumentalities as railroads, highways, waterways, and airports.

The Act also applies to employees engaged in the production of goods for interstate commerce, such as:

- Employees producing, manufacturing, mining, handling, transporting, or in any other manner working on goods shipped in commerce; and
- Employees engaged in any "closely related process or occupation directly essential" to the production of such goods.

The "closely related" and "directly essential" language was inserted in the 1949 amendments to the FLSA to narrow the coverage of "fringe" production workers. Certain fringe workers are still covered under the FLSA. (For a more detailed discussion on this subject, see Chapter 2 under Fringe Employees.)

Although the EPA relies on the FLSA case law for coverage principles, there are significant differences. For example, the white-collar exemption under the FLSA for professional employees does not apply under the EPA. One federal court stated that the professional employees of a state university medical school are covered by the EPA, despite the FLSA exemption, because Title IX of the Education Amendments of 1972 makes the FLSA exemption inapplicable to equal pay claims. *(Friedman v. Weiner)*

Employers

An employer under the EPA is defined as "any person acting directly or indirectly in the interest of an employer in relation to an employee and includes a public agency." The Act specifically excludes "any labor organization (other than when acting as an employer), or any one acting in the capacity of officer or agent of such labor organization."

Subsequent to the passage of the EPA, the U.S. Supreme Court ruled in *National League of Cities v. Usery* that Congress lacked authority under the Commerce Clause to extend coverage of the FLSA to state and local governments. *National League of Cities* was decided in 1976, and following this decision, numerous circuit courts held that this decision did not affect Congress' extension of the EPA to a "public agency." *(Usery v. Dallas Indep. School Dist.; Usery v. John J. Kane Hosp.)*

In 1985, the U.S. Supreme Court ruled in *Garcia v. San Antonio Metropolitan Transit Authority* that the FLSA in fact did extend to state and local governments without violating the Tenth Amendment to the Constitution's protection of state sovereignty. This decision created a consistent, cohesive federal statutory scheme of wage-hour regulations over all sectors; federal, state, local, and private sector employers.

Under FLSA case law, employers are covered under two concepts; the enterprise coverage theory, and the establishment standard. Although these concepts were alluded to earlier in this chapter, they are discussed in detail below.

"Enterprise" Coverage

Under the 1961 FLSA amendments, Congress specifically acknowledged the necessity of the enterprise concept for FLSA coverage to reach subsidiary branches of an employer's operations. In the absence of the enterprise concept, these branches might otherwise be exempt from FLSA coverage, either based on the minimum-employee test or the dollar-volume standard. The Act extends coverage to employees, not specifically exempted otherwise, who are employed by certain enterprises engaged in interstate commerce or in the production of goods for commerce. The enterprise must:

- Have two or more employees engaged in interstate commerce or in the production of goods for commerce, including handling, selling, or otherwise working on goods that have moved in or were produced for commerce by any person; and
- Meet the appropriate dollar-volume test specified for the five types of enterprises and establishments falling under the enterprise test for coverage. Currently, the minimum dollar-volume test is $362,500 per annum for retail and service establishments not covered by the FLSA prior to December 31, 1981. There is a general $250,000 dollar-volume test for enterprises engaged in the laundry or dry cleaning business, construction or reconstruction, the operation of hospitals, institutions or schools, or for public agencies. The dollar-volume test has been "grandfathered" with each revision in the minimum amount established, so that companies covered under a lower limit will not be deemed exempt under a higher limit.

"Establishment" Coverage

Prior to 1974, the FLSA covered certain retail or service stores in a chain based on an establishment test for coverage. The 1974 FLSA amendments phased out the establishment test incrementally, so that today, retail and service establishments are subject only to the general $362,500 dollar-volume test for businesses.

The establishment concept still applies, however, in EPA enforcement. The Act specifically prohibits discrimination on the basis of sex between employees "within any establishment in which such employees are employed." The employee bringing an EPA action has the burden to show that the allegedly unlawful wage disparity exists between employees within the same establishment. A federal district court illustrated the parameters of an establishment when it ruled that predominantly male pursers on an airline's international flights are not employed within the same establishment as the lower-paid and predominantly female cabin attendants on the airline's domestic flights. (*Maguire v. Trans World Airlines*)

EXCEPTIONS TO COVERAGE

As noted earlier, the EPA specifically excepts four categories of wage differentials, if they are:

- Based on a bona fide seniority system; or
- Based on a bona fide merit system; or
- Based on a system which measures earnings by quantity or quality of production; or
- Based on any factor other than sex.

According to the Wage-Hour Administrator, the first three bases are not limited to formal, written programs. If the criteria of a particular system or plan have been communicated to the employees, the employer may rely on that system or plan. However, a formal, written plan will serve both parties more effectively in an EPA dispute.

The fourth base, sex-based wage differentials, will be in violation of the Act according to the Wage-Hour Administrator. Regardless of the proffered basis for a wage differential, the Wage-Hour Division will examine the elements of any particular system or plan that allegedly discriminates on the basis of sex to determine whether the differential is sex-based or otherwise. As in FLSA enforcement, "titles" or labels will not determine the validity of a particular wage plan or system..

In examining the validity of wage differentials, courts have held:

- A hospital maintained an unlawful wage differential between janitors and maids, since all work was within the general cleaning function and there were only insubstantial or minor differences in the degree of effort, skill, or responsibility of the respective jobs; *(Brennan v. South Davis Community Hosp.)*
- An insurance company did not violate the Act by paying more to a male underwriter than to a female underwriter, since the differential was based on two different salary programs, neither of which had sex discrimination as its purpose or effect; *(EEOC v. Aetna Ins. Co.)* and
- An employer violated the Act when it paid a newly hired male employee $10,000 more than it paid a female worker, despite the employer's belief that it expected to gain greater profits from his work, since the employer failed to show that the male's work was actually more profitable. *(EEOC v. Hay Assoc.)*

Employers have come under scrutiny in the context of Equal Pay Act allegations for their job classification systems, "red circling" rates, merit-pay plans, and other wage and benefit programs.

The "factor other than sex" prong of the four statutory exceptions in the Act has provided a wide range of examples where employers have demonstrated that some sex-neutral element of the job warranted a wage differential. (The EPA creates this exception with the language "any other factor other than sex," the first "other" in the exception apparently resulting from a clerical error by the drafters.) Such sex-neutral elements as experience *(Trent v. Adria Laboratories, Inc.)*, training programs *(Hodgson v. First Victoria Nat'l Bank)*, and economic benefit to the employer *(Hodgson v. Anclote Manor Found.)* have been found to justify an employer's wage differential for certain work. On the other hand, the "market force" theory—that employers must pay more to acquire male workers in certain industries, and may pay less to female workers because this is what the "market will bear"—has been soundly rejected. *(Hodgson v. Brookhaven Gen. Hosp.; Brennan v. Victoria Bank & Trust Co.)*

With regard to fringe benefits, the Wage-Hour Administrator has stated that unequal insurance benefits provided for male and female employees is lawful, if the premiums paid or costs incurred by the employer are equal. Similarly, unequal premiums paid or costs incurred by the employer are lawful, if the benefits provided are equal. (WH AdminOp, Oct. 14, 1965).

The Act bars unions from causing or attempting to cause an employer to discriminate against an employee in a manner that would violate the equal pay standard. The union can be held liable in damages for such conduct. *(Hodgson v. Sagner, Inc.; Hodgson v. Baltimore Regional Joint Bd., Clothing & Textile Workers)*

However, an employer that was found to have violated the Act may not obtain contributions from the union to alleviate some of its back-pay liability, where the union that negotiated the discriminatory contract clauses was not sued by the aggrieved employees who sued the employer. *(Northwest Airlines v. Transport Workers)*

PENALTIES

As an amendment to the FLSA, the Equal Pay Act carries the same penalties for violations as FLSA violations: a two-year limitations period for nonwillful violations; a three-year limitations period plus liquidated damages for willful violations; and prejudgment interest and costs, where appropriate. *(Hill v. J.C. Penney Co.)*

REMEDIES

As stated earlier, an employer may not cure its equal pay violation by reducing the wage rate of the higher-paid employee to the rate of the lower-paid employee. The employer is required to raise the lower rate to equal the higher rate.

An employer may not cure a violation where males and females work in different classifications by merely permitting lower-paid female workers to transfer into the higher-paid male classifications as vacancies occur. *(Corning Glass Works v. Brennan; Schultz v. American Can Co.)*

Finally, an employer hoping to avoid a longer limitations period and liquidated damages liability may not rely on the advice of its attorney nor on the apparent complexity of the law to defend against a claim of "willfully" violating the Act. *(Hill v. J.C. Penney Co.)*

5
WALSH-HEALEY PUBLIC CONTRACTS ACT

The Walsh-Healey Public Contracts Act (WHA; WHM 90:201) predates the Fair Labor Standards Act of 1938 by two years. As originally designed, the WHA established employment standards for contractors furnishing or manufacturing materials, articles, or equipment for the U.S. government. In tandem with the National Recovery Act, the WHA was intended to move the country out of the depths of the Great Depression by directly aiding the common man by regulating the wage rates that had to be observed when doing business with the federal government.

Although the National Recovery Act was eventually ruled unconstitutional, the WHA is alive and well, and was most recently amended by Congress via the Department of Defense Authorization Act of 1986, which repealed the WHA's eight-hour day limit after which overtime rates had been mandatory. Currently, overtime pay at the rate of one-and-one-half times the regular rate of pay is required only for hours worked in excess of 40 per week.

In addition to regulating hours of work and wages for work performed under government contract, the Act addresses child labor, convict labor, and hazardous working conditions.

REQUIREMENTS

Under the WHA, all contractors who agree to undertake performance contracts for the federal government for the manufacturing or furnishing of materials, supplies, articles, and equipment in any amount exceeding $10,000 must stipulate that:

- All employees on the project, with certain exceptions, will be paid not less than the prevailing minimum rate determined by the Secretary of Labor for similar work in the locality;
- No employee will be permitted to work in excess of 40 hours in any week without the payment of overtime at a rate of time-and-one-half the employee's regular rate of pay for all hours in excess of 40 per week;
- No male worker under 16 years of age or female worker under 18 years of age will be employed on the contract;
- No convict laborer will be employed on the contract; and
- No part of the contract will be performed under working conditions that are unsanitary, hazardous, or dangerous to the health and safety of the employees.

The Secretary of Labor is authorized to permit an increase in the maximum hours of labor specified in the contracts executed under the Act, provided he establishes a rate of pay for overtime compensation that is not less than one-and-one-half times the basic hourly rate of pay received by any affected employee. The Secretary is also authorized to establish prevailing wage rates on an industrywide basis.

As administered by the Department of Labor's Wage-Hour Division, the WHA also applies to employees of manufacturers and "regular dealers" supplying the federal government with material, supplies, articles, or equipment on a contract whose value exceeds $10,000. Since the Act covers manufacturing and other public contract statutes cover "servicing" and "construction" and "alteration" and "repair," the courts have had to distinguish between these performances.

A typical dispute may involve large-scale repair of an engine; the issue becomes: "When does extensive 'repair' constitute wholesale 'manufacture'?" The Davis-Bacon Act (DBA), with the Contract Work Hours and Safety Standards Act, applies to mechanics and laborers engaged in the construction, alteration, or repair of public buildings or public works under contract with the federal government. Similarly, the McNamara-O'Hara Service Contract Act (Service Contract Act) governs service contracts performed for the federal government, and requires employers to pay employees the wages and fringe benefits prevailing in the locality, but in no event will the employees receive less than the minimum wage set under the Fair Labor Standards Act.

With this complex statutory scheme in mind, it becomes clear that some acts may be "cheaper" than others for the contractor performing under a government contact. This situation creates the incentive to operate, and ultimately to litigate, the extent of coverage of one federal contract act over another.

Where the government contract exceeds the $10,000 minimum amount, the WHA requires all primary and most secondary contractors (subcontractors or "subs") to comply with the standards unless their contracts are specifically exempt from the Act. The WHA, and certain regulations, have exempted such contracts as "open-market" agreements: contracts for the sale of perishables and other specified agricultural products, contracts for transport by common carrier, contracts for public utilities, and service contracts and rental agreements. (Contract exemptions will be discussed later in this chapter.)

All employees who actually work on the materials supplied under the government contract are covered by the WHA, including those engaged in manufacturing, fabricating, assembling, handling, supervising, or shipping. Employees who perform any preparatory work or other work necessary for the performance of the contract are also covered. If the contractor fails to segregate the work performed on the government contract from noncontract work, the WHA deems all employees as employed on the government contract and covered under the Act. As with the FLSA, all executive, administrative, and professional employees are exempt. Additionally, the WHA exempts all office and custodial workers from coverage. (Employee exemptions will be discussed in detail later in this chapter.)

COVERED CONTRACTS

Section 1 of the Act governs coverage over contracts and uses such phrases as "manufacturing," "furnishing," "fabrication," and "production." Such terms are inherently inartful, and changing needs and technology may make yesterdays "manufacturing" become tomorrow's "repair."

In a series of Wage-Hour Administrative Opinions, the Wage-Hour Division has interpreted these phrases in a way that the Act was found to cover contracts:

- For the "construction" of sled-targets and position buoys. The Administrator rejected a plea that the items were exempt because they were not "manufactured," since they were in fact "produced," "fabricated" and "furnished" to the government; *(In re Anderson & Cristofani)*
- For the reconditioning of tools. Where the work requires a complete or substantial rebuilding, it is regarded as "manufacturing"; (WH AdminOp, Oct. 22, 1941)
- For the erecting or installing of articles or equipment after delivery, such as the installation of generators requiring a prepared foundation; (WH AdminOp, 1941) and
- For the maintenance, servicing, and repair of government vehicles, since such a contract assumes that the contractor will provide a substantial amount of parts and supplies. (WH AdminOp, Oct. 7, 1964)

The Act also applies to the "construction, alteration, furnishing, or equipping of any naval vessel."

The Act specifies a dollar-amount of $10,000, and administrative practice has established several rules for applying this standard to individual contracts. For example, the stated price of the contract controls, even if prompt payment may reduce the amount due on the contract to less than the statutory minimum. Similarly, a postexecution reduction in contract price, even where both parties mutually agree on the reduction, will not remove the contract from the Act's coverage. *(United States v. Ozmer)*

If the contract price exceeds the statutory minimum, individual component parts of the contract and separate manufacturers are all covered, even if each component would sell for less than $10,000. Not surprisingly, where several contracts, each less than the statutory minimum, are awarded simultaneously by the government's acceptance of a single bid, then each contract is covered as if it met the statutory minimum. (WH AdminOp, May 3, 1957)

Contracts for indefinite amounts are covered, if they *may exceed* the $10,000 figure. When a contract's price is undetermined because of exigent circumstances, most commonly the "needs of the government," these open-ended contracts also fall under the Act. *(In re Norris, Inc.; In re Pelham's)* Additionally, purchase-notice agreements, also known as "supply" contracts, are covered.

COVERED CONTRACTORS

The Act covers a manufacturer whose contract with the government exceeds $10,000. The Wage-Hour Administrator has interpreted this phrase to encompass a person, corporation, partnership, or other, that owns, operates, or maintains a factory or establishment that produces on its premises the materials, supplies, articles, or equipment which is the basis for the contract. A prime contractor may be held liable for the violations of his subcontractor. *(United States v. Davison Fuel & Dock Co.)*

The Act also applies to a "regular dealer" in commodities, and the dealer's participation in a contract may expose a manufacturer who is not directly on the contract to liability under the contract. *(In re Negri)*

However, a regular dealer who contracts to furnish goods to the government may not be held liable for the failure of his manufacturing supplier to comply with the Act's wage and overtime provisions. *(United States v. New England Coal & Coke Co.)*

On the other hand, a substitute manufacturer, or successor contractor, who subcontracts part of the work he is obligated to perform may not be found liable for the violations of the "sub-substitute" manufacturer. *(In re Lyon & Borah, Inc.)*

PERSONAL LIABILITY

Section 2 of the Act provides that liability shall extend to the "party responsible." This provision has been used to impose personal liability on employer/contractor officials who would otherwise escape liability. The test for determining when personal liability should attach is whether the official *controlled* and *managed* the company during the relevant time in which the contract was performed. Under this test, employer officials were found liable, even though they did not sign the government contract, where they owned a majority of the stock and exercised exclusive control and supervision over the affairs of the contractor. (*In re A-AN-E Mfg. Corp.*)

On the other hand, a personnel director was found not to be personally liable, since he was not an officer of the contractor, had no property interest in it, and did not determine labor policy or control or manage the contractor's affairs.

However, financial interest of corporate officers, standing alone, is insufficient to bring these individuals within the meaning of "party responsible," such that personal liability would attach. (*United States v. Hudgins-Dize Co., Inc.*)

EXEMPTIONS

After it has been ascertained that an employer meets the Act's criteria for coverage (e.g., type of contract, dollar amount), the employer may attempt to fall within any of a number of exemptions contained both in the Act and in the regulations promulgated under the Act. There are three avenues for avoiding the Act's provisions: (*a*) subcontractor or successor employer exemptions; (*b*) employee exemptions, and (*c*) contract exemptions.

The Act specifically exempts open-market contracts (contracts which authorize the work to be done at rates currently available on the open market); contracts for the purchase of perishables, including dairy, livestock, and nursery products; agricultural or farm products processed for first sale by the original producers; contracts by the Secretary of Agriculture for the purchase of agricultural products; contracts for transportation by common carriers under published tariffs; and contracts with common carriers subject to the Federal Communications Act of 1934.

Under the regulations, the list of exempt contracts includes contracts for the construction of public works; rental of real or personal property; public utilities; delivery of newspapers, magazines, or periodicals by the publisher to sales agents or publisher representatives; and exclusive services.

The Secretary of Labor is authorized to exempt any contract that may impair the federal government's ability to conduct business, following a determination to that effect by the head of the federal agency involved in the contract. This authorization was used during World War II, but has fallen into disuse in recent years. (For further information, consult Walsh-Healey rulings and Interpretations No. 3, issued in 1955 and last amended in 1963, WHM 99:151.)

Most of the confusion/litigation in this exemption scheme has involved the exemptions for specified employee classifications and for specified contracts. These will be examined in detail.

Subcontractor/Successor Exemption

Generally, the Act does not apply to work performed by a manufacturer other than the original contractor, unless that work would *normally* have been performed by the contractor itself. Thus, subcontractors who actually fill part or all of the government contract are not covered by the Act if it is the "regular practice" in the industry for the prime contractor to purchase such goods rather than to manufacture them.

Where, however, a contractor subcontracts part of the work to another manufacturer, the producer of the commodities not manufactured by the original contractor is a "substitute manufacturer" who is considered fully covered by the Act. A prime contractor is liable for damages arising from violations committed by its substitute manufacturer.

Employee Exemptions

The Act covers *all* employees under a government contract, except office, supervisory, custodial, and maintenance workers who do any work in preparation for or that is necessary for performance of the contract. The Wage-Hour Division maintains an extensive list of workers who are not "directly working in production" but who are nevertheless covered by the Act. The line of demarcation appears to be whether the employee is doing *any work connected with* the manufacture, fabrication, assembling, handling, supervision, or shipment of materials, supplies, or equipment required under a government contract under the Act. If there is no work done in connection with such a contract, the employee most likely will not be covered by the Act. Employees performing commercial work on a contract who are separated from employees performing work on a government contract, for example, will be treated as exempt, provided the contractor's records keep such employees separate from the employees on the government contract.

The list of employees who are exempt by virtue of their not being directly involved in production under a government contract covered by the Act includes employees who only perform office work and whose work is not connected with the production of goods under the contract; custodial employees whose work is directed to the maintenance of the plant or facility and who are not involved in any work necessary for the fulfillment of the government contract; executive, administrative, and professional employees, as defined by the Wage-Hour Administrator under FLSA enforcement (exempt only from Walsh-Healey overtime provisions); foremen and instructors who do not operate machinery, perform manual work, or handle materials involved in a government contract; chief inspectors who are compensated on a salary basis and have a high degree of responsibility and authority; experimental workers who are not connected with the fulfillment of a government contract; requisition clerks who do nothing but prepare material orders and route orders through the plant; marine workers, if they are "seamen" under the FLSA; and convict laborers. However, paroled, pardoned, or discharged criminals, or prisoners participating in a work-release program are not deemed convict laborers for the purposes of this exemption.

Contract Exemptions

Several types of government contracts are exempt from the wage, hour, and child-labor provisions of the Act:

- Contracts for the construction of public works, which are covered by the Davis-Bacon and Contract Work Hours acts and the Anti-Kickback Law (Copeland Act);
- Contracts for agricultural or farm products processed for first sale by the original producer;
- Contracts made by the Secretary of Agriculture for the purchase of commodities or the products thereof;
- Contracts for the purchase of such materials, supplies, articles, or equipment "as may usually be bought in the open market" (the so-called open-market exemption). This exemption is construed by the Public Contracts Administrator as applying only to such purchases as the government *usually makes* in the open market, including purchases without ads for bids and purchases which the procurement agency is authorized to buy in the open market;
- Contracts for the "carriage of freight or personnel by vessel, airplane, bus, truck, express, or railway line where published tariff rates are in effect";
- Contracts exclusively for *personal* services;
- Contracts for the rental of real or personal property;
- Contracts for perishables, including dairy, livestock, and nursery products;
- Contracts for public utility services;
- Contracts for the furnishing of service by radio, telephone, telegraph, or cable companies subject to the Federal Communications Act of 1934; and
- Contracts to sales agents or publisher representatives for the delivery of newspapers, magazines, or periodicals by the publisher itself.

The Act also contains an exemption for "stockpiling" of goods, where the contractor "customarily" maintains a stockpile of material that cannot be identified as to the time work was done on any item in the pile.

RECORDKEEPING

The Act requires the contractor to maintain complete payroll records for each employee working on the government contract. These records must comply with FLSA requirements, and for purposes of Walsh-Healey compliance, must also contain injury-frequency rates, a record of the sex of each employee, and the number which identifies the contract on which each employee works.

ENFORCEMENT

The Secretary of Labor is authorized to investigate and decide cases involving alleged violations of the Act. This authority has been delegated to the Wage-Hour Administrator for daily enforcement purposes. Employers are liable for any under-payment of base wages or overtime and a penalty of $10 for each day an underage minor is employed.

The Defense Contract Administration Services is responsible for conducting compliance reviews, pre-award reviews and complaint investigations for covered federal contractors performing defense work. (See Appendix J for list of regional offices.)

Serious and willful violations of the Act may subject a contractor to the blacklist penalty which bars the receipt of a government contract by that contractor for a period of three years.

Back-pay claims under the WHA, like those under the FLSA, are governed by the Portal-to-Portal Pay Act, including limitations periods and liquidated damages liability. (See Chapter 3 for more on this issue.)

The WHA may apply to both the "manufacture" of equipment and the "installation" of equipment on the job site. Where more than an incidental amount of installation work is required, however, the Davis-Bacon Act (DBA) may enter the picture. Whether the WHA or DBA should govern such installation work will be determined by the Solicitor of Labor, who has issued "interpretative guidelines" in the past.

Similarly, if a contractor manufacturers goods under a government contract and the goods are shipped across state lines, the contractor will be subject both to the WHA and the FLSA. (WH AdminOp, Oct. 11, 1941) The Supreme Court rejected a a contractor's claim that the two laws could not apply concurrently, finding that the two laws are not mutually exclusive. (*Powell v. U.S. Cartridge Co.*)

6
McNamara-O'Hara
Service Contract Act

The McNamara-O'Hara Service Contract Act of 1965 (Service Contract Act or SCA; WHM 90:225) covers contracts with the federal government for the provision of services to the government. This differs from the Walsh-Healey Act, which covers contracts for the furnishing or manufacturing of goods, materials, and equipment to the federal government; and from the Davis-Bacon Act, which covers contracts for the provision of construction or supplies for construction of public buildings or public works.

Service employees generally include persons engaged in a recognized trade or craft or in a manual labor occupation. Such employees working under an SCA-covered contract must be paid the wages and fringe benefits prevailing in the locality, as determined by the Secretary of Labor. The Act allows the contractor to provide the service employee with any equivalent combination of fringe benefits or to make differential payments in cash.

The Act authorizes the Secretary of Labor to withhold accrued payments due on any contract to the extent necessary to pay covered workers the difference between wages and benefits required by the contract and those actually paid. Other sanctions against a noncomplying contractor include contract termination and debarment.

The Secretary of Labor is authorized to maintain a lawsuit against the contractor for any underpayments to SCA-covered employees. The Secretary is also authorized to determine if "unusual circumstances" exist to warrant a lesser penalty than the three-year blacklist penalty under the debarment provision of the Act. The courts have ruled that only the Secretary is authorized to bring an action under the Act, while individual employees are restricted to administrative proceedings.

COVERAGE

The SCA covers all contracts with the federal government exceeding $2,500 in amount, whose primary purpose is the providing of *services* to the government. (In August 1986, Congress considered raising the minimum dollar amount on SCA coverage from $2,500 per contract to $1 million. The change, embodied in the Department of Defense authorization bill, S.2638, was defeated. Additional attempts may be made in the future to raise the threshold, however.)

Covered Contracts

The Act applies to contracts the "principal purpose" of which is the furnishing of services to the United State through the use of service employees. Unless specified otherwise, any contract with the government that is not for construction or supplies is a contract for services, according to the Wage-Hour Administrator. In a series of Administrative Opinions, the Division has determined that the SCA covers contracts for:

- Equipment or vehicle rental including the equipment or vehicle operator;
- Surveying;
- Mapping;
- Spraying operations;
- Cafeteria and dormitory services;
- Car-washing, wheel-packing, chassis lubrication, vehicle maintenance, and storage;
- Office-equipment repair;
- Landscaping and grounds maintenance;
- Laundry services for the Armed Services;
- Subsurface exploration, involving drilling for soil samples and rock cores;
- Mail transportation;

- Shipping and storing of household goods;
- Printing and duplicating services, but only if the principal object of the contract is for services and the furnishing of printed or duplicated matter is secondary to the contract's main purpose;
- Computer maintenance and watch repair;
- Fire protection services;
- Engineering, design, programming, and testing;
- Furnishing hotel accommodations to military personnel;
- Inspection and maintenance services;
- Veterans' convalescent care in nursing homes; and
- Garbage removal.

This is only a partial list of covered contracts under the current $2,500 threshold. Suffice to say that, with a low threshold, few contracts for services for the government will ever be lower than the $2,500 minimum.

Section 7 of the Act concerns exemptions from SCA coverage. Where the Act is silent, and in line with the Administrator's pronouncements, certain operations may be regarded as covered in the absence of specific exclusions. These operations include:

- Galvanizing of steel products;
- Design functions;
- Motion-picture production; and
- Preparing title certificates for real property transactions.

Section 7 of the Act provides a list of exemptions from SCA coverage. This list includes:

- Contracts for constructing or repairing public works or public buildings;
- Contracts covered by the Walsh-Healey Act;
- Contracts for the carriage of freight or personnel where published tariffs are in effect;
- Contracts for the furnishing of services by radio, telephone, telegraph, or cable companies;
- Contracts for public utility services;
- Contracts for employment where an individual or indi-

viduals are to provide direct services to a federal agency; and

- Contracts with the U.S. Postal Service for the operation of a postal contract station.

The Wage-Hour Division, in determining which contracts are covered under the Act, has also established which contracts are not covered. The Division's list of exempt contracts includes contracts for:

- Medical services at a hospital under a Medicare program;
- Renting of parking spaces;
- Creating topographic maps;
- Renting of motor vehicles;
- Managing, operating, and maintaining research centers and a job corps center for women;
- Relocating persons under an agreement with a local re-development agency under the Federal Urban Renewal Program, even though the federal government pays all the expenses of moving an occupant displaced by urban renewal; and
- Tree-trimming, tree removing, and landscaping functions that are part of an urban renewal project.

In many of these instances, the Division has treated a contract as exempt if the contract is not "entered into by the United States" as a contracting party. (WH AdminOp, Apr. 20, 1966, WHM 99:2114)

Covered Employees

Under the Act, service contractors are required to pay the wages and fringe benefits prevailing in the locality to all "service employees" engaged in contract performance, including guards, watchmen, and any person in a recognized craft or trade, in a skilled mechanical craft, or in unskilled, semiskilled, or skilled manual labor occupations. The Act extends to foremen and supervisors whose jobs primarily require trade, craft, or laboring experience.

In addition to those employees who actually perform the service required under the contract, the Act covers workers whose duties are "necessary" to contract performance. Such employees include office workers who do clerical work in connection with the contract, for example. (WH AdminOp, May 16, 1966, WHM 99:2114) Additionally, an individual who meets the definition of a service employee under the Act is also covered, regardless of the relationship existing between the individual and the contracting entity.

In 1976, Congress amended the Act by including in Section 8(b) a complete definition of "service employee":

> The term "service employee" means any person engaged in the performance of a contract entered into by the United States and not exempted under section 7, whether negotiated or advertised, the principal purpose of which is to furnish services in the United States (other than any person employed in a bona fide executive, administrative or professional capacity, as those terms are defined in part 541 of title 29, Code of Federal Regulations, as of July 30, 1976 and any subsequent revision of those regulations); and shall include all such persons regardless of any contractual relationship that may be alleged to exist between a contractor or subcontractor and such persons.

The language was intended to be all-inclusive. It obviates a series of Administrative Opinions issued by the Division that interpreted a publication by the Civil Service Commission (now the Office of Personnel Management, OPM) entitled "Handbook of Blue-Collar Occupational Families and Series." Under the present scheme, the OPM administers the Act. Whether a particular individual falls under the Act turns on whether he/she may be classified as a bona fide executive, administrative, or professional employee within the meaning of the FLSA.

PREVAILING WAGE STANDARD

The Act provides three bases for determining what rates will be paid to service employees:

- The wage rates for similar employment prevailing in the locality, as determined by the Secretary of Labor; or
- The rates established in a collective bargaining contract covering service employees including future wage increases; or
- The minimum wage rate under the FLSA, where no prevailing wage rate determination has been made.

The Act does not contain an overtime standard, but it states that all SCA contracts are covered by the Contract Work Hours and Safety Standards Act, which provides that in computing overtime compensation, the regular or basic rate of pay will be the same as that under the FLSA. The Secretary is required to establish prevailing wage rates for all contracts where five or more service employees are employed.

A primary element of an SCA prevailing wage case concerns the parameters of the locality which governs the wage rate determination. One federal court has held that "locality" should be given its ordinary and common meaning and that this phrase has a meaning under the SCA that is different from its meaning under the Walsh-Healey Act. Rejecting the Labor Secretary's claim that a nationwide locality was appropriate, the court advised that in 98 percent of cases, the Standard Metropolitan Statistical Area standard used by the EEOC was an adequate basis for establishing the locality. (*Southern Packaging & Storage Co. v. United States*)

Another court held that the prevailing rates should have been those for comparable employment in the area where the services were to be performed, rather than the location of the government installation which sought the contract. (*Descomp, Inc. v. Sampson*)

Finally, an administrative law judge determined that the locality was the county, not the federal enclave involved, where the appropriate criteria were:

- Comparability of similar employment in the surrounding area;
- The area in which the work force possessing similar skills resides; and
- An identifiable and related geographical area that may serve as a basis for making the required comparison. (*In re Applicability of Bargained Wages*)

SUCCESSORS

Section 4(c) of the Act binds successor contractors to the collective bargaining contract of the predecessor contractor, according to the Secretary of Labor. *(In re Eastern Serv. Mgmt. Co.)* However, successorship and seniority rights under the contract are not fringe benefits within the meaning of Section 4(c), and therefore a successor contractor did not violate the Act when he failed to hire some of the predecessor's employees and hired others at lower pay. *(Clark v. Unified Servs.)*

VARIANCE PROCEEDINGS

Section 4(c) also relieves a contractor from the obligation to comply with the contractually established wages and fringe benefits of the predecessor's contract, if the Labor Secretary finds that such wages and fringes are "substantially at variance with those which prevail for services of a character similar in the locality." *(In re Applicability of Bargained Wages)* The variance determination can therefore legally interfere with the collective bargaining process.

Where a contracting officer modified the prevailing wage rate on a construction project, a question was raised whether the federal government was bound by the modification based on the officer's erroneous interpretation of the regulation governing effective modifications. The court found that the contractor's request for an adjustment in the contract price was justified and that the government was bound to it since the officer's modification was not "palpably illegal" and there is nothing in writing saying that an officer is not authorized to make mistakes of law. *(Broad Ave. Laundry v. United States)*

WAGE PAYMENTS AND DEDUCTIONS

Noncompliance with the Act's wage provisions, either by nonpayment or underpayment, was found in the following rulings:

- Employees may not bargain away the payment of wages secured to them by the Act, and therefore, their signatures on erroneous time cards do not affect their entitlement;
- The contractor cannot attempt to comply with the Act by reallocating portions of payments made for other

hours which are in excess of the specified minimum wage; and

- Payments to employees of amounts in excess of the minimum wages required in one workweek may not be credited toward amounts required to be paid in another workweek, since workweeks stand independent of one another. *(In re Roman)*

An employer was found to have violated the prevailing minimum wage requirements, as a result of certain deductions, which lowered the employee's wages below the statutory minimum in the following decisions;

- Where the employer deducted the cost of uniform laundering for food service employees; *(In re Quality Maintenance Co.)* and
- Where the employer required a prospective employee to pay for the cost of a uniform required to be worn on the job. (WH AdminOp, July 7, 1974, WH-274, WHM 95:138)

Finally, the Act requires the contractor to maintain adequate records of hours worked and wages paid to service employees. This requirement has led to a series of rulings on whether the employer has complied with the Act:

- Where an employee performs work on a covered contract and on nongovernment work in the same workweek, the records must effectively segregate the types of work performed. If the records are inadequate, the employee must be paid according to the Act's requirements for all hours in any workweek if he works for any part of a day in that workweek on a covered contract; (WH AdminOp, Mar. 14, 1966, WHM 99:2435)
- Where a maintenance worker spent part of his time on government work and part of his time on nongovernment work, the employer was not allowed to apply a pro rata system of wage payment, as an alternative to adequate recordkeeping, since this did not constitute compliance with the Act; (WH AdminOp, July 19, 1968) and

● Failure to maintain adequate records of segregated work only requires the government to show the amount and extent of work as a matter of "just and reasonable inference," even though the result is only approximate. *(In re Roman)*

FRINGE BENEFITS

The Act requires the contractor to furnish such fringe benefits as the Secretary determines to be prevailing for such employees in the locality. A contractor may satisfy his obligation to furnish specific fringe benefits by providing any equivalent combination of benefits or by making equivalent or differential payments in cash.

Since a contractor may discharge his fringe benefit obligation by paying the employee an equivalent amount in cash, the question has frequently arisen whether the cash value of the payment was in fact equal to the fringe that would otherwise have been provided. For example, to find the hourly cash equivalent of a "one week paid vacation," the employee's rate of pay is multiplied by the number of hours of vacation, using a standard 8-hour day and 40-hour week, unless otherwise specified. The total annual amount is divided by 2080, the number of regular working hours in a 52-week period, to arrive at the cash equivalent. (WH AdminOp, Aug. 15, 1966).

Where the determination lists the holidays for which payment is required under the Act, the contractor must furnish the holiday off with pay. The contractor may substitute another day off with pay if the substitution is done according to a plan that has been communicated to the affected employees. The contractor may pay the employee cash equivalents for specific holidays. (WH AdminOp, Jan. 28, 1970, WHM 99:2351)

A contractor may meet the health and welfare benefits requirement by maintaining a self-insured plan, where the contractor has not refused to pay a claim or to provide an employee with a benefit required by the contract, and there has been no evidence of bad faith by the contractor. *(White Glove-Building Maintenance, Inc. v. Hodgson)* The contractor's notice of its self-insured plan to all new employees satisfies the requirement that the substitution be made according to a plan that has been communicated to the affected employees. *(White Glove-Building Maintenance, Inc. v. Brennan)*

Severance pay is a fringe benefit and must be included in the wage determination and the new government contract, unless after an administrative hearing, it is found to be inconsistent with the prevailing wages in the locality. *(Trinity Servs., Inc. v. Usery)*

FRINGE OFFSETS AND PAYMENTS

Under the Act a contractor may not:

- Obtain contributions toward fringe benefits from its employees to satisfy the fringe benefit standards set by the Secretary; (WH AdminOp, Apr. 7, 1966)
- Offset social security payments by decreasing its contribution to employee retirement funds; (WH AdminOp, Apr. 14, 1966) and
- Offset fringe benefit payments made for hours spent on nongovernment work against an employer's fringe obligation for work done on a government contract. (WH AdminOp, June 7, 1967)

Service employees of a contractor are entitled to receive fringe benefit payments for hours they do not work but for which they are paid even though such hours are holidays or vacation time. The Labor Department has ruled that the contractor does not have the prerogative to apply the wage determination in a manner that it considered reasonable. *(In re Emerald Maintenance, Inc.)*

Finally, as with the segregation of government- and nongovernment work, the Act requires adequate recordkeeping of fringe benefit payments that are made as cash equivalents in lieu of fringes. *(In re Aarid Van Lines)*

ENFORCEMENT

The Act may not be enforced through a private action, since the enforcement responsibilities are assigned exclusively to the Labor Secretary. *(Teamsters Local 427 v. Philco-Ford Corp.;*

Foster v. Parker Transfer Co.) Although the Act limits the right to bring an action to the Secretary, it provides a range of mechanisms for obtaining compliance and/or imposing liabilities and penalties. The Act authorizes:

- The withholding of amounts due under a contract sufficient to pay employees the difference between the wages and the benefits required under the contract and those actually received;
- Court action against the contractor, subcontractor, or surety bond to recover any remaining amount of under-payments;
- Termination of the contract with the contractor liable for any resulting cost to the federal government;
- Imposition of a debarment list (blacklist), banning a contractor from receiving a government contract for a period of three years, unless the Labor Secretary finds "unusual circumstances."

Where the Labor Secretary withholds sums due the contractor based on a finding of noncompliance with the wage and fringe benefit provisions of the Act, the amounts withheld are deposited in a special fund, and paid to the employees directly upon determinations of how much each is to receive.

The Secretary is authorized to maintain an action for deficiencies where amounts withheld are insufficient to cover underpayments due employees. Any money not disbursed to employees is turned over the the U.S. Treasury.

If the contractor violates any provision of the contract, the contracting agency may cancel the contract upon written notice to the contractor. The government may charge the original contractor with any added costs incurred in obtaining contract completion through a substitute contractor.

LIMITATIONS PERIOD

An important distinction between the SCA and other federal public contract acts is that the SCA contains its own statute of limitations rather than borrowing the two-year period from the FLSA.

The Portal-to-Portal Pay Act does not include the SCA within its coverage, and the Fourth Circuit reasoned that this omission by Congress was not inadvertent. Although this omission creates an inconsistency in enforcement of public contracts acts, the court ruled, the SCA limitations period is the six-year general statute of limitations under 28 U.S.C. Sec. 2415. *(United States v. Deluxe Cleaners & Laundry, Inc.)*

Although the SCA does not follow FLSA limitations periods (through the Portal Act), it does adopt FLSA case law in appropriate circumstances. Approving the imposition of pre-judgment interest on a noncomplying contractor, a federal district court held that silence on this issue within the SCA was not enough to defeat FLSA case law authorizing the grant of prejudgment interest in similar cases. *(United States v. Powers Bldg. Maintenance Co.)*

The SCA contains recordkeeping requirements similar to those in the Walsh-Healey Act, particularly with reference to the segregation of government and nongovernment work. These records must be made available for inspection by authorized representatives of the Wage-Hour and Public Contracts Divisions.

BLACKLIST PENALTY

The Act requires that a noncomplying contractor be placed on the debarment list for a period of three years. The 1972 amendments to the SCA limited the Secretary's authority to deviate from this penalty, such that variance may only be granted upon a finding by the Secretary of "unusual circumstances." *(In re Dokken)*

The Act does not define "unusual circumstances," but certain elements should be present to justify such a finding. These include:

- Where the violation is clear and the contractor's conduct is culpable, willful, or aggravated, relief is not appropriate;
- Where there is a legitimate dispute as to a contract term leading to the violation, a contractor should not be penalized for electing to litigate an issue in doubt;

- Where the contractor's conduct is not culpable, consideration should be given to the nature and gravity of the violation, its impact on the unpaid employees, and any good-faith conduct by the contractor to correct the violation and comply with the Act. *(In re Emerald Maintenance, Inc.)*

"Unusual circumstances" have been found in the following situations:

- Undercapitalization and poor bookkeeping; *(In re Glover)*
- No prior history of violations, a bona fide dispute, the contractor's position was not frivolous, and the amount in dispute was small; *(In re Taskpower Int'l, Inc.)*
- Confusion concerning the number of years of experience necessary to qualify for accumulating vacation benefits and the contractor's reliance on statements of the contracting officer; *(In re Myers & Myers, Inc.)* and
- Action by the contracting agency that resulted in substantial monetary loss to the contractor. *(In re Quality Maintenance Co.)*

Contractors have been debarred based on a failure to demonstrate "unusual circumstances" in the following cases:

- Financial difficulties; *(In re Van Elk)*
- Ignorance of legal requirements and a nonchalant approach to ending violations; *(In re McLaughlin Storage, Inc.)*
- Wage determination was at substantial variance with the prevailing rate in the locality but the contractor made no effort to have the determination corrected or modified; *(In re Electric City Linoleum, Inc.)* and
- Simple negligent conduct. *(In re Dynamic Enters., Inc.)*

ATTORNEY'S FEES

The SCA is silent on the matter of attorney's fees awards. However, Congress has provided for an award of reasonable attorney's fees "to the prevailing party in any civil action brought by or against the United States . . . in any court having jurisdiction of such action." (Equal Access to Justice Act, 28 U.S.C. Sec. 2412(b)

The U.S. Court of Appeals for the Federal Circuit had an opportunity to address the application of the Equal Access to Justice Act (EAJA) in the context of a contractor that successfully protested an action of a federal contracting agency.

A public contractor was denied an upward price adjustment in the contract by a contracting officer. The Armed Services Board of Contract Appeals upheld the denial, even though it conceded that the officer's decision was based on her erroneous interpretation of an SCA regulation.

The contractor successfully appealed the Board's ruling to the U.S. Court of Claims, which granted the price adjustment but said nothing about the cost of the litigation. *(Broad Ave. Laundry v. United States)* The contractor then filed its request for fees under EAJA with the U.S. Court of Appeals for the Federal Circuit.

The EAJA provides that an agency or a court, in any "adversary adjudication" or "civil action . . . brought by or against the United States, shall award to a prevailing party other than the United States fees and other expenses, unless the position of the agency or the United States 'was substantially justified or that special circumstances make an award unjust.' "

The contractor was clearly a prevailing party as a result of the Claims Court's decision in favor of the price adjustment. The issue to be resolved by the appeals court was the meaning of the "position of the government" language in EAJA. The court rejected the claim that the Act was intended to cover the government's position at the administrative proceeding before the Board. It held, instead, that the "position of the government" meant the government's stance in litigation. The position of the government was therefore "substantially justified" in litigation, the court concluded, and no attorney's fees were awarded.

7

DAVIS-BACON ACT

The Davis-Bacon Act of 1931 (DBA; WHM 90:251) along with the Anti-Kickback Law (Copeland Act) and Contract Work Hours and Safety Standards Act, establishes employment standards for laborers and mechanics on public construction projects let under federal contracts for amounts in excess of $2,000. In 1986, the Senate Armed Services Committee approved a defense authorization bill that would raise the threshold for application of the Davis-Bacon Act prevailing wage provisions on military construction projects funded under the legislation from $2,000 to $250,000. The amendment was defeated, but since the original $2,000 floor was established in 1935, additional attempts to raise it can be expected.

The DBA requires covered contracts to specify prevailing minimum wage rates for various classes of mechanics and laborers employed on the project. Covered contracts include highway building, dredging, demolition, cleaning, and painting and decorating of public buildings. Covered employees include all mechanics and laborers employed directly on the site of the project, including subcontractor employees. Employees of "materialmen" (companies that supply material for the work away from the construction site and that maintain establishments where their goods are sold to the general public) are exempt if they do not spend more than 20 percent of their worktime at the construction site.

COVERAGE

In an early dispute concerning coverage of the Act, a conflict arose between the Comptroller General and the Attorney

General over the status of workers performing dredging operations. The Secretary of Labor had originally found that these workers were akin to mechanics and construction laborers, and therefore subject to the Act. The Attorney General held, to the contrary, that these workers are more like "seamen" and should be covered by the Maritime Workers Act rather than the DBA. The Comptroller General settled the dispute by siding with the Labor Secretary on the ground that the administration and enforcement responsibilities were delegated to the Labor Department and the Labor Secretary's position must control. (Comp Gen Dec. B-105067, Nov. 6, 1951)

This dispute illustrates the difficulty in establishing the parameters of the Act's coverage. The Act extends coverage based on the type of work called for in the contract, the type of contract involved, and the type of contractor involved.

The Act covers any lease-purchase agreement with the government for buildings or conversions, extensions, additions, or remodeling of existing structures. (Labor Solic Op, Dec. 1954) However, the Act does not apply to construction, alteration, or repair of buildings for occupancy by the federal government under any term-lease or lease-option agreement, since these types of contracts evidence a lack of a *firm commitment* by the government to acquire more than a lease-hold interest in the property. (Comp Gen Dec. B-122382, July 18, 1962)

Demolition work as part of a contract for initial construction or demolition performed as part of "initial construction" (i.e., closely related or immediately incidental thereto, is covered by the labor standards provisions of the Act. (Asst. Labor Solic Op, June 20, 1961)

The Act has been interpreted to cover other contracts, including:

- The plugging of oil and gas wells and the removal of above-ground equipment in connection with the construction of a reservoir; (Solic Op, June 13, 1961)
- The spreading of oil on road surfaces during the construction of a highway, at the construction site; (Solic Ops, Oct. 8, 1962 and Nov. 6, 1962)
- The renting of equipment to a covered contractor, where the rental agreement calls for the employees of the rental

company to operate the equipment on the construction project at the worksite; *(In re Griffith Co.)*

- The cleaning operations on public buildings or works performed by the process of steam or sandblast cleaning; (Solic Op, July 17, 1961)
- Contracts performed under the Area Redevelopment Act of 1961 must comply with the DBA's prevailing minimum wages (and overtime provisions of the Contract Work Hours and Safety Standards Act); and
- Contracts performed under the Federal-Aid Highway Act of 1956 (Sec. 115 of the Act).

In each of these agreements, it was determined that the work in question essentially constituted an "integral part" of the prime contractor's performance of its government contract. *(Sansone Co. v. California Dep't of Transp.)* Although not determinative, the "integral part" element is important in establishing the scope of the Act's coverage. The Act does not cover contracts for:

- The preparation of materials for a construction project away from the construction site and delivery in final form at the worksite, if the workers do not spend more than 20 percent of their time at the worksite; (Solic Op, Oct. 1942)
- The delivery of crushed stone from a quarry to a construction site, where the workers unload the stone merely by lifting the "tailgate" on the truck and perform no other work at the site; (Asst. Solic Op, Oct. 11, 1961)
- The delivery of standard materials (e.g., concrete aggregate, hot mix, and sand) to a construction site, performed independently of the contract; *(Zachry Co. v. United States)*
- The prefabrication of component roof panels for the contract, where the prefabrication work normally cannot be done at the construction site; (Solic Op, Aug. 2, 1961)
- The supplies, including installing or maintaining work that is only incidental to the furnishing of such supplies. However, the Act covers contracts for installation involving substantial construction, for transportation of

supplies to or from the building site by the contractor or subcontractor, such as window frames or millwork;

- Servicing or maintenance work in a building that is completed or substantially completed; the Act covers servicing or maintenance performed as part of the construction or repair of the public buildings or works;
- The complete dismantling or demolition of a construction site, where no construction is done by the dismantling or demolition company;
- Exploratory drilling;
- Construction work closely related to research and development, where the research work cannot be done separately, or where the construction work is the subject of the research;
- The construction or repair of vessels, aircraft, or other kinds of personal property; and
- Work outside the continental United States or a place not known or reasonably determinable at the time the contract is executed.

In addition, the Act does not cover preliminary survey work such as the preparation of metes and bounds prior to construction, especially if performed pursuant to a separate contract. Survey work done immediately prior to or during construction, performed as an aid to the crafts that are engaged in the actual construction project, is considered covered. (Solic Op, June 1960; Sec. Lab., Aug. 2, 1962)

Other work not regarded as Davis-Bacon work includes work performed off the construction site, whether done by contractors, subcontractors, or materialmen (Comp Gen Dec. B-148076, July 26, 1963) and certain types of installation work performed during the actual construction, that is only incidental to the actual construction. (Solic Op, Mar. 3, 1964)

The distinction between which contracts are covered and which are not is often characterized in terms of the work called for. Where the work brings the workers into close integration with ("integral part" of) the prime contractor's performance, the workers are classified as employees of a subcontractor covered under the Act. Where the workers do not perform work that is integral to the prime contractor's performance, they are classified as materialmen and not covered under the contract. But whether the examination focuses on the language in the contract or on the workers' classification, the determination turns on the actual nature of the work performed in relation to the prime contractor's performance.

Employees engaged in assembling major components of houses to be erected on nearby sites, for example, were deemed to be subcontractor employees, covered by the Act, even though they were employed in a mobile factory that could be located at a different site. The mobile factory operations are distinguishable from those of a factory producing prefabricated homes or components for a variety of customers, which may be regarded as a variant of the traditional materialman serving the construction industry. The employees performed work that was integrally related to the final assembly or conventional construction activities on the worksite, and thus constitute a part of the overall assembly or construction. (Solic Op, Aug. 27, 1969)

A variety of factors enters into the determination of whether a particular contract is covered by the Act, but the most decisive would appear to be the degree of integration or integral relations between the sub and prime contractors' performance.

In view of the variety of factors that can enter into the determination of whether a particular contract may be covered by the Act, it is advisable to contact the U.S. Labor Department, Davis-Bacon Office for clarification. (See Appendix J, Contract Standards Operations Division)

CONFLICT WITH OTHER LAWS

When a contract calls for installation work, there may be some doubt as to whether the amount of installation work is substantial enough to justify coverage by the DBA, or whether the installation is merely incidental to the construction project, thus warranting Walsh-Healey Act coverage. A contract calling for the installation of Minuteman missile equipment at a construction site was determined to be only "incidental" to the construction project, since it involved a minimal amount of time. Therefore, the Act did not apply. (Solic Op, Apr. 16, 1962)

But where the construction costs were the major part of an installation contract, or where the installation was complex and substantial, the installation contract was deemed to be within the Act's coverage. (Solic Ops, Nov. 6, 1961 and Nov. 30, 1961)

An employer who was the subject of an FLSA action by employees loading and unloading government goods at an Army reservation was unsuccessful in establishing that the Davis-Bacon Act covered, and thus shielded it, from FLSA liability. The court declared that only laborers engaged in the construction or repair of public works, and not employees of a private firm working on a government reservation, were covered by the DBA. It added that the DBA and FLSA statutes are not necessarily incompatible. *(Ortiz v. San Juan Dock Co., Inc.; Walling v. Patton-Tulley Transp. Co.)*

PREVAILING WAGES

Unlike the Walsh-Healey Act, the Davis-Bacon Act authorizes the Labor Secretary to establish prevailing wage rates on a contract-by-contract basis. The Secretary is required to conduct a survey of the wage rates prevailing in the "locality" and to set DBA rates for the contract according to those rates. Area and regional differentials are thus recognized in the setting of rates under the DBA.

The Secretary is also required to establish a scale of rates for the various classifications of workers on a particular project, rather than establishing one minimum prevailing wage rate for the project or industry. The classifications range from "helpers" to apprentices to laborers to journeymen, and each rate takes into consideration the locality. Thus the setting of such rates is a very complex and time-consuming process that has led to much litigation..

The constitutionality of the statutory mechanism for setting the prevailing wage rates for separate job classifications under the Act was contested and upheld in 1938. *(Gilioz v. Webb)* Similarly, the Supreme Court has declared that the Secretary's determination is not subject to judicial review. *(United States v. Binghamton Constr. Co.)* However, changes in the regulations implementing the process of setting the wage rates may be challenged, where the charging party demonstrates a substantial likelihood that it will prevail on the merits based on such things as improper promulgation of the regulations under the Administrative Procedure Act. *(Building & Constr. Trades v. Donovan)*

Because the Secretary's wage determinations are nonreviewable by a court, Congress established the Wage Appeals Board in 1964 to review:

- Wage determinations;
- Debarment cases;
- Controversies concerning payment of wages or proper classifications involving large sums of money or large groups of employees, or novel situations; and
- Adjustment of liquidated damages assessed under the Contract Work Hours and Safety Standards Act (WHM 90:271). Determinations of the Wage Appeals Board are reviewable on the grounds of lack of due process *(Framlau Corp. v. Dembling)* and fraud or gross error *(Southwest Eng'g Corp. v. United States)*.

Wage determination disputes usually arise at the time the rates are set, but do not get adjudicated until well after contract completion. Therefore, most disputes involve a contractor's attempt to gain reimbursement for what it regards as improperly high rates. In denying reimbursement, the U.S. Supreme Court has ruled that the rates established by the Secretary and included in the contract are not a representation or a warranty that such rates are prevailing in the local community. *(United States v. Binghamton Constr. Co.)*

Contractors have pursued reimbursement under three theories: *(a)* equitable adjustment, *(b)* mutual mistake of fact, and *(c)* redetermination of rates. The first two theories stem from basic contract law, and the third theory is the result of administrative practice by the Wage-Hour Division.

Under the equitable adjustment theory, a contractor was entitled to obtain $18,000 that a contracting officer had withheld following a downward redetermination of rates by the Labor Secretary. The rates had originally been set higher than what prevailed in the locality, and the contractor had originally submitted its bid based on the actual rates prevailing in the locality. The Court of Claims ruled that there was no equitable basis for the contracting agency to obtain the completed contract at a price less than that which it agreed to pay. The contractor was thus found equitably entitled to the reimbursement it sought. *(Burnett Constr. Co. v. United States)*

Under the mutual mistake of fact theory, the contractor obtained reimbursement based on the Labor Department's delay in adjusting the prevailing rates until after the contract was executed. The contractor incurred increased labor costs at the government's direction, and the court ruled that the parties had contracted under a mutual mistake of fact as to the maximum and minimum rates prevailing in the locality. The contract may be reformed to reflect the true intent of the parties. *(Poirier & McLane Corp. v. United States)*

Under the redetermination of rates concept, a contractor was denied an adjustment, even though he incurred higher labor costs due to higher rates set after the contract was executed. The contract contained a clause for payment of wages to be determined by the Secretary *after* the contract was executed, and the Court of Claims stated that this clause was not against public policy, since it had been included for the benefit of the workers, rather than for the benefit of the contractor. *(Bushman Constr. Co. v. United States)*

However, a union unsuccessfully sought to compel a state transportation department to incorporate the appropriate prevailing wages in bid solicitations for a construction project pursuant to the Act. The transportation department had included in the original solicitation the wage rates erroneously published in the Federal Register, and two federal agencies had notified the department of this fact 11 days before the scheduled date of opening of the bids. The court noted that the union had obtained all the substantive relief it sought prior to the instant action, and the union was merely seeking to preserve its status as a "prevailing party" for purposes of an award of attorneys' fees. *(Operating Eng'rs Local 3 v. Bohn)*

A final aspect of prevailing wage rate determinations involves Comptroller General rulings, such as:

- Obsolete rates may be adjusted by a change order; (Comp Gen Dec. B-106987, May 8, 1953)
- Issuance of a letter of inadvertence, acknowledging a mistake in the rate included in the contract, does not automatically authorize a change in the contract price; (Comp Gen Dec. B-129205, Nov. 15, 1957)
- Changed wage rates originally included in a contract to require payment of building instead of heavy-highway schedules represents a change in judgment, rather than a correction of inadvertent errors; (Comp Gen Dec. B-150293, Feb. 13, 1963)
- The Labor Secretary cannot restrict the use of spray painting work under a prevailing wage rate determination; (Comp Gen Dec. B-132044, June 10, 1957) and
- A Project Stabilization Agreement negotiated by construction industry employers and unions could be included in contracts for certain missile programs, in the interest of national defense, under the National Defense Contracts Act of 1958. The agreement covered all construction, fabrication, and related work covered by the Act at two military facilities, and called for the payment of fringe benefits and overtime pay. (Comp Gen Dec. B-148930, July 2, 1962)

FRINGE BENEFITS

Contributions to fringe benefit funds may not be counted toward satisfying the minimum prevailing wage rates in the contract under the Act, unless the wage rate determination specifically indicates that the fringes are included in the rates. The Act was amended in 1965 to allow contractors to combine wage payments and fringe contributions, if they added up to the total in the wage-fringe determination. However, this does not permit the contract to apply this "mix" formula to wage-only determinations. The Labor Solicitor issued a memorandum in 1965 to clarify the crediting of fringe benefit contributions in meeting Act wage determinations. (Solic Memo, Oct. 15, 1965)

ENFORCEMENT

In view of the Act's purpose of protecting the wage standards of workers performing under government contracts, the Act and the regulations provide for a variety of methods for ensuring that workers receive the prevailing wages set in the contract.

For example, noncompliance by the contractor entitles the contracting agency to cancel the contract and to seek money from the contractor for the extra costs incurred in finding a substitute performer on the contract. Similarly, the Comptroller General may pay the workers directly and seek reimbursement from the contractor for any deficiencies. The government may also set off payments due the contractor under one contract for deficiencies under another contract where the contractor has failed to pay the prevailing wages. Finally, the workers themselves may bring an action to recover unpaid wages under Section 3(b) of the Act. If the contract does not contain prevailing wages, however, there is no private right of action under the Act.

As with the FLSA and the Walsh-Healey Act, Davis-Bacon Act lawsuits are governed by the Portal-to-Portal Pay Act, including limitations period determinations and imposition of liquidated damages liability. (See Chapter 3 for further information.)

Employee Actions

The Act does not specifically confer on individual employees the right to bring an action for unpaid wages under a contract. On remand from the U.S. Supreme Court, however, the Court of Appeals for the Seventh Circuit made the definitive ruling on employee actions under the Act. It held:

- Laborers and mechanics are the "especial" beneficiaries of the Act, since the legislative history of the Act reveals that its fundamental purpose was to benefit laborers and mechanics by assuring they receive prevailing wages;
- The Act's grant of a right of action applies only to an action on a surety bond issued under the Miller Act, which requires the posting of a surety bond on most government contracts covered by the DBA;

- Employees have an implied right of action which effectuates congressional intent in passing the statute;
- The right to recover unpaid portions of the prevailing wage is based on congressional policy, despite the fact that an action for breach of an employment contract is traditionally a state-court action. *(McDaniel v. University of Chicago)*

An important aspect of this particular case, which led to the recognition of a private right of action, albeit "inferred," was that the statutory remedies available under the Act were ineffective in remedying the employees' injury from underpayments:

- No funds had been withheld from the contractor, so no monies could be forwarded to the employees or set off against another contract;
- No bond had been required against which the government could move on behalf of the employees;
- The government chose not to invoke the sanctions of contract termination or blacklisting. Had any of these circumstances not existed, the government would have had a means of using the statutory remedies to make "whole" the victims (employees) of the employer's noncompliance.

The existence of prevailing wages in the contract provides a basis for creating the inference of the private right of action. The absence of such wage rates destroys this inference, and allowing employees to sue under such circumstances would undercut the administrative mechanism created to assure consistency in the administration and enforcement of the Act. *(Universities Research Ass'n v. Coutu)*

Actions Against U.S. Government

Several unions successfully sued to compel the government to enforce the Act, claiming that Labor Department officials had failed to examine payroll records and conduct investigations to assure compliance with the Act; to send notices and hold hearings on charges of willful violations; to debar contractors who willfully violated the Act; and to withhold underpayments due employees from willful violators. The Tenth Circuit ruled that such actions are nondiscretionary duties under the Act and the regulations, and that mandamus and injunctive relief are available where dereliction of duty is alleged. *(Painters Local 419 v. Brown)*

Where the Comptroller General withholds funds from a contractor on the ground of noncompliance with the prevailing wage provisions, employees seeking to obtain money from the government must show that they had made a demand for payment from the Comptroller General, that there had been a determination of their right to payment by the official, and that the official had refused payment, as a condition precedent to maintaining an action in court against the government. *(Veader v. Bay State Dredging & Contracting Co.)*

The Act requires a federal contractor to maintain payroll records with sufficient particularity so that the contractor, if necessary, may demonstrate that there has been compliance with the Act's wage provisions. The contractor may dispute computations of the Labor Department, but it must have its own records to support its contentions. *(In re Woodside Village)*

A contractor that had submitted false records under the Act was debarred for three years from government contracting. The contractor's claim that its officers went beyond the scope of their duties and that the debarment penalty was thus inappropriate was unavailing. (Comp Gen Dec. B-145606, Aug. 1, 1961)

Receipt from the Labor Secretary of a notice of intent to initiate administrative enforcement procedures does not support a contractor's request to enjoin the Secretary, where the regulations provide levels of administrative proceedings that apparently are adequate to protect the contractor's rights, and in any event, there is no present harm to the contractor and no certainty that there will be future harm. *(Home Improvement Corp. v. Brennan)*

8
CONTRACT WORK HOURS
AND SAFETY STANDARDS ACT

The Contract Work Hours and Safety Standards Act of 1962 (CWHSSA; WHM 90:271) was enacted to supersede the collection of statutes that became law from 1892 to 1917, collectively entitled the Eight Hour Laws. Also called the Work-Hours Act, CWHSSA is intended to regulate the payment of overtime for all mechanics and laborers employed on any public works project under a government contract or a government-financed contract.

The CWHSSA, like the Eight Hour Laws, originally required payment of time-and-one-half for all hours worked in excess of eight in one day to laborers and mechanics on public works. CWHSSA extended this overtime requirement to a workweek maximum of 40 hours in any one week. Congress eliminated the eight-hour day limit, however, in an attempt to allow a more flexible work schedule for covered employees, by enacting the Department of Defense Authorization Act of 1986 (P.L. 99-145)

Although the eight-hour day maximum is no longer in effect, contractors are still required to comply with the Act's 40-hour per week overtime limit. Overtime is computed on the employee's "basic rate of pay," which is the equivalent of the FLSA's "regular rate" of pay. Consequently, weekly salaries and fluctuating workweek (Belo) plans may be applied in computing CWHSSA overtime pay. (See Chapter 2, FLSA, under Overtime for more information on Belo plans.)

The Act also provides that no covered employee shall be employed under working conditions that are "unsanitary, hazardous, or dangerous" to health and safety. Debarment, or the blacklist penalty, is available for willful or grossly negligent violations of the Act.

COVERAGE

Covered Contracts

The Act covers any contract that may require or involve laborers or mechanics on a public works project under a contract with the federal government or under a contract financed by the federal government. Section 103 specifies which contracts will be covered and provides a limitation on this coverage:

- A contract to which the United States or any agency or instrumentality thereof, any territory, or the District of Columbia, is a party;
- A contract that is made for or on behalf of the United States, any agency or instrumentality thereof, any territory, or the District of Columbia; and
- A contract for work financed in whole or in part by loans or grants from, or loans insured or guaranteed by, the United States or any agency or instrumentality thereof under any statute of the United States providing standards for such work. *Provided,* that the Act shall not apply to work where assistance from the United States or any agency or instrumentality is only in the nature of a "loan guarantee, or insurance."

The Act's legislative history indicates that this proviso was intended to exclude programs that involve only federal guarantees of private loans, such as home construction financed by the Federal Housing Authority or the Veterans Administration.

Under this proviso, municipal employees working on construction and beautification projects were found to be exempt from the Act. (WH AdminOp, Sept. 9, 1969)

Exempt Contracts

The Act specifically exempts contracts for transportation by land, air, or water *(Martinez v. Phillips Petroleum Co.)*; contracts for the transmission of intelligence; and contracts for the purchase of supplies or materials or articles ordinarily available in the open market ("Open market contracts"). The Act also states that it shall not apply to any contract covered by the Walsh-Healey Act.

Employee Coverage

The Act specifically covers all mechanics and laborers, including watchmen and guards, employed by any contractor or subcontractor in the performance of any part of the work contemplated by a covered contract. Workmen performing services in connection with dredging or rock excavation in any river or harbor of the United States or any territory or of the District of Columbia are also covered. The Act exempts any employee working as a "seaman," however.

HEALTH AND SAFETY STANDARDS

The Act authorizes the Secretary of Labor to set reasonable limits and to make such rules and regulations allowing reasonable variations, tolerances, and exemptions to and from any or all provisions of the Act as he may find necessary and proper in the public interest to prevent injustice or undue hardship or to avoid serious impairment of the conduct of government business.

The Assistant Secretary of Labor for Occupational Safety and Health is responsible for promulgating and administering the regulations governing health and safety standards under CWHSSA.

The Act also authorizes the Secretary to promulgate regulations providing for health and safety standards that must be observed in the performance of any contract or subcontract let under the Act. To this end, the Secretary may make inspections, hold hearings, issue orders, and make decisions that are deemed necessary to gain compliance.

The Secretary may apply to the federal courts to enforce compliance with safety and health standards. Where the contract has been canceled or the contractor has been debarred due to noncompliance, the contractor may seek review in the appropriate circuit court.

ENFORCEMENT

Under CWHSSA, the contractor who violates the Act may be liable directly to his employees for unpaid overtime and to the federal government for liquidated damages. The Act also provides criminal sanctions for willful violations, including a fine of $1,000 or six months imprisonment, or both.

The major source of disagreement under the Act's predecessor, the Eight Hour Laws, involved whether employees working for a covered contractor or subcontractor had a private right to bring an action for recovery of unpaid wages. The courts rejected any notion of a private right to sue *(Filardo v. Foley Bros. Inc.; McDaniel v. Brown & Root, Inc.)*—some decisions rejected a theory based on an implied right to bring an action, and others rejected a theory based on third-party beneficiary of the contract.

However, CWHSSA specifically grants employees the right to bring an action for wages. The two major sources of litigation under the Act have involved disputes over the debarment or blacklist penalty and over the imposition of liquidated damages.

LIQUIDATED DAMAGES

The Act provides that a noncomplying contractor will be assessed a penalty for liquidated damages in the amount of $10 per day for each calendar day on which a covered employee is permitted or required to work without receiving overtime pay for overtime work. The liquidated damages are withheld by and for the use of the federal government. The government withholds overtime pay on behalf of the employees, and the Comptroller General is authorized to pay these overtime wages directly to the employees.

If the amounts withheld under the contract are insufficient to reimburse the workers for their unpaid overtime, they are authorized to maintain private actions or interventions against the contractor and his sureties. The Act invalidates any agreement by the employees to accept less than the required wages or any voluntary refunds by them, as employer defenses to allegations of overtime violations.

A contractor who has had amounts withheld as liquidated damages may appeal this action to the head of the contracting agency, who has authority to issue a final order on the propriety of the withholding. The Secretary of Labor may accept or reject the contracting agency official's recommendation. The contractor has 60 days from the date of the Secretary's disposition of the case to appeal to the U.S. Court of Claims for review.

Most government contracts contain a standard Disputes Clause which establishes the time period within which a party to the contract must assert that a dispute has arisen. Most Dispute Clauses contain only a 30-day time period, even though the CWHSSA allows for 60 days to appeal. The 60-day period for appeal to the U.S. Court of Claims, however, is substantially shorter than the six-year limitations period characteristically allowed for ordinary contract disputes. The various boards of contract appeals have generally taken jurisdiction over such claims. *(In re Anaco Reproductions)*

A 1982 decision by the U.S. Court of Claims illustrates both the enforcement mechanisms for review of contracting agency determinations, and the application of the liquidated damages penalty. A contractor performing work under contracts covered by both the Service Contract Act and CWHSSA was assessed liquidated damages for underpayments under the latter statute. Following an investigation of the employer's recordkeeping and payroll practices, the Department of Labor recommended to the Secretary of the Army—the head of the contracting agency in this dispute—that the contractor be assessed liquidated damages. The Army Secretary imposed a penalty of $12,520 for the contractor's failure to exercise due care. The Court of Claims held that this finding by the Secretary was supported by substantial evidence. The court rejected the contractor's claim that its violations were "inadvertent notwithstanding exercise of due care." It concluded that the amount of damages was not so harsh as to constitute an "abuse of discretion" on the part of the Army Secretary. *(Inland Serv. Corp. v. United States)*

The Work-Hours Act, unlike the FLSA and the Walsh-Healey and Davis-Bacon acts, is *not* covered by the Portal-to-Portal Pay Act's "good-faith defense." Under CWHSSA's predecessor, the Eight Hour Laws, a contractor's reliance on rulings of the War Department was not a defense in an action by an employee to recover overtime pay allegedly due under the Law. *(Finnan v. Elmhurst Contracting Co.)*

DEBARMENT PENALTY

The CWHSSA does not specifically provide for the debarment (blacklist) penalty, but it does authorize the Labor Secretary to promulgate regulations to impose appropriate sanctions and measures to enforce the Act. Under the regulations (29 C.F.R. Sec. 5), the Secretary has prescribed this penalty for willful or aggravated violations of the Act. The Secretary's authority to impose debarment by promulgating a regulation, the propriety of inferring such a penalty where CWHSSA is silent and other statutes specify it, and the appropriateness of imposing it in a particular case, were all upheld by the U.S. District Court for the District of Columbia in 1961. *(Copper Plumbing & Heating Co. v. Campbell)*

OTHER LAWS

CWHSSA specifically exempts contracts covered by the Walsh-Healey Act. Since Walsh-Healey does not cover contracts below $10,000 in amount, CWHSSA will likely cover these contracts without running afoul of Walsh-Healey coverage.

Walsh-Healey applies to an employee in any workweek in which the employee devotes *any time* to work covered by the Act. However, CWHSSA applies only where the employee works on a government contract for more than 40 hours in the workweek. (WH AdminOp, Oct. 7, 1964)

9
OTHER FEDERAL LAWS

In addition to the major statutes that govern wages, hours recordkeeping, and safety-health standards that have been discussed in previous chapters, there is a plethora of minor statutes that affect these areas in one way or another. These statutes may only govern an area incidentally, rather than as a major intent of Congress, but employers must comply with them nevertheless.

ANTI-KICKBACK LAW (COPELAND ACT)

The Anti-Kickback Law (Copeland Act) of 1954 (WHM 90:281) is designed to protect employees' wages from illegal "kickback" arrangements in government-financed public construction. It covers contracts governed by Davis-Bacon and Work Hours acts. The Copeland Act prohibits anyone from compelling employees to return wages "by force, intimidation, or threat of procuring dismissal from employment, or by any other manner whatsoever." The Act prescribes a penalty of a $5,000 fine, up to five years' imprisonment, or both.

TITLE III, CONSUMER CREDIT PROTECTION ACT

Title III of the Consumer Credit Protection Act of 1968 (CCPA; WHM 90:141) covers all employees, regardless of the size of the employer's business. Congress enacted this law under its authority to regulate commerce. The law is intended to create a uniform treatment under the bankruptcy law. Therefore, only a minimal involvement in interstate commerce is necessary for an employer to fall under the Act's coverage. The Act regulates and makes consistent employer practices regarding garnishments of employee wages. It defines "earnings," "disposable earnings," and "garnishment," and it establishes restrictions on the amount of wages that can be garnisheed.

The maximum amount that may be garnisheed is determined under a formula. Under this calculation, the amount of wages that is subject to garnishment may not exceed (*a*) 25 percent of the employee's disposable earnings for any workweek, or (*b*) the amount by which his disposable earnings are greater than 30 times the federal minimum hourly wage, whichever is less. However, these limits on amounts that may be garnisheed do not apply where:

- The wage deduction is based on a court order for support or on an order of a court of bankruptcy; and
- Wage deductions for any debt due on any state or federal tax.

Under the CCPA, employers are barred from discharging any employee for the sole reason of having a "single" wage garnishment levied against his or her pay. An employer's violation of this prohibition will result in a $1,000 fine, up to one year in prison, or both.

Because of the large number of state laws that regulate in this area, Congress added a section in the Act stating that the states are not precluded from applying their own garnishment laws, where the state laws prescribe higher or stricter standards restricting garnishment than the CCPA. The Act does not protect an employee who is discharged for having more than a single garnishment.

Finally, any state may apply to the Secretary of Labor to have garnishments issued under state law exempted from CCPA restrictions, where the state law provides for restrictions that are substantially similar to the Act.

CHILD SUPPORT ENFORCEMENT ACT

The Child Support Enforcement Act of 1984 (WHM 90:143) revises the Social Security Act and requires all states to have child support withholding laws in effect by January 1, 1986.

Employers are required to withhold from employee wages any amounts determined to be due under support orders issued by a court or administrative body.

The Act prohibits employers from disciplining, discharging, or refusing to hire an individual because of a withholding order for support. Employees are entitled to advance notice and a hearing before any order becomes effective.

OCCUPATIONAL SAFETY AND HEALTH ACT

The Occupational Safety and Health Act of 1970 (OSHA; LRX 6201) covers all employers engaged in a business affecting commerce, but does not include the federal government or any state or political subdivision of a state. OSHA defines an employee as any individual employed in a business of the employer affecting commerce.

Although the Secretary of Labor has primary responsibility for enforcing OSHA, the Secretary of Health and Human Services and the Occupational Safety and Health Review Commission also have important duties under the Act. In addition, the states are free to conduct their own safety and health programs in areas where there are no federal standards.

The Act imposes on an employer the general duty to furnish each of its employees employment and a place of employment which are free from recognized hazards that are causing or are likely to cause death or serious physical harm to employees.

To constitute a violation of the employer's general duty, the hazard involved must be preventable by the employer and must therefore be foreseeable. The employer can satisfy this general duty by:

- Promulgating adequate safety rules;
- Enforcing such rules with reasonable sanctions adequate to deter violations;
- Providing adequate training and instruction to all employees involved in hazardous work;
- Providing adequate supervision to employees according to their experience and exposure to dangerous conditions; and

- Providing protective equipment and requiring use of such equipment, where necessary.

In establishing safety and health standards, Congress created the National Institute of Occupational Safety and Health (NIOSH). NIOSH is authorized to conduct research, develop innovative methods and techniques for identifying toxic substances, and set criteria for safe use.

The Act also authorizes "notice and comment" rulemaking, under the auspices of the Labor Secretary. Any person adversely affected by the standard may obtain review by the appropriate U.S. Court of Appeals.

The Labor Secretary is authorized to grant temporary variances, and variations, tolerances, and exemptions from any or all provisions of the Act due to national defense considerations. The Secretary is required to conduct investigations and to issue citations where appropriate.

For all violations, the Secretary must set a period of "abatement," by which time the employer must correct the infraction. However, the employer has several options:

- Challenging the determination and seeking to have the abatement order revoked or modified;
- Seeking to obtain a variance;
- Applying for a temporary variance, to gain time to comply with the abatement order; and
- Petitioning the Labor Secretary for revocation or modification of the order, on the ground that a good-faith attempt to comply has been unsuccessful because of factors beyond the employer's control.

Employers who violate the Act face a range of civil and/or criminal penalties that include fines of up to $10,000 and six months in jail for a first offense of willfully violating the Act, and a fine of up to $20,000 and one year imprisonment for each subsequent offense.

The Act encourages individual employees to contact the Occupational Health and Safety Administration when a violation is suspected. Employees are protected from retaliation for exercising their rights under the Act, such as filing complaints or testifying against their employer in a proceeding under the Act.

MISCELLANEOUS STATUTES

A variety of laws contain "employee protection" provisions that relate to wages-hours and/or safety-health issues in the workplace, even though the underlying purpose of the law may be to regulate in some other area. These federal statutes include the Energy Reorganization Act, the Surface Transportation Assistance Act of 1982, and the Rehabilitation Act of 1973.

Still other laws that touch on these areas of concern are the Employee Retirement Income Security Act of 1974, the Migrant and Seasonal Agricultural Worker Protection Act, the National Foundation on the Arts and Humanities Act, the Motor Carrier Act, the Mineral Land Act, the Area Redevelopment Act of 1961, the Merchant Marine Act, the Miller Act, and the Age Discrimination in Employment Act of 1967.

In addition to these laws, many states have their own statutory scheme to regulate wages, hours of work, and other aspects of the employee's compensation scheme, such as the accrual and payment of sick or vacation leave, payment upon termination of employment, and other items. (State minimum wage requirements appear in Appendix E; state maximum hours and overtime requirements appear in Appendix G.)

Last, but not least, employers may be obligated to pay certain wages and fringe benefits and scheduled increases under collective bargaining agreements or individual employment contracts.

APPENDIX A

DIRECTORY OF U.S. DEPARTMENT OF LABOR ADMINISTRATIVE AND REGIONAL OFFICES

U.S. DEPARTMENT OF LABOR
Administrative Offices

Address: U.S. Department of Labor Building, 200 Constitution Avenue, N.W., Washington, D.C. 20210. Telephone: (202) 523-8271

SECRETARY OF LABOR

William E. Brock, III, Secretary of Labor

(*Vacant*), Chief of Staff

Linda A. Townsend, Deputy Chief of Staff

David F. Demarest, Jr., Deputy Under Secretary for Public and Intergovernmental Affairs

Eunice Thomas, Special Assistant

Lyle Ryter, Special Assistant

Michael Volte, Special Assistant, Public Affairs

Chris H. Winston, Director, Information and Public Affairs

INSPECTOR GENERAL

James Brian Hyland, Inspector General

ADMINISTRATIVE LAW JUDGES

Nahum Litt, Chief Administrative Law Judge

Everette Thomas, Deputy Chief Administrative Law Judge

Robert Mahony, Associate Chief Administrative Law Judge

G. Marvin Bober, Associate Administrative Law Judge

BENEFITS REVIEW BOARD

Robert Ramsey, Chief Administrative Appeals Judge

EMPLOYEES' COMPENSATION APPEALS BOARD

Michael Walsh, Chairman

David Gerson & George Rivers

WAGE APPEALS BOARD

Alvin Bramow, Acting Chairman

Thomas X. Dunn & Stuart Rothman

UNDER SECRETARY OF LABOR

Dennis E. Whitfield, Under Secretary of Labor

Richard L. Baker, Special Assistant

DEPUTY UNDER SECRETARY FOR CONGRESSIONAL AFFAIRS

William J. Maroni, Deputy Under Secretary

Bruce C. Wood, Associate Deputy Under Secretary

DEPUTY UNDER SECRETARY FOR PUBLIC AND INTERGOVERNMENTAL AFFAIRS

David F. Demarest, Jr., Deputy Under Secretary

ASSISTANT SECRETARY FOR PENSION & WELFARE BENEFIT PROGRAMS

Dennis M. Kass, Assistant Secretary

David M. Walker, Deputy Assistant Secretary

ASSISTANT SECRETARY FOR POLICY, EVALUATION AND RESEARCH

Michael E. Baroody, Assistant Secretary

Gary B. Reed, Deputy Assistant Secretary for Program Economics and Research and Technical Support

Roland G. Droitsch, Deputy Assistant Secretary for Regulatory Economics and Economic Policy Analysis

ASSISTANT SECRETARY FOR ADMINISTRATION AND MANAGEMENT

Thomas C. Komarek, Assistant Secretary

Betty Bolden, Deputy Assistant Secretary

Comptroller

William R. Reise, Comptroller

ASSISTANT SECRETARY FOR MINE SAFETY AND HEALTH

David A. Zegeer, Assistant Secretary

Thomas J. Shepich, Deputy Assistant Secretary

DEPUTY UNDER SECRETARY FOR INTERNATIONAL AFFAIRS
Robert W. Searby, Deputy Under Secretary
Christopher Hankin, Associate Deputy Under Secretary for International Labor Affairs

BUREAU OF LABOR STATISTICS
Janet L. Norwood, Commissioner
Joseph P. Goldberg, Special Assistant (Labor)
Janis D. Murphey, Special Assistant (Business)

Office of Statistical Processing
Carl J. Lowe, *Acting* Associate Commissioner

Office of Systems & Standards
Carl Lowe, Associate Commissioner

Office of Wages & Industrial Relations
George L. Stelluto, Associate Commissioner

Office of Field Operations
Laura King, Associate Commissioner

Office of Employment Structure and Trends
Thomas J. Plewes, Associate Commissioner

Office of Productivity & Technology
Jerome A. Mark, Associate Commissioner

Office of Prices & Living Conditions
Kenneth V. Dalton, Associate Commissioner

Office of Occupational Safety & Health Statistics
William Eisenberg, *Acting* Associate Commissioner

Office of Publications
Henry Lowenstern, Associate Commissioner

Office of Administration and Internal Operations
William G. Barron, Jr., Associate Commissioner

Office of Research and Evaluation
Jack E. Triplett, Associate Commissioner

Office of Economic Growth
Ronald E. Kutscher, Assistant Commissioner

Office of Administration
William D. Stead, Assistant Commissioner

WOMEN'S BUREAU
Shirley Dennis, Director
Jill Houghton Emery, Deputy Director

DEPUTY UNDER SECRETARY FOR EMPLOYMENT STANDARDS
Susan R. Meisinger, Deputy Under Secretary
Lawrence W. Rogers, Jr., Acting Associate Deputy Under Secretary

DEPUTY UNDER SECRETARY FOR LABOR-MANAGEMENT RELATIONS AND COOPERATIVE PROGRAMS
Steven I. Schlossberg, Deputy Under Secretary
John R. Stepp, Associate Deputy Under Secretary
Philip G. Riccobono, Deputy Director

ASSISTANT SECRETARY FOR LABOR-MANAGEMENT STANDARDS
Salvatore R. Martoche, Assistant Secretary
Ronald J. St. Cyr, Deputy Assistant Secretary

Office of Management
Ernest J. German, Director
Charles G. George, Deputy Director

Program Operations
John J. Walsh, Deputy Assistant Secretary

Office of Elections
Richard Hunsucker

Office of Standards
John Kotch

ASSISTANT SECRETARY FOR OCCUPATIONAL SAFETY AND HEALTH ADMINISTRATION
John Pendergrass, Assistant Secretary

Frank White, Deputy Assistant Secretary

Candace Strother, Deputy Assistant Secretary

David Ziegler, Director, Administrative Programs

Jack McDavitt, Special Assistant for Press

ASSISTANT SECRETARY FOR EMPLOYMENT AND TRAINING ADMINISTRATION

Roger D. Semerad, Assistant Secretary/Administrator

Robert T. Jones, Deputy Assistant Secretary

Steven E. Some, Special Assistant for Public Affairs

Joyce Kaiser, Associate Assistant Secretary

Dennis Wyant, Deputy Assistant Secretary

Royal S. Dellinger, Administrator, Office of Regional Management

ASSISTANT SECRETARY FOR VETERANS' EMPLOYMENT AND TRAINING †

Donald E. Shasteen, Assistant Secretary

Garnett B. Prince, Jr., Deputy Assistant Secretary

Office of Veterans' Reemployment Rights

Joseph Juarez, Director

OFFICE OF THE SOLICITOR

George R. Salem, *Interim* Solicitor

George R. Salem, Deputy Solicitor for National Operations

Lydia Leeds, Director, Office of Management

Karen I. Ward, Associate Solicitor for Special Apellate and Supreme Court Litigation

Elizabeth Culbreath, Director, Administrative Appeals Unit

Judith E. Kramer, Executive Assistant

† Veterans' Employment and Training Services.

Division of Fair Labor Standards

Joseph Woodward, *Acting* Associate Solicitor

Joseph Woodward, Deputy Associate Solicitor

Division of General Legal Services

Ronald G. Whiting, Deputy Solicitor for Regional Operations

Alvin T. Bramow, Deputy Associate Solicitor

Division of Employment & Training Legal Services

William DuRoss III, Associate Solicitor

Division of Legislation & Legal Counsel

Seth D. Zinman, Associate Solicitor

Judith E. Kramer, Deputy Associate Solicitor

Division of Labor-Management Laws

John F. Depenbrock, Associate Solicitor

Donald Shalhoup, Deputy Associate Solicitor

Division of Civil Rights

James D. Henry, Associate Solicitor

Louis G. Ferrand, Jr., Deputy Associate Solicitor

Division of Occupational Safety & Health

Frank White, Associate Solicitor

John J. Hynan, Deputy Associate Solicitor

Division of Employee Benefits

Donald S. Shire, Associate Solicitor

Cornelius S. Donoghue, Deputy Associate Solicitor

Division of Plan Benefits Security

Robert Eccles, Associate Solicitor

Gregor B. McCurdy, Deputy Associate Solicitor

Division of Mine Safety and Health

Cynthia L. Attwood, Associate Solicitor

Edward P. Clair, Deputy Associate Solicitor

Office of The Solicitor: Regional Offices

Region I

JFK Federal Building, Rm. 1803, Boston, MA 02203. Albert H. Ross, Regional Solicitor, Tel.: (617) 223-6706.

Connecticut	**New Hampshire**
Maine	**Rhode Island**
Massachusetts	**Vermont**

Region II

Room 3500, 1515 Broadway, New York NY 10036. Tel.: (212) 944-3322. Francis V. LaRuffa, Regional Solicitor, Tel.: (212) 944-3322.

Canal Zone	**Puerto Rico**
New York	**Virgin Islands**
New Jersey	

Region III

14480 Gateway Bldg., 3535 Market St., Philadelphia PA 19104. Marshall H. Harris, Regional Solicitor; Kenneth L. Stein, Deputy Regional Solicitor, Tel.: (215) 596-5157.

District of	**Pennsylvania**
Columbia	**Virginia**
Delaware	**West Virginia**
Maryland	

Region IV

1371 Peachtree Street, NE, Room 500, Atlanta GA 30367. Mrs. Bobbye D. Spears, Regional Solicitor, Tel.: (404) 347-4811.

George D. Palmer, Associate Regional Solicitor, 1929 Ninth Avenue South, Birmingham, AL 35256 Tel.: (205) 254-0208.

Carl Gerig, Associate Regional Solicitor, 280 U.S. Courthouse, 801 Broadway, Nashville, TN 37203, Tel.: (615) 251-5761.

Donald R. McCoy, Associate Regional Solicitor, Federal Building Rm. 407-B, 299 East Brow.ud Blvd., Fort Lauderdale, FL 33301, Tel.: (305) 527-7362.

Alabama	**Mississippi**
Florida	**North Carolina**
Georgia	**South Carolina**
Kentucky	**Tennessee**

Region V

Room 844, 230 South Dearborn Street, Chicago IL 60604. Herman Grant, Regional Solicitor, Tel.: (312) 353-7256.

William S. Kloepfer, Associate Regional Solicitor, Room 881, Federal Office Building, 1240 East Ninth Street, Cleveland OH 44199, Tel: (216) 522-3870.

Illinois	**Minnesota**
Indiana	**Ohio**
Michigan	**Wisconsin**

Region VI

555 Griffin Square Bldg., Suite 501, Griffin & Young Sts., Dallas, TX 75202. Tel.: (214) 767-4902. James E. White Regional Solicitor.

Arkansas	**New Mexico**
Louisiana	**Oklahoma**
	Texas

Region VII

Federal Office Building, Room 2106, 911 Walnut Street, Kansas City, MO 64106. Tedrick A. Housh, Jr., Regional Solicitor, Tel.: (816) 374-6441.

Iowa	**Missouri**
Kansas	**Nebraska**

Region VIII

1961 Stout Street, Room 1585, Denver, CO 80294. Henry C. Mahlman, Associate Regional Solicitor, Tel.: (303) 837-5521.

Colorado	**South Dakota**
Montana	**Utah**
North Dakota	**Wyoming**

Region IX

450 Golden Gate Avenue, Federal Office Building, Room 11071, San Francisco, CA 94102. Daniel W. Teehan, Regional Solicitor; Jeannie J. Meyer, Deputy Regional Solicitor, Tel.: (415) 556-4042.

John C. Nangle, Associate Regional Solicitor, Federal Building, Room 3247, 300 North Los Angeles Steet, Los Angeles, CA 90012. Tel.: (213) 688-4980.

Arizona   **Hawaii**
California   **Nevada**

Region X

Robert A. Friel, Associate Regional Solicitor, 8003 Federal Office Building, 909 First Avenue, Seattle WA 98174, Tel.: (206) 442-0940.

Alaska   **Oregon**
Idaho   **Washington**

APPENDIX B

CHART OF FLSA WHITE-COLLAR EXEMPTION TESTS

CHART OF WHITE-COLLAR EXEMPTION TESTS

EXECUTIVES

Tests: All six must be met.

A. Primary duty is the management of (1) the enterprise in which he is employed, or (2) a customarily recognized department or subdivision thereof.

B. Customarily and regularly directs the work of **two or more** other employees.

C. Has authority to hire or fire other employees or to make recommendations as to hiring, firing and the advancement, promotion, or change of status of employees.

D. Customarily and regularly exercises discretionary powers.

E. Receives payment on a salary basis at a rate of not less than: (1) $155 a week in the 50 states; $130 a week if employed by other than the Federal Government in Puerto Rico, the Virgin Islands, and American Samoa.

F. Does not devote more than 20 percent of the hours worked in the workweek to activities which are not **directly and closely related** to the performance of exempt work; with the exception of

(1) executive employees in retail or service establishments who may devote up to 40 percent of the hours worked in the workweek to activities not directly or closely related to executive activities,

(2) an employee who owns at least 20-percent interest in the enterprise in which he is employed, and

(3) an employee who is in sole charge of an independent establishment or a physically separated branch establishment.

Streamlined Tests for High-Paid Executives

Executive employee paid at least $250 ($200 if employed by other than the Federal Government in Puerto Rico, the Virgin Islands, and American Samoa) weekly may qualify for exemption if he meets these tests:

(1) primary duty consists of the management of the enterprise in which he is employed or of a customarily recognized department or subdivision thereof; and

(2) such duty includes the customary and regular direction of the work of two or more other employees in the establishment or department.

ADMINISTRATIVE EMPLOYEES

Tests: A, B, D, and E must all be met along with one of the three tests in C.

A. Primary duty is the performance of office or nonmanual work directly related to management policies or general business operations of his employer or his employer's customers, or the performance of functions in the administration of a school system or educational establishment or institution, or of a department or subdivision thereof, in work directly related to academic instruction or training; and

B. Customarily and regularly exercises discretion and independent judgment; and

CHART OF WHITE-COLLAR EXEMPTION TESTS—Cont'd.

C. (1) Regularly and directly assists a proprietor, or an employee employed in a bona fide executive or administrative capacity, **or** (2) performs under only general supervision work along specialized or technical lines requiring special training, experience, or knowledge, **or** (3) executes under only general supervision special assignments and tasks; and

D. Does not devote more than 20 percent of his hours worked in the workweek to activities which are not directly and closely related to the performance of the work described in subsections (A) through (C) above; with the exception of administrative employees in retail or service establishments who may devote up to 40 percent of the hours worked in the workweek to activities not directly and closely related to administrative activities; **and**

E. Receives payment on a salary or fee basis at a rate of not less than: (1) $155 a week in the 50 states: (2) $125 if employed by other than the Federal Government in Puerto Rico, the Virgin Islands, and American Samoa, **or** in the case of academic administrative personnel, is compensated for his services at either of the rates above or on a salary basis in an amount which is at least equal to the entrance salary for teachers in the school system or educational establishment or institution by which he is employed. (3) Administrative employees employed on a fee basis for less than a normal 40 hour week must be compensated at an hourly rate of not less than $3.875 ($3.125 if employed by other than the Federal Government in Puerto Rico, the Virgin Islands and American Samoa). These figures represent the hourly rate at which such employees would ordinarily be compensated to reach the minimum salary rates, based on a 40 hour week, to qualify for exemption.

Streamlined Tests for High-Paid Administrative Employees

Administrative employees paid at least $250 ($200 if employed by other than the Federal Government in Puerto Rico, the Virgin Islands, and American Samoa) weekly may qualify for exemption if they meet these tests:

(1) primary duty is the performance of office or nonmanual work directly related to management policies or general business operations of his employer or his employer's customers; and

(2) such duty includes work requiring the exercise of discretion and independent judgment.

PROFESSIONAL EMPLOYEES

Tests: One of the alternate requirements under A and all of the requirements B, C, D, E must be met.

A. Employee must have as his primary duty **either** (1) work requiring knowledge of advanced type in a field of science or learning, **or** (2) original and creative work in an artistic field, **or** (3) teaching, tutoring, instructing, or lecturing in the activity of imparting knowledge as a teacher certified or recognized as such in the school system or educational establishment or institution by which he is employed.

B. Work requires the consistent exercise of discretion and judgment.

C. Work must be (1) predominantly intellectual and varied in character as opposed to routine mental, manual, mechanical, or physical

CHART OF WHITE-COLLAR EXEMPTION TESTS—Cont'd.

work; and (2) of such a character that the output produced or the result accomplished cannot be standardized in relation to a given period of time.

D. Time spent in activities not "an essential part of and necessarily incident" to professional duties may not exceed 20 percent of employee's own weekly hours worked.

E. Receives payment on a salary or fee basis at a rate of not less than (1) $170 a week in the 50 states; $150 if employed by other than the Federal Government in Puerto Rico, the Virgin Islands, and American Samoa. The salary requirements in this paragraph E need not be met in the case of an employee (a) who holds a valid license or certificate permitting the practice of law or medicine or any of their branches and is actually engaged in the practice thereof, or (b) who holds the requisite academic degree for the general practice of medicine and is engaged in an internship or resident program pursuant to the practice of medicine or any of its branches, or (c) who is employed and engaged as a teacher. (2) Professional employees employed on a fee basis for less than a normal 40 hour week must be compensated at an hourly rate of not less than $4.25 ($3.74 if employed by other than the Federal Government in Puerto Rico, the Virgin Islands and American Samoa). These figures represent the hourly rate at which such employees would ordinarily be compensated to reach the minimum salary rate, based on a 40 hour week, to qualify for exemption.

Streamlined Tests for High-Paid Professional Employees

Professional employees paid at least $250 ($200 if employed by other than the Federal Government in Puerto Rico, the Virgin Islands, and American Samoa) weekly may qualify for exemption if they meet either of these tests:

(1) primary duty consists of the performance of work either requiring knowledge of an advanced type in a field of science or learning, or teaching, including work that requires the consistent exercise of discretion and judgment; or (2) primary duty consists of the performance of work in a recognized field of artistic endeavor, including work that requires invention, imagination, or talent.

OUTSIDE SALESMEN

Tests: Two must be met.

A. Employed for the purpose of and is customarily and regularly engaged away from his employer's place of business in (1) making sales or (2) obtaining orders or contracts for services or for the use of facilities for which a consideration will be paid by the client or customer.

B. Hours of work of a nature other than described in the first test must not exceed 20 percent of the hours worked in the workweek by nonexempt employees of the employer. Work performed incidental to and in conjunction with the employee's own outside sales, including incidental deliveries and collections, shall not be regarded as nonexempt work.

APPENDIX C

CHART OF FLSA EXEMPTIONS FROM MINIMUM WAGE AND OVERTIME

NONAGRICULTURAL INDUSTRIES AND OCCUPATIONS: EXEMPTION CHART

(Agricultural exemption chart appears at WHM 91:547.)

INDUSTRY OR OCCUPATION	OVERTIME EXEMPTION	MINIMUM-WAGE EXEMPTION
Airlines	Exemption except for employees engaged in activities not necessary to or related to air transportation.	None.
Amusement & recreational establishments	Exemption if (a) establishment doesn't operate more than 7 months during calendar year, or (b) its average receipts during any 6 months of prior calendar year don't exceed one third of its average receipts for the other 6 months of the year. 1977 amendments added organized camps or religious or nonprofit educational conference centers as exempt establishments, but specifically deny exemption to concessioners in national parks, refuges, and forests, with exception of facilities operating in these areas that are directly relating to skiing.	Exemption under same terms as overtime exemption.
Apprentices i.e., one who is at least age 16 and is hired to learn a skilled trade in conformity with established apprenticeship standards).	None.	Subminimum rates may be paid under special certificate.
Auto, farm implement, boat, aircraft dealers	Exemption for salesmen, partsmen, and mechanics primarily selling or servicing autos, trucks, or farm implements, if employed by nonmanufacturer primarily selling to ultimate consumer. Exemption for salesmen primarily selling trailers, aircraft, or boats if employed by nonmanufacturer primarily selling to ultimate consumer.	None.
Domestic Service Workers in Private Household	Exemption if not covered by the Social Security Act nor employed for more than 40 hours per week for one employer. Babysitters employed on a casual basis and persons employed to provide companion services are exempt. Live-in domestics are exempt from overtime.	Exemption if not covered by the Social Security Act nor employed for more than eight hours per week in the aggregate. Babysitters employed on a casual basis and persons employed to provide companion services are exempt.
Drivers and drivers' helpers	Exempt if making local deliveries and compensated on trip rate basis.	None.

Checklist II—Other Industries and Occupations—Contd.

INDUSTRY OR OCCUPATION	OVERTIME EXEMPTION	MINIMUM-WAGE EXEMPTION
Foreign employment	Exemption for services performed within a foreign country.	Exemption under same terms as overtime exemption.
Forestry or logging	Exemption if employer has 8 employees or less.	None.
Gasoline stations	Exemption for stations with annual sales of less than $250,000.	Exemption under same terms as overtime exemption.
Handicapped workers (i.e., one whose earning capacity has been impaired by age or physical or mental deficiency or injury).	None.	Subminimum rates may be paid under special certificate.
Holly-wreath manufacture	Exemption for homeworkers engaged in making of wreaths composed principally of natural evergreens.	Exemption under same terms as overtime exemption
Hospital and nursing homes	Hospital may use work period of 14 days, rather than 7 days, in computing overtime if employees agree in advance and 1½ times regular rate is paid for hours over 8 per day, and 80 in 14-day period. Otherwise, overtime rate applies after 40 hours per week.	None
Hotels, motels, & restaurants (Other than those qualifying for retail-service exemptions)	Exemption for hotel, motel, and restaurant employees (other than hotel maids and custodial employees (provided they are paid 1½ times regular rate for hours over 44 hours per week effective January 1, 1976. Exemption is repealed effective January 1, 1979.	None

Checklist II—Other Industries and Occupations—Contd.

INDUSTRY OR OCCUPATION	OVERTIME EXEMPTION	MINIMUM-WAGE EXEMPTION
Learners (i.e., a beginner at a skilled occupation).	None.	Subminimum rates may be paid under special certificates.
Messengers	None.	Special certificates for employment at subminimum rates are authorized, but none has been issued.
Motion picture theaters	Exemption.	None.
Motor carriers	Exemption for employees whose hours of service are subject to regulation by Dept. of Transportation.	None.
Newsboys delivering newspapers to the consumer	Exemption.	Exemption.
Newspapers	Exemption for employees of paper with 4,000 or less circulation, major part of which is in county in which paper is published or in contiguous counties (paper may be printed elsewhere).	Exemption under same terms as overtime exemption.
Outside Salesman	Exempt.	Exempt.
Petroleum distributors	Exemption for any employee of independently owned & controlled local enterprise engaged in wholesale or bulk distribution of petroleum products, *provided* he is paid 1½ times the *statutory* minimum rate for work between 40 and 56 hours per week and 1½ times his *regular* rate all work in excess of 12 per day and 56 per week.	None.
Professional, executive, and administrative personnel	Exempt if they meet regulatory tests.	Exemption under same terms as overtime exemption.
Radio & TV broadcasters	Exemptions for announcers, news editors, and chief engineers of radio or TV station whose major studio is located in (1) city of 100,000 or less that is not part of a metropolitan area of more than 100,000, or (2) city of 25,000 or less, even in such metropolitan area if it is located at least 40 airline miles from principal city in area.	None.

Checklist II—Other Industries and Occupations—Contd.

INDUSTRY OR OCCUPATION	OVERTIME EXEMPTION	MINIMUM-WAGE EXEMPTION
Railroad, steamship companies	Exemption for employees of employer subject to Part I of Interstate Commerce Act, i.e., common carriers engaged in (a) transporting passengers or property wholly by rail, or partly by rail and partly by water when both are used under common control, management, or arrangement for continuous carriage or shipment; or (b) transportation of oil or other commodities, except water and natural or artificial gas, by pipeline or partly by pipeline and partly by railroad or water.	None.
Retail-service establishments (other than laundry-dry-cleaning establishment, hospital, nursing home, school for handicapped or gifted children, preschool elementary or secondary school, or college	Exemption if (a) more than 50% of establishment's annual sales is intrastate, and (b) at least 75 percent of its annual dollar sales is not for resale and is recognized as retail in the industry. Under the 1977 amendments to the FLSA, the test for coverage of employees of enterprises comprised of one or more retail or service establishments is raised to $362,500 in three steps as follows: ● July 1, 1978 .... $275,000 ● July 1, 1980 .... 325,000 ● Dec. 31, 1981 362,500	Exemption under same terms as overtime exemption.
Retail commission salesmen	Exemption provided employee's regular rate (including salary and commissions) is more than 1½ times the statutory minimum, and more than half his compensation comes from commissions.	None.
Retail-manufacturing units (e.g., bakeries, ice-cream parlors, candy shops)	Exemptions for establishments if (a) it meets tests for retail-service establishments, (b) it is recognized in industry as retail establishment, (c) more than 85 percent of its dollar volume of annual sales is made intrastate; (d) the goods are made or processed and sold in the same establishment.	None
Seamen	Exemption for all seamen, whether on U.S. or foreign vessels.	Exemption only for seamen on foreign vessels.
Students in agriculture	None.	Sec. of Labor may permit employment of students part-time (20 hours a week or less) and full-time during vacations at 85 percent of statutory minimum.
Students in higher educational institutions	None.	Same as above.

Checklist II—Other Industries and Occupations—Contd.

INDUSTRY OR OCCUPATION	OVERTIME EXEMPTION	MINIMUM-WAGE EXEMPTION
Students in retailing	None	Sec. of Labor may permit employment of students part-time (20 hours a week or less) and full-time during vacations at 85 percent of statutory minimum.
Substitute parents for institutionalized children	Exempt if employee and spouse are substitute parents for children residing in private non-profit educational institutions, receive jointly cash wages of $10,000 annually and reside in the same facilities as the children receiving free room and board.	None.
Taxicab drivers	Exemption for drivers employed by taxicab company.	None
Telephone exchanges	Exemption for employees of independently owned telephone company that has fewer than 750 stations.	Exemption under same terms as overtime exemption.

APPENDIX D

DIRECTORY OF U.S. DEPARTMENT OF LABOR EMPLOYMENT STANDARDS ADMINISTRATION, ADMINISTRATIVE AND REGIONAL OFFICES

Employment Standards Administration
Administrative Offices

Address: U.S. Department of Labor Bldg., 200 Constitution Avenue, N.W., Washington, D.C. 20210. Telephone: (202) 523-6191.

Office of Deputy Under Secretary
Susan R. Meisinger, Deputy Under Secretary
Debbie Bolden, Special Assistant
Ralph Muehlig, Special Assistant
Lawrence W. Rogers, Jr., *Acting* Associate Deputy Under Secretary

Office of Information
Linda Tavlin, Director

Equal Employment Opportunity Coordinator
Constance M. Davis, Coordinator

Office of Workers' Compensation Programs
Lawrence W. Rogers, Jr., Director
Richard A. Staufenberger, Deputy Director

Office of Management, Administration, and Planning
Carol Gandin, *Director*
John Fraser, Deputy Director

Office of State Liaison and Legislative Analysis
June Mitchell Robinson, Director

Office of Federal Contract Compliance Programs
Joseph N. Cooper, Director
Charles E. Pugh, Deputy Director

Operations Division
James Warren, Chief Veteran & Handicapped Worker Program
Richard Caliri, Deputy Director, Program Operations
Neil A. Montone, Division of Longshore & Harbor Workers' Compensation
John D. McLellan, Division of Federal Employees' Compensation

Wage and Hour Division
Paula V. Smith, Administrator
Herbert J. Cohen, Deputy Administrator

Donald M. Essig, Assistant to the Administrator
James Jones, Chief Management Support Staff

Office of Program Operations
Nancy Flynn, *Acting* Assistant Administrator
Nancy M. Flynn, Deputy Assistant Administrator

Fair Labor Standards Act Operations Division
Raymond Cordelli, Director
Stephanie R. Glyder, Chief Enforcement Branch
Arthur H. Korn, Chief Special Employment Branch

Farm & Child Labor Programs Division
Gordon L. Claucherty, Director
Charles I. Carter, Chief Child Labor Programs Branch
Solomon Sugarman, Chief Farm Labor Progams Branch

Wage Determinations Division
Alan L. Moss, Director
Raymond L. Kamrath, Chief Construction

Office of Policy Planning and Review
Charles Pugh, Assistant Administrator
Policy & Analysis Division
    William G. Blackburn, Director
Planning & Review Division
    Manuel J. Villarreal, Director

Contract Standards Operations Division
Sylvester L. Green, Director
    Rae Glass, Chief Construction Contract Operations Branch
    William W. Gross, Chief Service Contract Operations Branch

ESA Regional Offices

REGIONAL OFFICES SERVING VARIOUS STATES

Region No.	State	Region No.	State	Region No.	State
4	Alabama	3	Maryland	1	Rhode Island
10	Alaska	1	Massachusetts	4	South Carolina
9	Arizona	5	Michigan	8	South Dakota
6	Arkansas	5	Minnesota	4	Tennessee
9	California	4	Mississippi	6	Texas
8	Colorado	7	Missouri	8	Utah
1	Connecticut	8	Montana	1	Vermont
3	Delaware	7	Nebraska	3	Virginia
3	District of Columbia	9	Nevada	10	Washington
4	Florida	1	New Hampshire	3	West Virginia
4	Georgia	2	New Jersey	5	Wisconsin
9	Hawaii	6	New Mexico	8	Wyoming
10	Idaho	2	New York		*Territories and*
5	Illinois	4	North Carolina		*Possessions*
5	Indiana	8	North Dakota		
7	Iowa	5	Ohio	1	Canal Zone
7	Kansas	6	Oklahoma	10	Guam
4	Kentucky	10	Oregon	2	Puerto Rico
6	Louisiana	3	Pennsylvania	2	Virgin Islands
1	Maine				

Region I

Regional Administrator: Walter P. Parker
Address: JFK Federal Building, Room 1612C, Boston MA 02203
Tel.: (617) 223-4305

Wage and Hour Division
Assistant Regional Administrator: William L. Smith
Address: Same
Tel.: (617) 223-0995

Wage-Hour Area Offices
Boston
Address: Park Square Bldg., Room 462, 31 St. James Ave., Boston MA 02116
Tel.: (617) 223-6751

Hartford
Address: Federal Bldg., Rm. 305, 135 High Street, Hartford CT 06103
Tel.: (203) 244-2660

Portland
Address: Area Director, 66 Pearl St., Portland ME 04101
Tel: (207) 780-3344

Providence
Address: Area Director, John E. Fogarty, Fed. Bldg., 24 Weybosset St., Rm. 103, Providence RI 02903
Tel.: (401) 528-4378

Region II

Regional Administrator: Frank B. Mercurio
Address: 1515 Broadway, Rm. 3300, New York NY 10036
Tel.: (212) 944-3351

Wage and Hour Division

Assistant Regional Administrator: Raymond G. Condelli
Address: Same

Tel.: (212) 944-3348

Wage-Hour Area Offices
Albany
Address: Area Director, Leo W. O'Brien Federal Bldg., Rm. 822, Albany, NY 12207
Tel.: (518) 472-3596

Bronx
Address: Area Director, 400 East Fordham Rd., Rm. 302, Bronx NY 10458
Tel.: (212) 298-9472

Brooklyn
Address: Area Director, 271 Cadman Plaza East, Rm. 631, Brooklyn, NY 11201
Tel.: (212) 330-7662

Buffalo
Address: Area Director, Harry J. Gray, Federal Bldg., Rm. 617, 111 West Huron St., Buffalo NY 14202
Tel.: (716) 846-4891

Hempstead L.I.
Address: Area Director, 159 North Franklin St., Hempstead, L.I. NY 11550
Tel.: (516) 481-0582

New York City
Address: Area Director, 26 Federal Plaza, Rm. 2946, New York NY 10007
Tel.: (212) 264-8185

Newark
Address: Area Director, 970 Broad St., Rm. 836, Newark NJ 07102
Tel.: (201) 645-2279

Trenton
Address: Area Director, 402 East State St., Rm. 411, Trenton NJ 08603
Tel.: (609) 989-2247

(ESA Regional Offices—Continued)

Caribbean Office

Address: Area Director, F. Degetau Fed. Office Bldg., Rm. 403, Carlos Chardon St., Hato Rey PR 00918
Tel.: (809) 753-4442

Wage-Hour Area Offices

Hato Rey

Address: Area Director, F. Degetau Federal Office Bldg., Rm. 152, Carlos Chardon St., Hato Rey PR 00918
Tel.: (809) 765-0404, Ext. 263

Region III

Regional Administrator: James W. Kight
Address: Gateway Bldg. Rm. 15230, 3535 Market Street, Philadelphia, PA 19104
Tel.: (215) 596-1185

Wage and Hour Division

Assistant Regional Administrator: John A. Craven, Jr.
Address: Same
Tel.: (215) 596-1194

Wage-Hour Area Offices

Baltimore

Address: Area Director, Federal Office Bldg., Rm. 913, 31 Hopkins Plaza, Charles Ctr., Baltimore MD 21201
Tel.: (301) 962-2265

Charleston

Address: Area Director, 22 Capitol St., Suite 100, Charleston WV 25301
Tel.: (304) 343-6181, Ext. 448

Harrisburg

Address: Area Director, Federal Bldg., Rm. 774, 228 Walnut St., Harrisburg PA 17108
Tel.: (717) 782-4539

Hyattsville

Address: Area Director, Al Morrone Presidential Bldg., 6525 Belcrest Rd., Suite 904, Hyattsville MD 20782
Tel.: (301) 436-6767

Philadelphia

Address: Area Director, 600 Arch St., Rm. 4244, Philadelphia PA 19106
Tel.: (215) 597-4950

Pittsburgh

Address: Area Director, Federal Bldg., Rm. 1429, 1000 Liberty Avenue, Pittsburgh PA 15222
Tel.: (412) 644-2996

Richmond

Address: Area Director, Federal Bldg., Rm. 7000, 400 North Eighth St., Richmond VA 23240
Tel.: (804) 771-2995

Region IV

Regional Administrator: James E. Patching, Jr.
Address: 1371 Peachtree Street, NE, Atlanta GA 30367
Tel.: (404) 881-2818

Wage and Hour Division

Assistant Regional Administrator: Richard Robinette
Address: Same
Tel.: (404) 881-4801

Birmingham, AL

Assistant Regional Administrator: Sterling B. Williams
Address: 1931 Ninth Avenue South, Birmingham AL 35256
Tel.: (205) 254-1301

Wage-Hour Area Offices

Atlanta

Address: Area Director, Citizens' Trust Bldg., Rm. 1100, 75 Piedmont Ave., N.E., Atlanta GA 30303
Tel.: (404) 221-6401

Birmingham

Address: Area Director, 1931 Ninth Ave., south Birmingham AL 35256
Tel.: (205) 254-1305

Charlotte

Address: Area Director, BSR Bldg., Rm. 401, 316 East Morehead St., Charlotte NC 28202
Tel.: (704) 371-6120

Columbia SC

Address: Area Director, Federal Bldg., Rm. 1072, 1835 Assembly St., Columbia SC 29201
Tel.: (803) 765-5981

Fort Lauderdale

Address: Area Director, Federal Bldg., Rm. 307, 299 East Broward Blvd., Fort Lauderdale FL 33301
Tel.: (305) 527-7762

Jackson

Address: Area Director, Billy R. Jones Federal Bldg., Suite 1414, 100 West Capitol St., Jackson MS 39201
Tel.: (601) 960-4347

Jacksonville

Address: Area Director, 3947 Blvd. Ctr. Drive, Suite 121, Jacksonville FL 32207
Tel.: (904) 791-2489

Knoxville

Address: Area Director, 608 South Gay St., Rm. 202, Knoxville TN 37902
Tel.: (615) 637-9300, Ext. 4246

(ESA Regional Offices—Continued)

Lexington

Address: Area Director, Concord Square, Suite C, 1460. Newtown Rd., Lexington N.Y. 40505

Tel.: (606) 252-2312 Ext. 2575

Louisville

Address: Area Director, Federal Bldg., Rm. 187-E, 600 Federal Place, Louisville KY 40402

Tel.: (502) 582-5226

Memphis

Address: Area Director, Federal Office Bldg., Rm. 486, 167 North Main Street, Memphis TN 38103

Tel.: (901) 534-3418

Miami

Address: Area Director, Rm. 202, 1150 Southwest First St., Miami FL 33130

Tel.: (305) 350-5767

Mobile

Address: Area Director, 951 Government St. Bldg., Rm. 417, Mobile AL 36604

Tel.: (205) 690-2311

Montgomery

Address: Area Director, 474 South Court St., Montgomery AL 36104

Tel.: (205) 832-7450

Nashville

Address: Area Director, West End Bldg., Rm. 610, 1720 West End Ave., Nashville TN 37203

Tel.: (615) 749-5452

Orlando

Address: Area Director, Orlando Professional Ctr., Rm. 309, 22 West Lake Beauty Drive, Orlando FL 32806

Tel.: (305) 841-1026

Raleigh

Address: Area Director, Federal Bldg., Rm. 408, 310 New Bern Ave., Raleigh NC 27486

Tel.: (919) 755-4190

Savannah

Address: Area Director, Rm. 104 415 West Broughton St., Savannah GA 31401

Tel.: (912) 232-4321, Ext. 222

Tampa

Address: Area Director, Suite 402, Interstate Bldg., 1211 N. Westshore Blvd., Tampa FL 33607-4604

Tel.: (813) 228-2154

Region V

Regional Administrator: William Van Zanen

Address: 230 South Dearborn Street, Chicago IL 60604

Tel.: (312) 353-7280

Wage and Hour Division

Assistant Regional Administrator: Richard A. McMahon, Jr.

Deputy Assistant Regional Administrator: Barry J. Haber

Address: Same

Tel.: (312) 353-8845, 7250

Wage-Hour Area Offices

Chicago

Address: Area Director, Federal Building, Rm 412, 2305 Dearborn Street, Chicago, IL 60604

Tel.: (312) 353-8145

Cincinnati

Address: Area Director, Federal Office Bldg., Rm. 3525, 550 Main St., Cincinnati OH 45202

Tel.: (513) 684-2902

Cleveland

Address: Area Director, Federal Office Bldg., Rm. 817, 1240 East 9th St., Cleveland OH 44199

Tel.: (216) 522-3892, 3893

Columbus

Address: Area Director, 646 Federal Office Bldg., 200 N. High St., Columbus OH 43215

Tel.: (614) 469-5677

Grand Rapids

Address: Area Director, 82 Ionia St., N.W., Grand Rapids MI 49503

Tel.: (616) 456-2337

Indianapolis

Address: Area Director, Minton-CapeHart Building, Rm. 106, 575 N. Pennsylvania Street, Indianapolis IN 46204

Tel.: (317) 269-6801

(ESA Regional Offices—Continued)

Madison

Address: Area Director, Federal Center Bldg., Rm. 309, 212 E. Washington Ave., Madison WI 53703
Tel.: (608) 264-5221

Milwaukee

Address: Area Director, Henry Reuss Federal Plaza, 310 W. Wisconsin Avenue, Rm. 1280, Milwaukee WI 53203
Tel.: (414) 291-3585

Minneapolis

Address: Area Director, Bridge Place, Rm. 102, 220 South Second Street, Minneapolis MN 55401
Tel.: (612) 349-3701, 3702

South Bend

Address: Area Director, JMS Building, Rm. 523, 108 N. Main Street, South Bend IN 46601
Tel.: (219) 236-8331

Springfield

Address: Area Director, 524 South 2nd St., Rm. 630, Springfield IL 62701
Tel.: (217) 492-4060

Region VI

Regional Administrator: Bill A. Belt
Address: 555 Griffin Square Building, Dallas TX 75202
Tel.: (214) 767-6894

Wage and Hour Division
Assistant Regional Administrator: Alfred A. Ramsey
Address: Same
Tel.: (214) 767-6891

Wage-Hour Area Offices
Albuquerque

Address: Area Director, 505 Marquette Ave. N.W., Suite 1130, Albuquerque NM 87102
Tel.: (505) 766-2477

Baton Rouge

Address: Area Director, Hoover Bldg., Rm. 216-B, 8312 Florida Blvd., Baton Rouge LA 70806
Tel.: (504) 924-5160

Corpus Christi

Address: Area Director, Six Hundred Bldg., Rm. 714, 600 Leopard St., Corpus Christi TX 78473
Tel.: (512) 888-3156

Dallas

Address: Area Director, 1607 Main St., Suite 200, Dallas TX 75201
Tel.: (214) 767-6294

Fort Worth

Address: Area Director, 819 Taylor St., Rm. 7A12, Forth Worth TX 76102
Tel.: (817) 334-2678

Houston

Address: Area Director, 2320 La-Branch, Rm. 2101, Houston TX 77004
Tel.: (713) 226-4304

Little Rock

Address: Area Director, Federal Office Bldg., Rm. 3519, 700 West Capitol St., Little Rock AR 72201
Tel.: (501) 378-5292

New Orleans

Address: Area Director, Federal Bldg., Rm. 703, 600 South St., New Orleans LA 70130
Tel.: (504) 589-6171

San Antonio

Address: Area Director, U.S. Federal Bldg., Rm. A-621, 727 East Durango, San Antonio TX 78206
Tel.: (512) 229-6125

Tulsa

Address: Area Director, Center Mall Professional Bldg., 717 South Houston, Suite 306, Tulsa OK 74127
Tel.: (918) 581-7695

Region VII

Regional Administrator: Everett P. Jennings
Address: Federal Office Bldg., Rm. 2000, 911 Walnut Street, Kansas City MO 64106
Tel.: (816) 374-5381

Wage and Hour Division
Assistant Regional Administrator: Manuel J. Villarreal, Jr.
Address: Same
Tel.: (816) 374-5386

Wage-Hour Area Office
Des Moines

Address: Area Director, Federal Bldg., Rm. 643, 210 Walnut St., Des Moines IA 50309
Tel.: (515) 284-4625

Kansas City MO

Address: Area Director, Federal Office Bldg., Rm. 2900, 911 Walnut St., Kansas City MO 64106
Tel.: (816) 374-5721

Omaha

Address: Area Director, Federal Bldg., Rm. 436 110 North 14th St., Omaha NE 68102
Tel.: (402) 221-4682

(ESA Regional Offices—Continued)

St. Louis

Address: Area Director, 210 North Tucker Blvd., Rm. 563, St. Louis, MO 63101
Tel.: (314) 425-4706

Region VIII

Regional Administrator: Doyle I. Loveridge
Address: Federal Office Building, Rm. 1442, 1961 Stout Street, Denver CO 80294
Tel.: (303) 837-5903

Wage and Hour Division

Assistant Regional administrator: Loren E. Gilbert
Address: Same
Tel.: Same

Wage-Hour Area Offices
Denver

Address: Area Director, U.S. Custom House, Rm. 228, 721-19th St., Denver CO 80202
Tel.: (303) 837-4405

Salt Lake City

Address: Area Director, Federal Bldg., Rm. 4311, 125 South State St., Salt Lake City UT 84138
Tel.: (801) 524-5706

Region IX

Regional Administrator: William C. Buhl
Address: 450 Golden Gate Avenue, Rm. 10353, San Francisco CA 94102
Tel.: (415) 556-1318

Wage and Hour Division

Assistant Regional Administrator: Herbert Goldstein
Address: Same
Tel.: (415) 556-3592

Wage-Hour Area Offices
Glendale

Address: Area Director, 115 North Central Ave., Glendale CA 91203
Tel: (213) 240-5274

Los Angeles

Address: Area Director, Federal Bldg., Rm. 3251, 300 North Los Angeles St., Los Angeles CA 90012
Tel.: (213) 688-4957-4958

Phoenix

Address: Area Director, 2120 North Central Ave., Suite G-130, Phoenix AZ 85004
Tel.: (602) 261-4224, 4223

Sacramento

Address: Area Director 2800 Cottage Way, Rm. 1603-E, Sacramento CA 95825
Tel.: (916) 484-4447

San Francisco

Address: Area Director, Rm. 341, 211 Main St., San Francisco CA 94105
Tel.: (405) 556-6815, 6816

Santa Ana

Address: Area Director, 1600 North Broadway, Suite 440, Santa Ana CA 92706
Tel.: (714) 836-2156

Region X

Regional Administrator: Joe Garcia
Address: 909 First Avenue, Rm. 4141, Seattle WA 98174
Tel.: (206) 442-1536

Wage and Hour Division

Assistant Regional Administrator: Wilbur J. Olson
Address: Same
Tel.: (206) 442-2805

Wage-Hour Area Offices
Portland

Address: Area Director, 540 New Federal Bldg., 1220 Southwest 3rd Ave., Portland OR 97204
Tel.: (503) 221-3057

Seattle

Address: Area Director, Century Bldg., Rm. 510, 1520 Third Ave., Seattle, WA 98101
Tel.: (206) 442-4482

APPENDIX E

CHART OF STATE MINIMUM WAGES

Comparison Chart — State Minimum Wage

Most employees are covered by the federal minimum wage standard — currently $3.35 an hour — established by the Fair Labor Standards Act. However, most states also have enacted minimum wage laws. In some cases, these state laws establish a higher minimum wage standard than the federally imposed $3.35 minimum. Employers in these states generally are obliged to pay the higher state rate. In other cases, state laws may provide minimum wage protections for groups of employees not covered by the federal law. These laws typically either extend rights to the federal minimum rate to the unprotected groups or establish a lower minimum wage rate that employers must pay. State minimum wage requirements are established either by state legislatures or by wage boards authorized by the legislatures. Wage board orders usually are directed at wage rates for particular industries or occupational groups.

STATE	REQUIREMENTS AND PROVISIONS
Alabama	**Minimum Wage** — No state requirements.
Alaska	**Minimum Wage Established by State Law** — $3.85 an hour. Less than minimum wage for handicapped, apprentices, learners, and those employed in work therapy in certain residential drug or alcohol treatment programs if approved by Commissioner. Less than minimum wage for minors under 18 if working not more than 30 hours a week on part-time basis. Tips or gratuities may not be applied toward the minimum wage. **Employees Covered** — All employees, except: those in agriculture; babysitters and domestic workers; federal employees; voluntary workers for nonprofit charitable, cemetery, or educational organizations; newspaper deliverers; watchmen or caretakers for property not in productive use for four or more months; those in bona fide executive, administrative, or professional capacity; outside salespersons on commission; those searching for placer or hard rock minerals; certain employees of nonprofit educational or childcare facility serving as live-in parents. **Wage Board Orders** — None.
Arizona	**Minimum Wage Established by State Law** — No state requirements. However, state law allows minimum rate for minors under 18 to be set by a wage board for any substantial number of minors receiving unfair wages and wages that do not meet minimum cost of living necessary for health. Less than experienced minors' wage for minor learners and handicapped minors if recommended by a wage board. Less than minimum fair rate for handicapped minors, with license from Industrial Commission. **Employees Covered** — All minor employees under 18, except part-time employees who are: students, domestic workers, or agricultural workers. **Wage Board Orders** — None.
Arkansas	**Minimum Wage Established by State Law** — $3.15 an hour. Less than minimum wage for learners, apprentices, full-time students, and those handicapped by lack of skill, age, physical deficiency or injury, or otherwise, with special license from Labor Board. At least 85 percent of minimum wage for full-time students of state-accredited school working 20 hours or less during school session or 40 hours during vacation. Tips may be counted as part of the minimum wage up to $1.35 per hour for employees customarily receiving tips.

Comparison Chart — State Minimum Wage —Contd.

STATE	REQUIREMENTS AND PROVISIONS
Arkansas— Contd.	**Employees Covered** — All employees of employer of five or more workers, except: those covered by FLSA; those working in bona fide executive, administrative, or professional capacity; outside salespersons on commission; employees of federal, state, or local government, except public schools and educational, charitable, religious or nonprofit school districts where no employer-employee relationship exists; independent contractors; workers for agricultural employers not using more than 500 worker-hours of agricultural labor in any quarter of preceding year; members of agricultural employer's immediate family; certain hand-harvest laborers; those in range production of livestock; and certain forestry and lumber workers. **Wage Board Orders** — None.
California	**Minimum Wage Established by State Law** — None. See wage board orders. However, state law requires at least 85 percent of minimum wage for student employees and counselors of organized camp, regardless of hours worked. **Wage Board Orders** — Minimum wage of $3.35 an hour for industries listed below. At least 85 percent of minimum wage for: learners 18 or older in first 160 hours, if no previous experience; minors if number doesn't exceed 25 percent of regular workers (except during school vacation); and up to three minor workers of employers with less than 10 workers. Less than minimum wage for handicapped by special license on joint application of employer and employee to Industrial Welfare Commission. Tips may not be credited toward the minimum wage, but certain rates for meals and lodging may be applied with employee's voluntary written agreement. The minimum wage applies to the following industries and occupations: manufacturing; personal service; canning, freezing, preserving; professional, technical, clerical, mechanical, and similar occupations; public housekeeping; laundry, linen supply, dry cleaning, and dyeing; mercantile; farm products, after harvest; transportation; amusement and recreation (except full-time ride operators of traveling carnivals); broadcasting; motion picture industry; on-farm preparing of agricultural products for market; agricultural occupations (except sheepherding); and household occupations. **Employees Covered** — All employees covered by wage board orders, including minors, except: those in administrative, executive, or professional capacity paid at least $900 a month and licensed or certified by state in certain occupations; federal, state, or local government employees; outside salespersons; employer's parent, spouse, child, or legally adopted child; and persons exempted by individual order.
Colorado	**Minimum Wage Established by State Law** — None. See wage board orders. **Wage Board Orders** — A minimum wage of $3.00 an hour for all employees in the laundry and dry cleaning, retail trades, public housekeeping, beauty services, food and beverage, medical profession, and janitorial industries. At least 85 percent of minimum wage for unemancipated minors and handicapped (if certified impairment) in above industries. Tips may be considered as up to 40 percent of minimum wage of employee regularly receiving more than $30 a month in tips, with signed written report from employee. Deductions from wages may be made for: reasonable cost or fair market value for employee's full maintenance on seven-day-a-week basis; reasonable cost or fair market value (but not employer profit) of meals; or reasonable cost of lodging not exceeding $15 a week.

Comparison Chart — State Minimum Wage —Contd.

STATE	REQUIREMENTS AND PROVISIONS
Colorado— Contd.	**Employees Covered** — All employees, including emancipated minors under 18, except: certain medical occupations; teachers; supervisors; resident managers; outside salespersons; employees of federal, state, or local government; student employees in college dormitory or club; students enrolled in work experience study (special education) program; and unpaid workers in institutional laundry.
Connecticut	**Minimum Wage Established by State Law** — $3.37 an hour. At least 85 percent of minimum wage for learners, beginners, and minors under 18 for first 200 hours, then regular wage rate, except for institutional training programs exempted by Labor Commissioner. At least 85 percent of minimum wage for minors age 14-18 working in agriculture, but 70 percent if working for employer with eight or fewer workers during preceding calendar year. Less than minimum wage for physically or mentally handicapped and for learners and apprentices in established programs, with permission of Commissioner. **Employees Covered** — All employees, except: those working in camps or resorts open no more than six months a year; domestic workers; those in bona fide executive, administrative, or professional capacity; federal employees; volunteers in activities of educational, charitable, literary, or nonprofit organization without employer-employee relationship; head resident or resident assistant of college or university; outside salespersons; and employees of nonprofit theater operating no more than seven months in calendar year. **Wage Board Orders** — Tips may be credited for up to 23 percent of the minimum wage for hotel employees and not more than 35 cents an hour for other employees customarily receiving tips, when recorded on weekly basis. Cost of board (85 cents for full meal, 45 cents for light meal), lodging ($4 for private room, $3 for shared room), uniforms, and protective apparel may be deducted from minimum wage.
Delaware	**Minimum Wage Established by State Law** — $3.00 an hour. Less than minimum wage for handicapped, learners, and apprenticeships, with permission of Department of Labor. Gratuities may be credited up to one-third of minimum wage for employees regularly receiving more than $30 a month in gratuities and tips. **Employees Covered** — All employees, except: agricultural and domestic workers; those in bona fide executive, administrative, or professional capacity; outside salespersons on commission; volunteers of educational, charitable, religious, or nonprofit organization; federal employees; and those working in fish and seafood industry up through first processing. **Wage Board Orders** — None.
District of Columbia	**Minimum Wage Established by State Law** — None. See wage board orders. **Wage Board Orders** — $3.35-$4.75 an hour, depending on industry and employee status. Industry: $3.50 an hour for retail trade; $3.70 an hour for laundry and dry cleaning; $3.80 an hour for hotel, restaurant, apartment building, and allied occupations; $3.90 for clerical, semi-technical, and certain miscellaneous occupations; $3.95 an hour for manufacturing, wholesale trade, printing and publishing; $4.50 an hour for beauty culture; and $4.75 for building services. Certain credits for meals and lodging may be applied to minimum wage, depending on industry. Employee status: $3.35-$3.70 an hour for adult learners under certain conditions and depending on the industry; $3.35 an hour for minors under 18 in most industries, but full rate for minors employed by higher education institutions. Less than minimum wage for handicapped, with certificate from Wage-Hour Board.

Comparison Chart — State Minimum Wage —Contd.

STATE	REQUIREMENTS AND PROVISIONS
District of Columbia—Contd.	**Employees Covered** — All employees, except: U.S. and D.C. government workers; unpaid volunteers with educational, charitable, religious, or nonprofit organizations; lay members in religious activities within religious organizations; casual babysitters; those in bona fide executive, administrative, or professional capacity; outside salespersons; and those in home newspaper delivery.
Florida	**Minimum Wage** — No state requirements.
Georgia	**Minimum Wage Established by State Law** — $3.25 an hour. Less than minimum wage to certain organizations and businesses to employ handicapped and others who cannot compete effectively, with authorization of Commissioner of Labor. **Employees Covered** — All employees, except: those subject to FLSA; employees of employers with five or fewer workers; farm owners, share croppers, and land renters; domestic workers; those working for employers with sales of $40,000 or less a year; those paid wholly or partially in tips; high school and college students; and newspaper carriers. **Wage Board Orders** — None.
Hawaii	**Minimum Wage Established by State Law** — $3.35 an hour. Less than minimum wage for learners, apprentices, those impaired by old age or physical or mental handicap, certain students, and paroled wards of state youth correctional facility, with rule provided by Director of Labor and Industrial Relations. Twenty cents an hour less than minimum wage allowed for employees regularly receiving more than $20 a month in tips, if combined wages and tips are at least 50 cents an hour more than minimum wage. **Employees Covered** — All employees, except: those with guaranteed monthly salary of $1,000; workers in small coffee harvesting operations; domestic workers; houseparents in charitable organizations; employer's relatives (brother, sister, brother-in-law, sister-in-law, son, daughter, spouse, parent, parent-in-law); those employed in bona fide executive, administrative, supervisory, or professional capacity; outside salespersons or collectors; those in fish or aquatic farming industry prior to first processing; seamen; on-call, fixed stand vehicle drivers; golf caddies; student employees of nonprofit school; seasonal employees of certain nonprofit youth camps; and automobile or truck salespersons for licensed dealer. **Wage Board Orders** — None.
Idaho	**Minimum Wage Established by State Law** — $2.30 an hour. Less than minimum wage for handicapped, learners, and apprentices, with license from Director of Labor and Industrial Services. Less than minimum wage for minors under 16 working part-time or at odd jobs not exceeding four hours per day with one employer. Tips may not be counted toward minimum wage, although commissions and reasonable cost (as defined by Employment Security Agency) of meals, lodging, or other facilities furnished employee may be deducted. **Employees Covered** — All employees, except: employees of federal, state, or local government; of any labor organization (other than when acting as employer); those in bona fide executive, administrative, or professional capacity; agricultural and domestic workers; outside salespersons; and seasonal employees of nonprofit camp. **Wage Board Orders** — None.

Comparison Chart — State Minimum Wage —Contd.

STATE	REQUIREMENTS AND PROVISIONS
Illinois	**Minimum Wage Established by State Law** — $3.35 an hour. At least 70 percent of minimum wage for learners up to six months of learning. Less than minimum wage for handicapped, with permit from Director after public hearing. Gratuities may be credited for up to 40 percent of minimum wage, with evidence to Director that employee received tips. **Employees Covered** — All employees, except: those working for employers with less than four employees exclusive of parent, spouse, child, or immediate family member; certain agricultural workers; domestic workers; outside salespersons; members of religious corporations or organizations; certain camp counselors; and students of accredited Illinois colleges and universities employed under FLSA provisions. **Wage Board Orders** — None.
Indiana	**Minimum Wage Established by State Law** — $2.00 an hour. At least 50 percent of minimum wage for those with age, mental, or physical handicap, with rate to be determined by wage adjustment board. Less than minimum wage for minors under 17. Amount of gratuities credited toward minimum wage to be determined by board, but not to exceed 50 percent of minimum wage. **Employees Covered** — All employees, except those employed by employers with three or fewer workers during workweek; those subject to FLSA; self-employed persons; those performing services not in course of employing unit's business; those working on commission; persons employed by parent, spouse, or child; members or volunteers of religious order or charitable organization; student nurses; apprentice funeral directors and embalmers; hospital interns and residents; students working for their school; physically or mentally handicapped persons working for nonprofit organizations; insurance agents on commission; those working in camping, recreation or guidance facilities run by charitable, religious, or educational nonprofit organizations; those in executive, administrative, or professional capacity earning $150 a week; outside salespersons; those not employed for more than 10 weeks in any four consecutive 3-month periods; those subject to Motor Carrier Act or to state public service commission regulations; and certain agricultural workers. **Wage Board Orders** — None.
Iowa	**Minimum Wage** — No state requirements.
Kansas	**Minimum Wage Established by State Law** — $1.60 an hour. At least 80 percent of minimum wage for learners and apprentices upon hiring, 90 percent after two months, and full minimum wage after three months, with permit from Secretary of Human Resources. At least 85 percent of minimum wage for handicapped and patient laborers at state institutions or hospitals, with one-year permit from Secretary. Gratuities may be credited for up to 40 percent of minimum wage for employees customarily receiving and retaining them. **Employees Covered** — All employees, except: those covered by FLSA; agricultural and domestic workers; those in bona fide executive, administrative, or professional capacity; outside salespersons on commission; federal employees; unpaid volunteers for nonprofit organization; part-time workers age 18 or under and age 60 or over; and students under 18 working between academic terms. **Wage Board Orders** — None.

Comparison Chart — State Minimum Wage —Contd.

STATE	REQUIREMENTS AND PROVISIONS
Kentucky	**Minimum Wage Established by State Law** — $3.35 an hour. Less than minimum wage for handicapped or for sheltered workshop employees upon certificate from Commissioner. At least 85 percent of minimum wage for students for maximum of 20 hours a week, then minimum wage for hours over 20. Gratuities may count for up to 50 percent of minimum wage for employees regularly receiving more than $20 a month in tips, if weekly records show employees retained tips. **Employees Covered** — All employees, except: agricultural workers; those in bona fide executive, administrative, supervisory, or professional capacity; outside salespersons or collectors as defined by Commissioner; federal employees; domestic workers; employees of retail stores, service industries, hotels, motels, and restaurants with average annual sales less than $95,000 for preceding five years; employer's parent, spouse, child, or immediate family member; babysitter or live-in companion to sick or elderly if principal duties not housekeeping; newspaper deliverers; certain emergency employees; those in nonprofit camp, or religious or nonprofit educational conference center operating no more than seven months a year. **Wage Board Orders** — None.
Louisiana	**Minimum Wage** — No state requirements.
Maine	**Minimum Wage Established by State Law** — $3.65 an hour. Less than minimum wage for physically handicapped by age or otherwise and for learners and apprentices for fixed period of time, with license from Director of Labor and Industry. Tipped employees must receive wages of at least $2.01 an hour, with combined wages and tips ($1.54 in 1986 and $1.64 in 1987) at least equaling the minimum wage. **Employees Covered** — All employees, except: agricultural workers, as defined by state law and FUTA (but not including those working on farms with over 300,000 laying birds); domestic workers; unsupervised sales persons on commission; those in nonpolitical public-supported or educational nonprofit organization; summer camp counselors, or employees under 19 in camps operated by or belonging to non-capital stock corporations under state law; those in fish and seafood industry up through first processing; switchboard operators in public telephone exchange with less than 750 stations; unsupervised homeworkers; family members who live with or are dependent upon employer; those in bona fide executive, administrative, or professional capacity earning $175 weekly; taxicab drivers; service employees with more than $20 a month in tips. **Wage Board Orders** — None.
Maryland	**Minimum Wage Established by State Law** — $3.35 an hour. Less than minimum wage for minors under 16 employed by one or more employers more than 20 hours a week, or employees 62 or over not working more than 25 hours a week. At least 80 percent of minimum wage for apprentices and learners, with amount set by Commissioner. Less than minimum wage for physically or mentally handicapped, with certificate from Commissioner of Division of Labor and Industry or from U.S. Department of Labor if filed within 10 days of receipt. Tips may count for up to 40 percent of minimum wage for employees regularly receiving more than $30 a month in tips, if they retain tips and are informed of rules. Reasonable cost for board, lodging, or other facilities customarily furnished employee may be deducted from wages.

Comparison Chart — State Minimum Wage —Contd.

STATE	REQUIREMENTS AND PROVISIONS
Maryland— Contd.	**Employees Covered** — All employees, except: those in bona fide executive, administrative, or professional capacity; volunteers in educational, charitable, religious, or nonprofit organization where no employer-employee relationship exists; those in establishment selling food and drink for consumption on premises with annual gross income of $250,000 or less; employees of movie theaters; those processing or packaging poultry, seafood, or fresh produce or horticultural commodities; outside salespersons and those on commission; employer's parent, spouse, child, or other immediate family member; students in public school special education programs for mentally, emotionally, or physically handicapped employed as part of training; non-administrative day camp personnel; and certain agricultural workers. **Wage Board Orders** — None.
Massachusetts	**Minimum Wage Established by State Law** — $3.55 an hour; $3.65 eff. 7/1/87; $3.75 eff. 7/1/88. Less than minimum wage for those handicapped by age or physical or mental deficiency, with certificate from Commissioner of Labor and Industries. Wages set less than minimum rate: $1.25 an hour for ushers, ticket sellers, and ticket takers; $36 a week for janitors and caretakers of residences when furnished living quarters; certain rates for golf caddies; $1.60 an hour for agricultural employees, except minors under 18 and employer's parent, spouse, child, or other immediate family member. Tips may be credited for up to 40 percent of the minimum wage for employees receiving more than $20 a month in tips (except service employees in mercantile occupations and public housekeeping — wage board orders), unless employee challenges. See also wage board orders. **Wage Board Orders** — At least 80 percent of minimum wage for the following student employees, with permit from Commissioner: apprentices and learners enrolled in vocational or technical course and employed part-time pursuant to the program, for period fixed by Commissioner; students employed by school or summer camp; those employed at school, hospital, or other training establishment as part of formal training; and high school minors working in hospital ward or school dining hall or dormitory, if ratio of one minor to five adult employees. Credits for meals ($1.00 breakfast, $1.75 lunch, $1.75 dinner) and for lodging ($20 a week single, $25 double, $30 triple occupancy) may be deducted from wages, but no deduction for uniforms. (However, state law says Commissioner may set board and lodging rates for agricultural workers and other defined classes.) **Employees Covered** — All employees, except: minors under 18 in domestic service in employer's home; those being rehabilitated or trained in charitable, educational, or religious institutions; members of religious orders; agricultural, floricultural, and horticultural workers; those in professional service; and outside sales persons not reporting to or visiting office daily.
Michigan	**Minimum Wage Established by State Law** — $3.35 an hour. Less than minimum wage for those under 18 or over 64 years of age. Less than minimum wage for handicapped covered by blanket wage deviation certificate. **Wage Board Orders** — Credit for tips, meals, and lodging may be applied for a total of 25 percent of the minimum wage. Certain rates for agricultural piecework are set by the Wage Deviation Board. **Employees Covered** — All employees of employers with two or more employees within calendar year, except: those subject to FLSA, if higher minimum rate; those employed in summer camps not more than four months; employees of fruit, pickle, or tomato growers; and transient agricultural workers contracting for harvest on piecework basis.

Comparison Chart — State Minimum Wage —Contd.

STATE	REQUIREMENTS AND PROVISIONS
Minnesota	**Minimum Wage Established by State Law** — $3.35 an hour; $3.02 for minors under 18, but less for minors working under 20 hours for municipal recreation program. Gratuities of employees tipped $35 a month or more may be credited for up to five percent of the minimum wage in 1987 (but zero percent eff. 1/1/88), with signed statement from employee at time credit is taken. **Wage Board Orders** — Minimum wage of $2.07 an hour for apprentices and learners for first 300 hours. At least 50 percent of minimum wage for handicapped, with permit from Labor Standards Division. Credit for $1.15 per meal and $1.50 per night's lodging may be deducted from the minimum wage. **Employees Covered** — All employees, except: certain agricultural workers; seasonal staff members of licensed nonprofit children's camp; those in bona fide executive, administrative, or professional capacity, if meet certain criteria; salespersons with at least 80 percent sales off premises; volunteers to nonprofit organization; elected officials or volunteer workers for any political subdivision; police or firefighters; public employees ineligible to participate in public retirement association; babysitters; seasonal workers in carnival, circus, fair, or ski facility; state conservation officers; those with qualifications and hours under control of U.S. Department of Transportation; seafarers, as defined; employees supervising children in single facility residence that is extension of county home school; and those in religious orders.
Mississippi	**Minimum Wage** — No state requirements.
Missouri	**Minimum Wage** — No state requirements.
Montana	**Minimum Wage Established by State Law** — $3.35 an hour. Less than minimum wage for apprentices and learners for no more than 30 days. $3.05 an hour but no overtime rate or $635 a month for agricultural workers. $750 a month for firefighters, except during probation or training period. At least 50 percent of minimum wage for learners under 18 for 180 days, and for retired or semi-retired residential employees working part-time. Deductions for board, lodging, or other facilities furnished employee may not exceed 40 percent of total wages paid. **Employees Covered** — All employees, except: students in distributive education program of accredited agency; those performing menial chores in private home; caretakers of children directly employed by household head; employer's relatives dependent on employer for half or more support; volunteers in non-profit organization; handicapped whose work is incidental to training or evaluation program or who are severely impaired and unable to compete; those in bona fide executive, administrative, or professional capacity; and federal employees. **Wage Board Orders** — None.
Nebraska	**Minimum Wage Established by State Law** — $1.60 an hour; 90 cents an hour for employees compensated primarily by tips. **Employees Covered** — All employees, except: those working for employers with 3 or fewer workers (not including seasonal workers of 20 or fewer weeks in calendar year); babysitters in private home; those in bona fide executive, administrative, professional, or supervisory capacity; employees of federal, state or local government; those engaged in activities of educational, charitable, religious, or nonprofit organization where services voluntarily given or no employer-employee relationship exists; apprentices and learners; primary and secondary students working after school or on vaca-

Comparison Chart — State Minimum Wage —Contd.

STATE	REQUIREMENTS AND PROVISIONS
Nebraska— Contd.	tion; veterans in training under Veterans Administration supervision; employer's child or parent; physically or mentally disabled person employed in rehabilitation program and receiving any form of government aid or welfare. **Wage Board Orders** — None.
Nevada	**Minimum Wage Established by State Law** — $2.75 an hour. At least 85 percent of minimum wage for minors age 18 or under. $2.30 an hour for]agricultural workers. Tips may not be credited toward minimum wage. No more than $1.50 a day for meals may be credited toward minimum wage (agricultural workers excluded), with employee consent. **Employees Covered** — All employees, except: casual babysitters; live-in domestic workers; outside salespersons on commission; agricultural workers for employer who used no more than 500 worker-hours of labor in any quarter of preceding calendar year; and taxicab and limosine drivers. **Wage Board Orders** — None.
New Hampshire	**Minimum Wage Established by State Law** — $3.45 an hour; $3.55 eff. 1/1/88; and $3.65 eff. 1/1/89. At least 75 percent of minimum wage for employees with less than six months experience and for minors 16 years or under, if application filed with Labor Commissioner within 10 days of hire. Less than minimum wage for those with earnings impaired by age or by physical or mental handicap, including those in sheltered workshop, with rate set by Commissioner. Less than minimum, or no rate, for students in work-study programs, with rate set by Commissioner if circumstances warrant. Tips may be credited for up to 50 percent of minimum wage for workers paid more than $20 a month in tips; no more than $4.30 a day or $30 a week for room and board may be credited. **Employees Covered** — All employees, except: employer's child, grandchild, or ward; spouse working on voluntary basis; agricultural and domestic workers; outside salespersons; newscarriers; employees of summer camp for minors; and nonprofessional ski patrols or golf caddies. **Wage Board Orders** — None.
New Jersey	**Minimum Wage Established by State Law** — $3.35 an hour. Less than minimum wage for minors under 18 not possessing special vocational graduate permit. Less than minimum wage for learners, apprentices, and students, and for those with earning capacity impaired by age or by physical or mental handicap, with permit from Office of Wage and Hours Compliance. At least 85 percent of minimum wage for full-time students working for their schools. Credits applied toward minimum wage for tips, meals, and lodging vary by occupation. See also wage board orders. **Employees Covered** — All employees, except: those working for nonprofit or religious summer camp, conference, or retreat; part-time child caretakers in employer's home; outside salespersons; motor vehicle salespersons; volunteers working at agricultural fair for nonprofit or religious organization and receiving only incidental benefits. **Wage Board Orders** — Also exempt from minimum wage: those in executive, administrative, or professional capacity, as defined; volunteer firefighters, rescue workers, and other public protectors; volunteers caring for sick, aged, destitute, etc., in religious, educational, charitable, hospital, etc., activities; and patients in charitable programs receiving inconsequential pay.
New Mexico	**Minimum Wage Established by State Law** — $3.35 an hour. $2.85 for minors under 18. $2.01 for employees receiving more than $40 a month in tips. Reasonable value of room, board, utilities, and supplies may be deducted from wages of agricultural workers.

Comparison Chart — State Minimum Wage —Contd.

STATE	REQUIREMENTS AND PROVISIONS
New Mexico— Contd.	**Employees Covered** — All employees, except: those in executive, administrative, professional, or supervisory capacity; domestic workers; public employees; volunteers working for educational, charitable, religious, or nonprofit organization; salespersons and employees on commission, piece-work, or flat-rate schedule; apprentices and learners; employees of ambulance services; non-college students working after school or during vacation; persons under 18 who are not students or high school graduates; G.I. bill trainees; certain agricultural workers; resident employees of charitable, religious, or nonprofit group home for mentally, emotionally, or developmentally disabled; and certain seasonal employees of youth camps, with certificate from Labor Commissioner. **Wage Board Orders** — None.
New York	**Minimum Wage Established by State Law** — $3.35 an hour. See also wage board orders. **Employees covered** — All employees, except: babysitters and live-in companions; farm workers; those in bona fide executive, administrative, or professional capacity; outside salespersons; taxicab drivers; volunteers, learners, apprentices, students or handicapped working for nonprofit religious, charitable, or educational institution; those whose work is incidental to charitable aid received from charitable or religious organization and not under contract of hire; members of religious orders; employees of summer camp or conference of religious, charitable, or educational institution not more than three months a year; counselors in children's camp; students employed by nonprofit group in college or university; and public employees. **Wage Board Orders** — Less than minimum wage for handicapped in rehabilitation program approved by Commissioner (except wage orders covering farm workers). Minimum wage of $3.35 an hour for farm workers, if payroll $3,000 or more. Students not deemed working if obtaining supervised experience in another institution to fulfill curriculum requirements. Certain allowances for tips, gratuities, meals, and lodging for employees in the hotel and restaurant industries.
North Carolina	**Minimum Wage Established by State Law** — $3.35 an hour. At least 90 percent of minimum wage for full-time students, apprentices, learners, and messengers. Less than minimum wage for handicapped whose earning capacity is impaired by age or physical or mental deficiency, when regulated by Commissioner. At least 85 percent of minimum wage for no more than 52 weeks for those unemployed for at least 15 weeks and receiving aid to families with dependent children or supplementary social security benefits, with eligibility certificate from Employment Security Commission. At least 85 percent of minimum wage for seasonal employees, as defined. Tips may count for up to 50 percent of minimum wage; no employee's tips may be reduced more than 15 percent when pooled. Up to $10 a week for lodging and $15 a week for meals may be deducted from wages. **Employees Covered** — All employees, except: agricultural and domestic workers; babysitters; pages in state legislature and governor's office; bona fide volunteers in medical, educational, religious, or nonprofit organization where no employer-employee relationship; those confined in public penal, correctional, or mental institution; performers for TV, radio, or film; employees of outdoor drama theaters except ushers, ticket takers, and parking attendants; those working in children's summer camp or seasonal religious or nonprofit educational conference center; employees in seafood industry through first sale; employer's spouse, child, parent, or qualified dependent under state tax laws; those in bona fide executive, administrative, profes-

Comparison Chart — State Minimum Wage —Contd.

STATE	REQUIREMENTS AND PROVISIONS
North Carolina— Contd.	sional, or outside sales capacity; employee of employer with two or fewer workers in any workweek; and public employees, including those in seasonal recreation program. **Wage Board Orders** — None.
North Dakota	**Minimum Wage Established by State Law** — A minimum of $300 a month for full-time state employees. Less than minimum wage for those physically impaired by age or otherwise, with license from Labor Commissioner. See also wage board orders. **Wage Board Orders** — Minimum wage of $2.80 an hour for workers in public housekeeping; $2.95 for those in manufacturing; $3.10 an hour for employees of mercantile businesses; and $3.10 for those in professional, technical, clerical, and similar occupations. Certain rates apply for apprentices and learners. Tips for employees in public housekeeping not counted as part of minimum wage. **Employees Covered** — All employees in occupations covered by wage board orders, except outside salespersons on commission.
Ohio	**Minimum Wage Established by State Law** — $2.30 an hour. $1.50 for employees of employer with less than $150,000 in gross annual sales. At least 80 percent of minimum wage for learners for no more than 90 days, and for students at state-approved cooperative vocational education programs for no more than 180 days. At least 85 percent of minimum wage for apprentices for no more than 90 days, with license from Director of Industrial Relations. Less than minimum wage for those with earning capacity impaired by physical or mental deficiencies or injuries, with license from Director. Tips may count for up to 50 percent of minimum wage for workers given more than $20 a month in tips; notice of policy required on menus. **Employees Covered** — All employees, except: hand harvest laborers on piece-work basis or under 16 and working for parents, under certain conditions; federal employees; babysitters or live-in companions; those delivering newspapers to consumers; outside salespersons on commission; those in bona fide executive, administrative, or professional capacity; agricultural workers for employer using no more than 500 worker-hours during any calendar quarter of preceding calendar year; employer's parent, spouse, child, or other immediate family member; volunteers providing personal services in health institution; police and firefighters; students working part-time or seasonally for state political subdivision; employees of camp or recreational area for minors owned and operated by nonprofit organization. **Wage Board Orders** — Not applicable.
Oklahoma	**Minimum Wage Established by State Law** — $3.35 an hour. $2.00 an hour for those working for employer with 10 or fewer employees in one location or who grosses less than $100,000 annually. Credit toward minimum wage for tips, gratuities, meals, and lodging not to exceed 50 percent of said wage; reasonable cost of uniforms also may be credited. **Employees Covered** — All employees, except: minors under 18; employees of state, or of concessionaire; farm workers connected with raising or harvesting any farm commodity or with operating or managing a farm; domestic workers; federal employees; volunteers working for charitable, religious, or nonprofit organization; newspaper vendors or carriers; employees of any carrier subject to Part I of Interstate Commerce Act; those in bona fide executive, administrative, or professional capacity; outside salespersons; those under 18 not graduates of vocational or high school; students under 22; employees of feed store operated primarily for farmers and ranchers; and reserve force deputy sheriffs. **Wage Board Orders** — None.

Comparison Chart — State Minimum Wage —Contd.

STATE	REQUIREMENTS AND PROVISIONS
Oregon	**Minimum Wage Established by State Law** — $3.35 an hour. At least 75 percent of minimum wage for student-learners in vocational training programs, with authorization of Commissioner. Less than minimum wage for handicapped and aged, with permit from Bureau of Labor. Less than minimum wage for specific employees, including, but not limited to, mentally and physically handicapped who cannot perform all of job within entry level time, with authorization of Commissioner. Blanket approval for less than minimum wage for handicapped in sheltered workshops, etc., under certain conditions. Tips not counted as part of minimum wage, but reasonable deductions allowed for room, board, facilities, and services. **Employees Covered** — All employees over 18, except: those donating services to public employer or religious, charitable, educational, public service, or similar nonprofit organization; certain agricultural workers; domestic workers; those in administrative, executive, or professional capacity earning more than $650 a month salary; federal employees; students working for their school; outside salespersons; taxicab operators; those employed in own home; those domiciled at place of employment to be available for emergencies or occasional duties; those paid to be available for duty during specific hours; those domiciled at multi-unit accomodation designed to provide other people with lodging for purpose of maintenance, management, or assistant management; seasonal employees of camp with gross annual income less than $275,000; and those employed at nonprofit conference ground or center operated for charitable or religious purposes. **Wage Board Orders** — None.
Pennsylvania	**Minimum Wage Established by State Law** — $3.35 an hour for all hours worked, whether hourly, salaried, commissioned, piece rate, or on other basis; but separate arrangement for off-premises, unsupervised personnel, with approval of Secretary of Labor and Industry. At least 85 percent of minimum wage for learners and students, with certificate from Secretary. Less than minimum wage for handicapped with license from Secretary. Tips and gratuities may count for up to 40 percent of minimum wage, provided employees informed of provision, customarily receive more than $30 a month in tips, and retain own tips or pool among selves. Reasonable cost of room, board, and other facilities may be deducted. **Employees Covered** — All employees, except: farm laborers; domestic workers; newspaper deliverers to consumers; employees of weekly, semi-weekly, or daily publication with circulation under 4,000 and mostly within county where published or contiguous counties; those in bona fide executive, administrative, or professional capacity, including academic administrative personnel and elementary and secondary teachers; outside sales personnel, including certain retail and service personnel; voluntary workers for educational, charitable, religious, or nonprofit organization where no employer-employee relationship exists; certain seasonal workers; students working in nonprofit educational institution where enrolled; employees of public amusement or recreational establishment, organized camp, or religious or nonprofit educational conference center, under certain conditions; golf caddies; telephone company switchboard operators; and employees not subject to civil service laws: elected office holders and their personal staff and advisors. **Wage Board Orders** — None.
Puerto Rico	**Minimum Wage Established by State Law** — At least 50 percent of minimum wage for apprentices, except those whose rate is fixed by Apprenticeship Council, with permit from Secretary of Labor. At least 50 percent of minimum wage for those with earning capacity impaired by age, physical disability, injury, or other reason, with permit from Secretary. See also wage board orders.

Comparison Chart — State Minimum Wage —Contd.

STATE	REQUIREMENTS AND PROVISIONS
Puerto Rico — Contd.	**Wage Board Orders** — Minimum wage rates from 55 cents to $3.35 an hour for 40 industries set by Minimum Wage Board. **Employees Covered** — All employees in 40 specified industries, except: domestic workers (except chauffeurs); federal, commonwealth, capital, and municipal employees (except those working for commonwealth agencies operating as private enterprises); and managers, executives, and professionals.
Rhode Island	**Minimum Wage Established by State Law** — $3.55 an hour; $3.65 eff. 7/1/87. At least 75 percent of minimum wage for minors age 14-15 working 24 hours or less a week; full minimum wage for those working over 24 hours a week. At least 90 percent of minimum wage for full-time students under 19 working for nonprofit organization. Less than minimum wage for learners and apprentices during first 90 days and for handicapped, with license from Director of Labor. Tips may count for up to 35 percent of minimum wage, except for bus boys (unless receive gratuities directly from customers) and taxicab drivers. **Employees Covered** — All employees, except: agricultural and domestic workers; volunteers for educational, charitable, religious, or nonprofit organization where no employer-employee relationship; news carriers for home delivery; shoe shiners; golf caddies; bowling alley pin setters; ushers in theaters; outside salespersons; employer's parent, spouse, or child under 18; and those working between May 1 and October 1 for resort establishment regularly serving meals to general public and open not more than six months a year. **Wage Board Orders** — None.
South Carolina	**Minimum Wage** — No state requirements.
South Dakota	**Minimum Wage Established by State Law** — $2.80 an hour. Less than minimum wage for employees under 18 years. Tips may be credited for up to 30 percent of minimum wage for employees regularly receiving more than $25 a month in tips, room, board, and other considerations, with consent of employee. **Employees Covered** — All employees, except: babysitters; and outside salespersons. **Wage Board Orders** — None.
Tennessee	**Minimum Wage** — No state requirements, except that blind employees paid by state shall not be paid less than federal minimum wage.
Texas	**Minimum Wage Established by State Law** — $1.40 an hour; $3.05 for agricultural workers. Less than minimum wage for hand harvesters, as set by Commissioner. Not less than $30 a week for agricultural workers living in quarters furnished by employer, with less for employee's family members. At least 60 percent of minimum wage for handicapped and those over 65, except agricultural workers, with medical certificate. Less than minimum wage for Department of Mental Health and Mental Retardation clients working in institution as part of therapy or being trained in sheltered workshop. Tips, meals and lodging may count for up to 50 percent of minimum wage, if customarily received. Cost of meals and lodging may be deducted from wages if customarily furnished and stated separately on earnings statement.

Comparison Chart — State Minimum Wage —Contd.

STATE	REQUIREMENTS AND PROVISIONS
Texas— Contd.	**Employees Covered** — All employees, except: members of religious orders and Christian Science readers on duty; those under 18 not vocational or high school graduates; students under 20, except those in agriculture; those in bona fide executive, administrative, or professional capacity; outside salespersons and collectors on commission; switchboard operators in certain independent companies; babysitters and domestic workers; those in jail; volunteers for nonprofit organization where no employer-employee relationship exists; family members; certain handicapped workers under 21; employees of certain amusement or recreational establishments; those working for Boy or Girl Scouts of America, or nonprofit camp; employees of dairy farm; agricultural workers not covered by state unemployment compensation act; and employee and spouse working for nonprofit educational organization as residential parents to children and receiving room and board without cost. **Wage Board Orders** — None.
Utah	**Minimum Wage Established by State Law** — None. See wage board orders. **Wage Board Orders** — $2.75 an hour for minors in Salt Lake, Weber, Utah, and Davies Counties, and cities with population of 5,000 or more; $2.50 in all other areas. Ten cents less than minimum wage for first 80 hours for inexperienced employees with less than 400 hours in industry. Twenty cents less than minimum wage for students working part-time or during vacation. Less than minimum wage for minors who are handicapped, learners, and apprentices, with license from Commissioner. Tips may count for up to 25 percent of minimum wage for employees receiving at least $30 a month in tips and gratuities. **Employees Covered** — Minors in restaurant, retail trade, public housekeeping, and laundry, cleaning, dyeing, and pressing industries.
Vermont	**Minimum Wage Established by State Law** — $3.45 an hour, $3.55 eff. 7/1/87, and $3.65 eff. 7/1/88, after employee has worked 90 days. Deductions from the minimum wage allowed for board, lodging, apparel, rent, utilities, or other items as may be usual. See also wage board orders. **Employees Covered** — All employees of employer with two or more workers, except: agricultural and domestic workers; federal or state employees; those in public-supported nonprofit organization, except laundry workers, nurses aides or practical nurses; those in bona fide executive, administrative, or professional capacity; home deliverers of newspapers or advertising; outside salespersons; and students working during school year or vacation. **Wage Board Orders** — Minimum wage of $3.35 an hour for employees in hotel, motel, restaurant, tourist, retail, wholesale, and service occupations; less than minimum wage for handicapped in these occupations, with permit from Commissioner. Less than minimum wage for learners in retail, wholesale, and service industries, with permit from Commissioner. For employees receiving $2.01 or more an hour in tips, a maximum of $1.34 an hour may be counted toward the minimum wage for service workers in hotel, motel, tourist, and restaurant occupations. Certain deductions from minimum wage in retail, wholesale, and service industries allowed for meals and lodging, but not for cost of uniform.

Comparison Chart — State Minimum Wage —Contd.

STATE	REQUIREMENTS AND PROVISIONS
Virginia	**Minimum Wage Established by State Law** — $2.65 an hour. Less than minimum wage for those under 16 or over 64, persons whose earning capacity is impaired by physical or mental deficiency, and students and apprentices in bona fide educational or apprenticeship programs. Amount deducted from wages for tips shall be determined by employer, unless employee able to show actual amount is less. Reasonable cost of meals and lodging may be deducted, if customarily furnished. **Employees Covered** — All employees of employers with at least four workers (excluding employer's spouse, parent, or child), except: county or municipal employees; farm laborers or employees; domestic workers; those working in primarily public-supported charitable institutions; volunteers in educational, charitable, religious, or nonprofit organization where no employer-employee relationship exists; newsboys; shoe shiners; golf caddies; babysitters; theater ushers, cashiers, and concession and door attendants; outside salespersons on commission; taxicab drivers and operators; employer's child or ward under 18; those confined in state or local penal, corrective, or mental institutions; employees of children's summer camp; those employed on piece-rate basis; full-time students under 18 not employed more than 20 hours a week; students of any age enrolled in full-time work study program or equivalent at educational institution; and minors under 18 under jurisdiction of a juvenile and domestic relations district court. **Wage Board Orders** — None.
Washington	**Minimum Wage Established by State Law** — $2.30 an hour. At least 85 percent of minimum wage for learners 18 or over, and 75 percent for student learners, 18 or over. Less than minimum wage for handicapped, with permit from Director. See also wage board orders. **Employees Covered** — All employees, except: volunteers registered with state or federal volunteer program; volunteers for educational, religious, governmental, or non-profit charitable organization; those in bona fide executive, administrative, or professional capacity; commissioned outside salespersons; and independent contractors controlling own manner and means of work. **Wage Board Orders** — Minimum wage of $2.00 for employees of employers covered by Industrial Welfare Commission's wage rate determination. Minimum wage of $1.75 an hour for minors under 18. Certain minimum rates for workers in seasonal recreational camps. Tips and gratuities not to be considered part of minimum wage.
West Virginia	**Minimum Wage Established by State Law** — $3.35 an hour. Less than minimum wage for those 62 years or over if receiving social security old-age or survivors benefits. Tips may count for 20 percent of minimum wage, and credit of $1.00 a day for meals allowed for full-time workers. Reasonable deductions allowed for board and lodging, as provided in regulations by Commissioner of Labor. **Employees Covered** — All employees of employers with six or more workers in one location or establishment, unless 80 percent of workers covered by FLSA, except: federal employees; volunteers in educational, charitable, religious, fraternal, or nonprofit organization with no employer-employee relationship; newsboys; shoe shiners; golf caddies; bowling alley pin setters and chasers; outside salespersons; employer's spouse, parent, or child; those in bona fide professional, executive, or administrative capacity; on-the-job trainees; severely physically and mentally handicapped employed in nonprofit sheltered workshop; employees of children's camp; agricultural workers, as defined by FLSA; state firefighters; theater ushers; students working part-time; employees of motorbus carriers; and certain employees of state legislature.

Comparison Chart — State Minimum Wage —Contd.

STATE	REQUIREMENTS AND PROVISIONS
West Virgin-ia— Contd.	**Wage Board Orders** — None.
Wisconsin	**Minimum Wage Established by State Law** — None. See wage board orders. **Wage Board Orders** — Minimum wage of $3.25 an hour, including minors 17 and under engaged in street trades. $2.90 an hour for all other minors 17 and under. $3.05 an hour for agricultural workers, but $2.70 for those 17 and under. At least 75 percent of minimum rate for handicapped and student learners age 14-18 in bona fide training program, with license from Department of Industry, Labor, and Human Relations. Certain rates for caddies and employees of nonprofit seasonal camps. At least 50 percent of minimum wage for workers in sheltered workshops that are not work activities centers or for training or evaluation programs, with license from Department. Minimum wage of $1.95 for adults receiving tips, and $1.65 for minors under 17, with employee consent. Certain credits also allowed for tipped adults and minors furnished meals and lodging. **Employees Covered** — All employees, except: home newspaper deliverers; those in direct retail sales to consumers; real estate agents and salespersons strictly on commission; casual domestic workers employed 15 hours or less a week; and certain live-in companions.
Wyoming	**Minimum Wage Established by State Law** — $1.60 an hour. Up to 50 percent of tips may be counted as part of the minimum wage of employees customarily receiving more than $20 a month in tips, so long as wages paid are not less than $1.10 an hour. **Employees Covered** — All employees 18 years and over, except: agricultural workers; those in executive, administrative, or professional capacity; public employees; those in educational, charitable, religious, or nonprofit organization where no employer-employee relationship exists or on voluntary basis; outside salespersons solely on commission; drivers of ambulances or other vehicles on call at any time; and part-time and piece workers working 20 hours a week or less. **Wage Board Orders** — None.

APPENDIX F

COEFFICIENT TABLE FOR COMPUTING OVERTIME

Coefficient Table for Computing Overtime

The coefficient table below (WH-134) was prepared by Wage-Hour and Public Contracts Divisions to simplify overtime computations. The accompanying text is the official explanation of how the table was constructed and how it may be used.

In determining the extra half-time that is due for overtime pay, the method of calculation commonly used is to divide the straight-time earnings by the total number of hours worked and multiply the results by the number of overtime hours divided by two. For instance, in weeks in which overtime is due after 40 hours, the computation would be :

$$\text{for } 47\tfrac{3}{4} \text{ hours, } \frac{\text{Earnings}}{47\tfrac{3}{4}} \times \frac{7\tfrac{3}{4}}{2};$$

$$\text{for 48 hours, } \frac{\text{Earnings}}{48} \times \frac{8}{2}; \text{ and}$$

$$\text{for 50 hours, } \frac{\text{Earnings}}{50} \times \frac{10}{2}.$$

The following tables contain the decimal equivalents of the fraction, $\dfrac{\text{O.T. Hours}}{\text{Total Hrs.} \times 2}$

For example, the decimal for :

$$47\tfrac{3}{4} \text{ hours } \frac{7\tfrac{3}{4}}{47\tfrac{3}{4} \times 2} = \frac{7.75}{95.5} = .081;$$

$$\text{for 48 hours is } \frac{8}{48 \times 2} = \frac{1}{12} = .083; \text{ and}$$

$$\text{for 50 hours it is } \frac{10}{50 \times 2} = \frac{1}{10} = .1 .$$

U.S. DEPARTMENT OF LABOR
EMPLOYMENT STANDARDS ADMINISTRATION
WAGE AND HOUR DIVISION

COEFFICIENT TABLE FOR COMPUTING EXTRA HALF-TIME FOR OVERTIME

This Form has been prepared for use by employers who may find the coefficient table to be a time-saver when computing the extra half-time for hours worked over 40 in a workweek.

Hours 40	Even	1/4	1/2	3/4	1/10	2/10	3/10	4/10	6/10	7/10	8/10	9/10
		0.003	0.006	0.009	0.0012	0.0025	0.0037	0.0049	0.0074	0.0086	0.0098	0.0110
41	0.012	.015	.018	.021	.0134	.0146	.0157	.0169	.0192	.0204	.0215	.0227
42	.024	.027	.029	.032	.0249	.0261	.0272	.0283	.0305	.0316	.0327	.0338
43	.035	.038	.040	.043	.0360	.0370	.0381	.0392	.0413	.0423	.0434	.0444
44	.045	.048	.051	.053	.0465	.0475	.0485	.0495	.0516	.0526	.0536	.0546
45	.056	.058	.060	.063	.0565	.0575	.0585	.0595	.0614	.0624	.0633	.0643
46	.065	.068	.070	.072	.0662	.0671	.0680	.0690	.0708	.0717	.0726	.0736
47	.074	.077	.079	.081	.0754	.0763	.0772	.0781	.0798	.0807	.0816	.0825
48	.083	.085	.088	.090	.0842	.0851	.0859	.0868	.0885	.0893	.0902	.0910
49	.092	.094	.096	.098	.0927	.0935	.0943	.0951	.0968	.0976	.0984	.0992
50	.100	.102	.104	.106	.1008	.1016	.1024	.1032	.1047	.1055	.1063	.1071
51	.108	.110	.112	.114	.1086	.1094	.1101	.1109	.1124	.1132	.1139	.1146
52	.115	.117	.119	.121	.1161	.1169	.1176	.1183	.1198	.1205	.1212	.1219
53	.123	.124	.126	.128	.1234	.1241	.1248	.1255	.1269	.1276	.1283	.1289
54	.130	.131	.133	.135	.1303	.1310	.1317	.1324	.1337	.1344	.1350	.1357
55	.136	.138	.140	.141	.1370	.1377	.1383	.1390	.1403	.1409	.1416	.1422
56	.143	.144	.146	.148	.1435	.1441	.1448	.1454	.1466	.1473	.1479	.1485
57	.149	.151	.152	.154	.1497	.1503	.1510	.1516	.1528	.1534	.1540	.1546
58	.155	.157	.158	.160	.1558	.1564	.1569	.1575	.1587	.1593	.1599	.1604
59	.161	.162	.164	.165	.1616	.1622	.1627	.1633	.1644	.1650	.1656	.1661
60	.167	.168	.169	.171	.1672	.1678	.1683	.1689	.1700	.1705	.1711	.1716
61	.172	.173	.175	.176	.1727	.1732	.1737	.1743	.1753	.1759	.1764	.1769
62	.177	.179	.180	.181	.1779	.1785	.1790	.1795	.1805	.1810	.1815	.1820
63	.183	.184	.185	.186	.1830	.1835	.1840	.1845	.1855	.1860	.1865	.1870
64	.188	.189	.190	.191	.1880	.1885	.1890	.1894	.1904	.1909	.1914	.1918
65	.192	.193	.195	.196	.1928	.1933	.1937	.1942	.1951	.1956	.1960	.1965
66	.197	.198	.199	.200	.1974	.1979	.1983	.1988	.1997	.2001	.2006	.2010
67	.201	.203	.204	.205	.2019	.2024	.2028	.2033	.2041	.2046	.2050	.2054
68	.206	.207	.208	.209	.2063	.2067	.2072	.2076	.2085	.2089	.2093	.2097
69	.210	.211	.212	.213	.2106	.2110	.2114	.2118	.2126	.2131	.2135	.2139
70	.214	.215	.216	.217	.2147	.2151	.2155	.2159	.2167	.2171	.2175	.2179
71	.218	.219	.220	.221	.2187	.2191	.2195	.2199	.2207	.2211	.2214	.2218
72	.222	.223	.224	.225	.2226	.2230	.2234	.2238	.2245	.2249	.2253	.2257
73	.226	.227	.228	.229	.2264	.2268	.2271	.2275	.2283	.2286	.2290	.2294
74	.230	.231	.232	.232	.2301	.2305	.2308	.2312	.2319	.2323	.2326	.2330
75	.233	.234	.235	.236	.2337	.2340	.2344	.2347	.2354	.2358	.2361	.2365
76	.237	.238	.239	.239	.2372	.2375	.2379	.2382	.2389	.2392	.2396	.2399
77	.240	.241	.242	.243	.2406	.2409	.2413	.2416	.2423	.2426	.2429	.2433
78	.244	.244	.245	.246	.2439	.2442	.2446	.2449	.2455	.2459	.2462	.2465
79	.247	.248	.249	.249	.2472	.2475	.2478	.2481	.2487	.2491	.2494	.2497
80	.250	.251	.252	.252	.2503	.2506	.2509	.2512	.2519	.2522	.2525	.2528
81	.253	.254	.255	.255	.2534	.2537	.2540	.2543	.2549	.2552	.2555	.2558
82	.256	.257	.258	.258	.2564	.2567	.2570	.2573	.2579	.2582	.2585	.2587
83	.259	.260	.261	.261	.2593	.2596	.2599	.2602	.2608	.2611	.2613	.2616
84	.262	.263	.263	.264	.2622	.2625	.2628	.2630	.2636	.2639	.2642	.2644
85	.265	.265	.266	.267	.2650	.2653	.2655	.2658	.2664	.2666	.2669	.2672

TO CONVERT INTO WEEKLY EQUIVALENT: Multiply SEMIMONTHLY salary by 0.4615; MONTHLY salary by 0.2308; ANNUAL salary by 0.01923.

TO CONVERT INTO STRAIGHT-TIME HOURLY EQUIVALENT FOR 40 HOURS: Multiply WEEKLY salary by 0.025; SEMIMONTHLY by 0.01154; MONTHLY salary by 0.00577; ANNUAL by 0.00048.

TO CONVERT INTO TIME AND ONE-HALF HOURLY RATE BASED ON 40 HOUR WEEK: Multiply WEEKLY salary by 0.0375; SEMIMONTHLY by 0.0173; MONTHLY salary by 0.00866; ANNUAL by 0.000721.

CAUTION: Be sure straight-time earnings are not below legal minimum

(SEE INSTRUCTIONS ON REVERSE SIDE)

Form WH-134
(Rev. Aug. 1974)

APPENDIX G

CHART OF STATE
MAXIMUM HOURS-OVERTIME

State Maximum Hours and Overtime Laws — Comparison Chart

STATE	REQUIREMENTS AND PROVISIONS
Alabama	**Maximum Hours before Overtime** — No general provision. **Overtime Pay** — 1½ times regular pay or compensatory time for hours in excess of 8-hour day or 40-hour week for state law enforcement officers. **Employees Covered** — No general provision. **Maximum Work Hours Allowed** — *Truckdrivers:* 10-hour day followed by 8-hour rest, plus certain provisions. **Day of Rest** — No minor, apprentice, or servant may be required to perform any labor on Sunday, except customary domestic duties or works of charity; merchants, shopkeepers, druggists excepted, may not keep stores open on Sunday. Certain other specific operations exempted. **Meal Period** — No general provision.
Alaska	**Maximum Hours before Overtime** — 8-hour day, 40-hour week. *Special rule:* 10-hour day, 40-hour week for workers with flexible work hour plan if part of collective bargaining agreement or signed employer-employee agreement filed with state Department of Labor. **Overtime Pay** — 1½ times regular pay for hours in excess of maximum hours. **Employees Covered** — All employees, *except:* those of employer with less than 4 workers; those in executive, administrative, or professional capacity; outside salespersons, as defined; those employed in making dairy products and handling or preparing for market agricultural or horticultural products; agricultural employees; those employed in certain newspapers with circulation under 1,000; certain switchboard operators; taxicab employees; certain retail or service workers handling telegraphic, telephone or radio messages; seamen; forestry and lumbering workers of firms with 12 or fewer workers; outside buyers of raw poultry or dairy products; casual employees, as defined; and nonprofit hospital workers. **Maximum Work Hours Allowed** — *Underground Mines:* 12-hour day, 56-hour week for up to 14 weeks during mining season (as defined) for those in mines with 12 or fewer workers. **Day of Rest** — No general provision. **Meal Period** — No general provision.
Arizona	**Maximum Hours before Overtime** — No general provision. **Overtime Pay** — 1½ times regular pay for hours in excess of maximum for law enforcement officers and security personnel in municipal correctional institution. **Employees Covered** — No general provision. **Maximum Work Hours Allowed** — *Laundries:* 8-hour day and 48-hour week, with certain exceptions. *Mines:* 8-hour day for workers and hoisting engineers in mines or other kind of underground workings (except in emergencies and during shift changes if not more than once in two weeks), and furnace persons at smelters. *Public Works Contractors:* 8-hour day for manual or mechanical laborers, except in emergencies. *Motor Transportation:* 10-hour day (or 10-hour aggregate in any 24 hours, followed by 8 hours off) for truck and bus operators and their helpers, except for unforeseen delays and emergencies. *Railroads:* 16 hours followed by 9 hours rest, except for emergencies and actual necessity. **Day of Rest** — No general provision. **Meal Period** — No general provision.
Arkansas	**Maximum Hours before Overtime** — 40-hour week. *Special rule:* 48-hour week for employees of hotel, motel, restaurant, and tourist attraction with annual sales volume less than $362,500. **Overtime Pay** — 1½ times regular pay for hours in excess of maximum. **Employees Covered** — All employees, *except* agricultural workers. **Maximum Work Hours Allowed** — *Saw Mills:* 10-hour day for workmen and laborers in saw and planing mills. *Motor Transportation:* 12 consecutive hours followed by 8 hours rest for drivers, except when wrecks or washouts. *Railroads:* 16 consecutive hours followed by 8 hours rest for trainmen, except in emergency or on passenger train; 8 hours in 24 hours for railroad telegraph and telephone operators handling movement of trains. **Day of Rest** — On Sunday, unlawful for any person to sell, offer for sale, or employ others to sell certain specified goods. Law inapplicable to sale of goods for

State Maximum Hours and Overtime Laws — Comparison Chart —Contd.

STATE	REQUIREMENTS AND PROVISIONS
Arkansas (Contd.)	charitable or governmental purposes, or the advertising for sale of personal property. Person who conscientiously observes a day other than Sunday as a day of rest and abstains on that day from the sale of items prohibited also exempted. **Meal Period** — Establishments with six or more employees must grant one hour for meal periods if lunch room is not required on premises.
California	**Maximum Hours before Overtime** — For employees in *manufacturing; personal service; professional, technical, clerical, mechanical and similar occupations; public housekeeping; laundry, linen supply, dry cleaning, and dyeing; mercantile; amusement and recreation; and broadcasting* occupations: 8-hour day, 40-hour week, and 6-day week (but 10-hour day and 4-day week with written agreement of 2/3 of affected workers). For workers in *canning, freezing, and preserving; farm products, after harvest; and preparing agricultural products for market, on the farm:* 8-hour day and 40-hour week. For *agricultural* workers: 10-hour day, but 8 hours on seventh day. For employees of *manufacturing* operating continuously: 12-hour day and 3-day week, with option of alternating with 12-hour day and 4-day week for average workweek of 42 hours over 2-week period, with agreement of 2/3 of affected workers. For *hospital* employees: 12-hour day and 3-day week, or 9-hour day and 5-day week, with written agreement of 2/3 of affected employees. For employees of *acute or extended care hospital:* 80 hours in 14-day period, with written agreement. For employees *caring for aged* in home with fewer than eight beds: 54-hour, 6-day week, except in emergencies. For those in *motion picture industry:* 8-hour day, 40-hour week, 5-day week, with certain exceptions. For employees selling *retail drugs or compounding prescriptions:* except registered pharmacists: 9-hour day, or 108 hours in 12 days or two consecutive weeks. For employees of *ski facility:* during month of ski activity: 56-hour week. For those employed in: *manufacturing; personal service; canning, freezing, and preserving; professional, technical, clerical, mechanical and similar occupations; public housekeeping; laundry, linen supply, dry cleaning, and dyeing; mercantile; amusement and recreation; broadcasting; and preparing agricultural products for market, on the farm:* 7-day week, if hours don't exceed 30 a week and 6 a day. **Overtime Pay** — 1½ times regular pay for hours in excess of maximum. *Hospitals:* Twice the regular pay for hospital workers, under certain conditions. *Agriculture:* Twice the regular rate for agricultural workers in excess of 8 hours on seventh day. *Manufacturing; Personal Service; Canning, Freezing, and Preserving; Professional, Technical, Clerical, Mechanical, and Similar Occupations: Laundry, Linen Supply, Dry Cleaning, and Dyeing; Mercantile Occupations; Farm Products, after Harvest; Amusement and Recreation; Broadcasting; and Preparing Agricultural Products for Market, on the Farm:* Twice the regular pay for hours in excess of 12 hours a day and eight hours on seventh day. Twice the regular pay for working over 8 hours on additional days for those with 4-day week, 10-hour day agreement. **Employees Covered** — Manufacturing; personal service; canning, freezing, and preserving; professional, technical, clerical, mechanical, and similar occupations; public housekeeping; laundry, linen supply, dry cleaning and dyeing; mercantile; farm products, after harvest; transportation; amusement and recreation; broadcasting; motion picture industry; agricultural products for market; agricultural occupations; and household employees. *Exceptions:* manufacturing and transportation employees covered by collective bargaining agreements, if provided premium overtime rate (manufacturing employees), and if agreement is in accordance with Railway Labor Act (transportation workers); manufacturing, canning, freezing, preserving, and public housekeeping occupations with hours regulated by U.S. Department of Transportation; mercantile or professional, technical, clerical, mechanical, and similar occupations with earnings over 1½ times the minimum wage if more than half of wages from commissions; ambulance drivers and attendants in transportation and public housekeeping on 24-hour shifts under certain conditions; adult employees giving children 24-hour care; camp counselors; resident managers and employees caring for aged in homes with fewer than eight beds; taxicab drivers; airline employees temporarily working up to 60 hours a week at own request; motion picture projectionists; professional

State Maximum Hours and Overtime Laws — Comparison Chart —Contd.

STATE	REQUIREMENTS AND PROVISIONS
California (Contd.)	actors; radio/TV announcers, news editors, or chief engineers in station in town of 25,000 or less; sheepherders; licensed fishing employees; agricultural workers for employer with five or fewer agricultural employees in calendar year (except those working more than half of time as irrigators). **Maximum Work Hours Allowed** — *Mines:* 8-hour day, but 12 hours in 24 hours if stipulated by collective bargaining agreement. *Motor Transportation:* 10 hours (or 10 hours over 15-hour period), followed by 8 hours off duty for drivers; but 12 hours over 15 hours, followed by 8 hours off, for drivers transporting merchandise, freight, materials, and other property. *Railroads:* 12 hours followed by 10 hours off duty, or 8 hours off duty in 24 hours, for all trainmen. 9 hours in 24 hours for employees directing train movements in stations operating continuously, except for 4 additional hours not more than 3 days a week in emergencies. *Food Preservation:* 72 hours in seven days, followed by 24 hours off duty, for employees in canning, freezing, and preserving, and in occupations concerned with farms products after harvest. *Other:* 72-hour week in professional, technical, clerical, mechanical, and similar occupations, except in emergency, as defined. **Day of Rest** — Every person employed in any occupation of labor is entitled to one day's rest in seven with a few specified exceptions. If work requires employee to work seven or more consecutive days, days of rest may be accumulated if equivalent time off is allowed during calendar month. Requirement applies to collective bargaining agreements unless agreement expressly provides otherwise. Exemption may be granted when total hours of employment do not exceed 30 in any week or 6 in any one day. **Meal Period** — One-half hour between third and fifth hour of each day's shift for employees of plants or mills that process or manufacture any lumber or allied wood products.
Colorado	**Maximum Hours before Overtime** — 12-hour day and 40-hour week. Two or more weeks may not be averaged out for overtime. *Special rule:* 8-hour day and 80-hours in 14 consecutive days for employees of hospitals and nursing homes electing to pay overtime pursuant of FLSA. **Overtime Pay** — 1½ times regular pay for hours in excess of the maximum. **Employees Covered** — All employees, *except:* salespersons, partspersons, and mechanics employed by automobile, truck, or farm implement (retail) dealer; salespersons employed by trailer, aircraft, or boat (retail) dealer. **Maximum Work Hours Allowed** — *Cement and Plaster Factories:* 8-hour day; but 16 hours in 24 hours, followed by 8 hours of rest, in emergencies or change of shifts. *Hazardous Occupations:* 8-hour day for employees working in underground and open mines or workings, smelters, reduction works, stamp or concentrating mills, chlorination or cyanide processes, and coke ovens, except in emergencies. *Public Works:* 8-hour day for mechanics and workers, except in emergencies affecting life or property. *Retail Drug Selling:* 9-hour day, or 108 hours in two weeks, for employees of drug stores, laboratories, or offices selling drugs at retail or filling prescriptions, in town with 5,100 or more population, except in specified emergencies. *Railroads:* 16 hours, followed by 10 hours of rest, for railroad conductors, engineers, firemen, brakemen, telegraphers, or any trainmen. **Day of Rest** — No general provision. **Meal Period** — No general provision.
Connecticut	**Maximum Hours before Overtime** — 40-hour week. 48-hour week for employees in hotel, restaurant, or bowling establishment or in institution (other than hospital) for care of sick, aged, or mentally ill residents. 80-hour, 14-day work period for hospital employees, with employee agreement. **Overtime Pay** — 1½ times regular pay for hours in excess of maximum. **Employees Covered** — All employees, *except:* drivers or helpers with hours set by Interstate Commerce Commission; employees subject to Railroad Labor Act; seamen; announcers, news editors, and chief engineer of TV/radio station; those in bona fide executive, administrative, or professional capacity; outside salespersons; those working no more than 54 hours a week and whose regular pay exceeds

State Maximum Hours and Overtime Laws — Comparison Chart —Contd.

STATE	REQUIREMENTS AND PROVISIONS
Connecticut (Contd.)	two times the minimum wage or whose monthly compensation is more than half from commissions; taxicab drivers if paid 40 percent or more of meter fares; milk and bakery route salespersons; all agricultural employees; permanent municipal police and firefighters; and firefighters of private nonprofit firm under contract with municipality. **Maximum Work Hours Allowed** - 8-hour day, 48-hour and 6-day week for persons over 65 (except with their consent), handicapped, and disabled veterans (except with their consent and doctor's certification) for employees in mercantile establishment. 9-hour day and 48-hour week for persons over 65 (except with their consent), handicapped, and disabled veterans (except with their consent and doctor's certification) for employees in manufacturing, mechanical, hair, amusement, recreation, shoe shining, photographic gallery, or restaurant (except hotel) establishment. Certain exceptions during emergencies or peak periods for above employees in manufacturing, mechanical, or mercantile establishments, with permit from Commissioner. *Railroads:* 8-hour day for telegraph or telephone operators and dispatchers, but 12 hours when only one employee and 16 hours in emergencies. *Public Works:* 8-hour day and 40-hour week, except in emergencies. *Motor Carriers:* 12 hours followed by 8 hours off, or 16 hours in 24 hours followed by 10 hours off, except in emergencies. **Day of Rest** — Employer may not compel employee engaged in commercial occupation or industrial process to work more than six days in calendar week. No person who conscientiously believes that a particular day of week ought to be observed as the Sabbath may be required by employer to work on such day. No person, firm, or corporation shall engage or employ others in work, labor, or business on Sunday except charitable, religious, or service organization; federal, state, municipal or local governmental agency; and person, firm, or corporation performing acts necessary for public safety or health. Inapplicable to certain specified business operations; the sale or furnishing of specified articles, if they are sold in ordinary course of business; or to isolated or occasional sales by persons not engaged in the sale, transfer, or exchange of property as a business. **Meal Period** — No general provision.
Delaware	**Maximum Hours before Overtime** — No state provision. **Overtime Pay** — No provision. **Employees Covered** — No provision. **Maximum Work Hours Allowed** — No provision. **Day of Rest** — No general provision. **Meal Period** — No general provision.
District of Columbia	**Maximum Hours before Overtime** — 40-hour week. *Special rule:* 160 hours during any 4-week period for automobile washers for employer with more than half of annual dollar sales volume from car washing. **Overtime Pay** — 1½ times regular pay for hours in excess of maximum. **Employees Covered** — All employees, *except:* federal or city employees; unpaid volunteers with educational, charitable, or nonprofit organization; lay persons active within religious organization; casual babysitters; those in bona fide executive, administrative, or professional capacity; outside salespersons; those in home delivery of newspapers; seamen; railroad employees; salespersons, partspersons, and mechanics engaged in retail auto, truck, or trailer sales; parking lot or garage attendants; air carrier employees voluntarily exchanging workdays for air travel benefits; companions of aged or infirm; and retail and service employees earning more than 11/2 times the minimum wage and receiving more than half of earnings from commissions. **Maximum Work Hours Allowed** — No provision. **Day of Rest** — No general provision. **Meal Period** — No general provision.
Florida	**Maximum Hours before Overtime** — No general provision. *Special rule:* 10-hour day for manual laborers, unless written contract requires otherwise. **Overtime Pay** — No general provision. Extra pay for hours in excess of maximum for manual laborers.

State Maximum Hours and Overtime Laws — Comparison Chart —Contd.

STATE	REQUIREMENTS AND PROVISIONS
Florida (Contd.)	**Employees Covered** — No general provision. **Maximum Work Hours Allowed** — *Railroads:* 13 hours followed by 8-hour rest, except when behind schedule or in emergencies. **Day of Rest** — No general provision. **Meal Period** — No general provision.
Georgia	**Maximum Hours before Overtime** — No general provision. *Special rule:* 10-hour day, 60-hour week for employees of cotton or woolen manufacturers (except engineers; firefighters; guards; mechanics; teamsters; yard employees; clericals; and repair employees). **Overtime Pay** — No provision. **Employees Covered** — No general provision. **Maximum Work Hours Allowed** — *Motor Carriers:* 10-hour day followed by 10 hour rest for drivers of motor contract and common carriers, except in emergencies. *Railroads:* 13-hour day followed by 10 hour rest, except in case of casualty. **Day of Rest** — Pursuit of business or work of ordinary calling forbidden on Lord's day, except works of necessity or charity. The operation of any business, with certain exemptions, on both the two consecutive days of Saturday and Sunday is declared a public nuisance; counties may exempt themselves by referendum. **Meal Period** — No general provision.
Hawaii	**Maximum Hours before Overtime** — 40-hour week. *Special rule:* 48-hour week for 20 weeks a year for employees of certain employers processing dairy products, sugar cane, agricultural and horticultural products, poultry, livestock, and seasonal fruits. **Overtime Pay** — 1½ times regular pay for hours in excess of maximum. **Employees Covered** — All employees, *except:* those with guaranteed monthly salary of $1,000; workers in small coffee harvesting; domestic workers; houseparents in charitable organizations; employer's relatives (brother, sister, brother-in-law, sister-in law, son, daughter, spouse, parent, parent-in-law); those employed in bona fide executive, administrative, supervisory, or professional capacity; outside salespersons or collectors; those in fish or aquatic farming industry prior to first processing; seaman; on-call, fixed stand vehicle drivers; golf caddies; student employees of nonprofit school; seasonal employees of certain nonprofit youth camps; and automobile or truck salespersons for licensed dealer. **Maximum Work Hours Allowed** — No provision. **Day of Rest** — No general provision. **Meal Period** — Lunch period of 45 minutes, not working time, allowed all government employees.
Idaho	**Maximum Hours before Overtime** — No general provision. *Special rule:* 10-hour day and 40-hour week for workers in or upon surface mines and workings, and in smelters, ore reduction works, and other places where metalliferous ores are treated. **Overtime Pay** — 1½ times regular pay for hours in excess of maximum. **Employees Covered** — No general provision. **Maximum Work Hours Allowed** — *Mines:* 8-hour day for workers in or upon underground mines and workings, and 10-hour day for workers in or upon smelters and other places where metalliferous ores are treated, except when life or property in imminent danger. **Day of Rest** — No general provision. **Meal Period** — No general provision.
Illinois	**Maximum Hours before Overtime** — 40-hour week. **Overtime Pay** — 1½ times regular pay for hours in excess of maximum. *Special rule:* Lower rate for bona fide executive, administrative, or professional employees of nonprofit organization, by regulation. **Employees Covered** — All employees, except: salespersons or mechanics in nonmanufacturing firm primarily selling or servicing automobiles, trucks, or farm implements; salespersons in nonmanufacturing firm primarily selling trac-

State Maximum Hours and Overtime Laws — Comparison Chart —Contd.

STATE	REQUIREMENTS AND PROVISIONS
Illinois (Contd.)	tors, boats, or aircraft; agricultural workers; government employees; those in bona fide executive, administrative, or professional capacity; commissioned employees, as defined by FLSA; and employee working in another employee's stead as part of worktime exchange agreement. **Maximum Work Hours Allowed** — *Motor Transportation:* 10 hours followed by 8 hours off duty and 60 hours in seven days for operators unless emergency permission from Department of Law Enforcement, except for: public utility operators in emergency or temporary necessity, drivers connected with packing and preserving perishable fruits and vegetables, those hauling materials to and from construction site within 50-mile radius, and driver-salespersons within 50 miles of principal business. *Municipal Firefighters:* 56 hours in any week of month for firefighters in towns over 10,000 in population. **Day of Rest** — At least 24 consecutive hours of rest in every calendar week in addition to regular period of rest allowed at the close of each working day. Inapplicable to part-time employees whose total work hours for one employer during calendar week do not exceed 20, and certain other specified employees. Emergency permits may be granted to employers authorizing longer hours during an emergency situation. Before operating on Sunday, employer must post in conspicuous place schedule containing list of employees required or allowed to work on Sunday, and designating day of rest for each. No employee shall be required to work on their designated day of rest. **Meal Period** — At least 20 minutes for meal period beginning no later than five hours after the start of work period for employees working for 7½ continuous hours or longer. Inapplicable to employees for whom meal periods are established through collective bargaining.
Indiana	**Maximum Hours before Overtime** — No general provision. **Overtime Pay** — No provision. **Employees Covered** — No general provision. **Maximum Work Hours Allowed** — *Railroads:* 12-hour day followed by 10 hours off duty, or 12 hours aggregate in 24 hours followed by 8 hours off duty, for firefighters, engineers, conductors, brakemen, switchmen, telegraph operators, and other employees engaged in movement of passenger or freight trains. *Motor Transportation:* certain rules for drivers, except drivers of farm trucks. **Day of Rest** — Person age 14 and over who is found on Sunday rioting, hunting, quarreling, at common labor, or engaged in his usual vocation - except works of charity and necessity - shall be fined from $1.00 to $10. Nothing shall be construed to affect those who observe conscientiously the Sabbath and certain specified others. **Meal Period** — No general provision.
Iowa	**Maximum Hours before Overtime** — No provision. **Overtime Pay** — No provision. **Employees Covered** — No general provision. **Maximum Work Hours Allowed** — *Motor Transportation:* 12 hours followed by 10 hours off duty, or 12 aggregate hours in 24 hours followed by 8 hours off duty, for operators. 12 hours in 24 hours for urban transit drivers. *Railroads:* 16 hours followed by 10 hours of rest, or 16 aggregate hours in 24 hours, for employees connected with movement of trains unless to protect life or property, except employees of sleeping car companies. **Day of Rest** — No general provision. **Meal Period** — No general provision.
Kansas	**Maximum Hours before Overtime** — 46-hour week. *Special rule:* 258 hours in 28-day period (or equivalent hour/day ratio for periods from seven to 27 days) for firefighters, law enforcement personnel, and security personnel in correctional institution unless covered under FLSA. 8-hour day for employees in lead and zinc mines, except in emergencies. **Overtime Pay** — 1½ times regular pay for hours in excess of maximum. **Employees Covered** — All employees, *except:* employees primarily selling motor vehicles for nonmanufacturing retail firm; prisoners; those covered by FLSA;

State Maximum Hours and Overtime Laws — Comparison Chart —Contd.

STATE	REQUIREMENTS AND PROVISIONS
Kansas (Contd.)	agricultural and domestic workers; those in bona fide executive, administrative, or professional capacity; outside salespersons on commission; federal employees; unpaid volunteers for nonprofit organization; part-time workers age 18 or under and age 60 or over; and students under 18 working between academic terms. **Maximum Work Hours Allowed** — *Mines:* 8-hour day for employees in lead and zinc mines, except in emergencies. *Railroads:* 16 hours followed by 8 hours of rest — except for train crews handling livestock or perishable freight and for sleeping car, baggage, or express employees — unless washout, wreck, or unavoidable blockade. *Motor Transportation:* Hours fixed by Public Utilities Commission. **Day of Rest** — Sunday labor prohibited except works of necessity or charity; not applicable to persons observing a different Sabbath. **Meal Period** — No general provision.
Kentucky	**Maximum Hours before Overtime** — 40-hour week. **Overtime Pay** — 1½ times regular pay for hours in excess of maximum. 1½ times regular pay for hours worked on seventh day of week, *except for:* those whose primary duty is to direct or supervise; employees of telephone exchanges with less than 500 subscribers; stenographers; bookkeepers; technical assistants of licensed professions; employees subject to Federal Railway Labor Act; seamen and those operating on navigable streams; those icing railroad cars; and employees of common carriers under supervision of bureau of vehicle regulation. **Employees Covered** — All employees, except: retail store employees engaged in selling, purchasing, and distributing goods; employees of restaurant, hotel, or motel; those providing 24-hour residential care on employer's premise in parental role to dependent, neglected, and abused children under care of licensed nonprofit childcare facility; agricultural workers; those in bona fide executive, administrative, supervisory, or professional capacity; outside salespersons or collectors as defined by Commissioner; federal employees; domestic workers; employees of retail stores, service industries, hotels, motels, and restaurants with average annual sales less than $95,000 for preceding five years; employer's parent, spouse, child, or immediate family member; babysitter or live-in companion to sick or elderly if principal duties not housekeeping; newspaper deliverers; certain emergency employees; those in nonprofit camp, or religious or nonprofit educational conference center operating no more than seven months a year. **Maximum Work Hours Allowed** — *Motor Transportation:* 12 hours followed by 8 hours off duty, or 16 hours in any 24 hours followed by 10 hours off duty, with 3 hours breaking continuity, for motor vehicle drivers, except in emergencies or for those under collective bargaining agreement. **Day of Rest** — Fines will be levied on any person who works on Sunday or employs any other person in labor or other business, whether for profit or amusement, unless work or the employment of others is in the course of ordinary household duties, a necessity or charity, or required in the maintenance or operation of public service, utility, or system. Inapplicable to religious society which observes another day as Sabbath, certain specified operations, or employers using continuous work scheduling that permits at least one day of rest each calendar week for each employee. **Meal Period** — Employers, except those subject to FRLA, shall grant employees a reasonable period for lunch, which shall be as close to the middle of the employee's scheduled shift as possible. Employee shall not be required to take lunch period sooner than three hours or later than five hours from commencement of shift; provision does not negate any provision of collective bargaining or mutual agreement between employer and employee.
Louisiana	**Maximum Hours before Overtime** — No state provision. **Overtime Pay** — No provision. **Employees Covered** — No provision. **Maximum Work Hours Allowed** — No provision. **Day of Rest** — No store or business opposed to being open on Sunday shall be required to open on Sunday, unless agreed to in lease agreement. New or used car or truck dealers may not be open on Sunday.

State Maximum Hours and Overtime Laws — Comparison Chart —Contd.

STATE	REQUIREMENTS AND PROVISIONS
Louisiana (Contd.)	**Meal Period** — No general provision.
Maine	**Maximum Hours before Overtime** — 40-hour week. **Overtime Pay** — 1½ times regular pay for hours in excess of maximum. **Employees Covered** — All employees, *except:* those processing, marketing, or storing agricultural products, meat, fish, and other perishable goods; seamen; employees of hotel, motel, eating establishment, nursing home, or hospital; public employees; automobile salespersons; agricultural workers, as defined by state law and FUTA (but not including those working on farms with over 300,000 laying birds); domestic workers; unsupervised salespersons on commission; those in nonpolitical public-supported or educational nonprofit organization; summer camp counselors, or employees under 19 in camps operated by or belonging to noncapital stock corporations under state law; those in fish and seafood industry up through first processing; switchboard operators in public telephone exchange with less than 750 stations; unsupervised homeworkers; family members who live with or are dependent upon employer; those in bona fide executive, administrative, or professional capacity earning $175 weekly; taxicab drivers; service employees with more than $20 a month in tips. **Maximum Work Hours Allowed** — No provision. **Day of Rest** — No place of business shall be kept open on Sunday except for work of necessity or charity, with certain specified exceptions. Isolated transactions by persons not engaged in sale, transfer, or exchange of property as a business are exempt. **Meal Period** — In absence of collective bargaining or other agreement, worker may be employed or permitted to work for no more than six consecutive hours at one time without at least 30 consecutive minutes of rest time, except in cases of emergency in which there is danger to property, life, public safety, or health. Rest time may be used as meal time. Inapplicable to place of employment where fewer than three employees are on duty at one time, and nature of work allows employees frequent breaks during work day.
Maryland	**Maximum Hours before Overtime** — 40-hour week. *Special rule:* 48 hours for employees of hotel, motel, restaurant, bowling alley, or institution (except hospital) caring for sick, aged, or mentally ill or defective persons. 60-hour week for agricultural workers. **Overtime Pay** — 1½ times regular pay for hours in excess of maximum. **Employees Covered** — All employees, *except:* employees of amusement or recreational establishments (except certain theater and music establishments) if not operated more than seven months in calendar year and if average receipts for any six months more than 1/3 of average receipts for other six months; those covered by Federal Motor Carrier Act or Part I of Interstate Commerce Act; salespersons, partspersons, or mechanics primarily selling or servicing automobiles, trailers, trucks, or machinery in nonmanufacturing firm; gasoline service station employees; taxicab drivers; country club employees; those working for nonprofit employer furnishing temporary at-home services for sick, aged, mentally ill, or handicapped; agricultural workers exempted by FLSA; those in bona fide executive, administrative, or professional capacity; volunteers in educational, charitable, religious, or nonprofit organization where no employer-employee relationship; those in establishment selling food and drink for consumption on premises with annual gross income of $250,000 or less; employees of movie theaters; those processing or packaging poultry, seafood, or fresh produce or horticultural commodities; outside salespersons and those on commission; employer's parent, spouse, child, or other immediate family member; students in public school special education programs for mentally, emotionally, or physically handicapped employed as part of training; nonadministrative day camp personnel; and certain other agricultural workers. **Maximum Work Hours Allowed** — *Railroads:* 8-hour day for telephone and telegraph operators handling train movements under "block system," except

State Maximum Hours and Overtime Laws — Comparison Chart —Contd.

STATE	REQUIREMENTS AND PROVISIONS
Maryland (Contd.)	when less than nine passengers or 20 freight trains each way in 24 hours. *Cotton and Wool Manufacturing:* 10-hour day for employees manufacturing cotton or woolen yarns, fabrics, or domestics, except during repairs, improvements, firing up, and readying machinery. *Tobacco Warehouses* (Baltimore only): hours from 7 a.m. to 12 noon and 1 p.m. to 6 p.m. for tobacco warehouse employees. **Day of Rest** — Sunday work is prohibited, works of necessity and charity excepted. Inapplicable to person who believes seventh day of week should be observed as Sabbath, refrains from labor on that day, and whose business is closed on such day; to person who believes Sabbath begins at sundown Friday and ends at sundown Saturday and whose business is closed during such period; and in certain specified counties. No person shall deal in certain specified articles of merchandise on Sunday. Special laws and exceptions listed for each county. Except in cases of emergency, nonmanagerial employees in retail establishments operating on Sunday shall be entitled to choose their sabbath as a day of rest upon filing of written notice with employer. **Meal Period** — No general provision.
Massachusetts	**Maximum Hours before Overtime** — 40-hour week. **Overtime Pay** — 1½ times regular pay for hours in excess of maximum. 11/2 times regular rate for Sunday labor in retail establishments, except for those working for employer with fewer than seven employees including proprietor, and those in bona fide executive, administrative, or professional capacity earning over $200 a week. **Employees Covered** — All employees, *except:* caretakers of residential property if furnished living quarters and paid at least $36 a week; golf caddies, news carriers, or child performers; those in bona fide executive, administrative, or professional capacity or training for such positions and earning more than $80 a week; outside salespersons and outside buyers; learners, apprentices, or handicapped, with special license; those catching or taking aquatic animal or vegetable life; public telephone switchboard operators; drivers and helpers under Interstate Commerce Commission or Railway Labor Act; those employed in business determined seasonal by Commissioner and existing not more than 120 days in any year; seamen; employees of passenger motor carrier, as defined; hotel, motel, and restaurant employees; garage and gasoline station workers; those working in hospital, home for the aged, nonprofit school, or summer camp operated by nonprofit charitable organization; agricultural laborers; employees in amusement park operating not more than 150 days a year; those being rehabilitated or trained in charitable, educational, or religious institutions; members of religious orders; agricultural, floricultural, and horticultural workers; those in professional service; and outside salespersons not reporting to or visiting office daily. **Maximum Work Hours Allowed** — *Railways:* 9-hour day within 11 consecutive hours for conductors, guards, drivers, motormen, brakemen, dispatchers, and gatemen of street, electric, or elevated railways. *Motor Transportation:* 12-hour day followed by 8 hours off duty, or 16-hours followed by 10 hours off duty, with 3 hours or more breaking continuity, for motor vehicle drivers. **Day of Rest** — For each seven consecutive days worked, employees must have 24 consecutive hours of rest, including unbroken period between 8 a.m. and 5 p.m., except in emergency for employees in workshop or manufacturing, mechanical, or mercantile establishments. Employees working on Sunday must be allowed 24 consecutive hours without work in the six days following, with certain specified exceptions. Sunday labor prohibited, except works of necessity or charity. **Meal Period** — No person shall be required to work for more than six hours a day without an interval of at least 30 minutes for a meal, with certain specified exceptions.
Michigan	**Maximum Hours before Overtime** — 40-hour week. *Special rules:* 80 hours within 14-day period for resident employees of public hospital or institution primarily engaged in care of sick, aged, or mentally ill or defective, except for executive, administrative, or professional employees. 216 hours in 28 days (or equivalent hour/day ratio for periods from seven to 27 days) for public fire

State Maximum Hours and Overtime Laws — Comparison Chart —Contd.

STATE	REQUIREMENTS AND PROVISIONS
Michigan (Contd.)	protection and law enforcement employees, including security personnel in correctional institution. **Overtime Pay** — 1½ times regular pay for hours in excess of maximum. **Employees Covered** — All employees, *except:* those in bona fide executive, administrative, or professional capacity; elected and appointed government officials; workers in amusement or recreational establishment operating not more than seven months in calendar year; employees in all branches of agriculture; those subject to FLSA; those employed in summer camps not more than four months; employees of fruit, pickle, or tomato growers; and transient agricultural workers contracting for harvest on piecework basis. Special rules for firefighters, law enforcement personnel, and employees of public hospitals and nursing homes. **Maximum Hours of Work** — *Motor Transportation:* 10 hours in any 15 hours followed by 8 hours off duty for drivers of motor trucks and truck tractors, except those operating government vehicles or operating within 50-mile radius of domicile, unless emergency, as defined. **Day of Rest** — Barber shops and pawn shops must be closed on Sunday. **Meal Period** — No general provision.
Minnesota	**Maximum Hours before Overtime** — 48-hour week. *Special rule:* 8-hour day and 80 hours in 14-day work period for employees in health care facility. **Overtime Pay** — 1½ times regular pay for hours in excess of maximum. **Employees Covered** — All employees, *except:* those subject to FLSA; sugar beet hand laborers on piece rate basis, when hourly pay exceeds minimum wage by 40 cents; salespersons, partspersons, and mechanics on commission or incentive basis for retail employer selling or servicing automobiles, trailers, trucks, or farm implements; those employed in farm silo construction or installing appurtenant equipment on unit or piece rate basis, when pay exceeds minimum wage; caretakers and other employees of residential building living on-site when available but not performing duties; companions of aged or infirm, under certain conditions; certain agricultural workers; seasonal staff members of licensed nonprofit children's camp; those in executive, administrative, or professional capacity, if meet certain criteria; salespersons with at least 80 percent sales off premises; volunteers to nonprofit organization; elected officials or volunteer workers for political subdivision; police or fire fighters; public employees ineligible to participate in public retirement association; babysitters; seasonal workers in carnival, circus, fair, or ski facility; state conservation officers; those with hours controlled by U.S. Department of Transportation; seafarers, as defined; employees supervising children in single facility residence that is extension of county home school; and those in religious orders. **Maximum Work Hours Allowed** — *Motor Transportation:* 12 hours for truck drivers, unless transporting own products or fresh vegetables between farms, canneries, and viner stations. *Railroads:* 14 hours followed by 9 hours rest (less if worker requests) for engineers and firemen. 16 hours out of 24, followed by 8 hours rest for those engaged in movement of trains, except in defined emergencies. **Day of Rest** — All trades, manufacturing, and mechanical employments are prohibited on Sunday, with certain specified exceptions. Violations are misdemeanors, but it is sufficient defense that another day of the week is kept uniformly as holy time and that the act complained of was done in such a manner as not to disturb others in observance of the Sabbath. **Meal Period** — No general provision.
Mississippi	**Maximum Hours before Overtime** — No state provision. **Overtime Pay** — No provision. **Employees Covered** — No provision. **Maximum Work Hours Allowed** — No provision. **Day of Rest** — Sunday work prohibited except for necessary household work and certain other specified business activities. Retail sales are prohibited on Sundays, with certain specified exceptions. **Meal Period** — No general provision.

State Maximum Hours and Overtime Laws — Comparison Chart —Contd.

STATE	REQUIREMENTS AND PROVISIONS
Missouri	**Maximum Hours before Overtime** — No state provision. **Overtime Pay** — No provision. **Employees Covered** — No provision. **Maximum Work Hours Allowed** — *Mining:* 8-hour day in 24 hours for workers engaged in mining or crushing rocks, or in reducing, roasting, refining, or smelting minerals in ores for mechanical, chemical, manufacturing, or smelting company. *Public Works:* 8-hour day in 24 hours for laborers and mechanics on public works in second class city. *Railroads:* 9-hour day in 24 hours for employees operating interlocking tower. **Day of Rest** — It is unlawful to sell or expose for sale at retail on Sunday a number of specified articles. County with population over 400,000 may exempt itself by referendum. **Meal Period** — No general provision.
Montana	**Maximum Hours before Overtime** — 8-hour day, 40 hour week. *Special rules:* 48-hour week for students employed in seasonal recreational area if furnished board, lodging. 80 hours in 14-day period for health care workers, with their consent. **Overtime Pay** — 1½ times regular pay for hours in excess of maximum. **Employees Covered** — All employees, *except:* farming and stock raising employees; those subject to U.S. Department of Transportation or Part I of Interstate Commerce Act; outside buyers of raw dairy and poultry products; salespersons, partspersons, or mechanics on commission or contract selling or servicing automobiles, trucks, mobile homes, recreational vehicles, or farm implements for retail establishment; salespersons selling trailers, boats, or aircraft for retail establishment; drivers and helpers making local deliveries and paid on delivery payment plan, with permit; agricultural workers; those engaged in supplying and storing water for agriculture; employees of country elevators with no more than five workers; taxicab drivers; spouses employed by nonprofit educational institution as resident children's parents and receiving board, lodging, and $10,000 a year; workers planting, tending, cruising, surveying, felling, or transporting trees or forestry products to mill, plant, or transportation terminal, if employed by employer with eight or fewer workers; municipal or county employees with collectively bargained workweek of 40 hours in 7-day period; public firefighters with collective bargaining agreement; police officers in third class city or police department employees in first or second class city working under chief's schedule; sheriff's or public safety employees working under established work period; students in distributive education program of accredited agency; domestic workers; caretakers of children directly employed by household head; employer's relatives dependent on employer for half or more support; volunteers in nonprofit organization; handicapped whose work is incidental to training or evaluation program or who are severely impaired and unable to compete; those in executive, administrative, or professional capacity; and federal employees. **Maximum Work Hours Allowed** — *Mining:* 8-hour day for workers in underground and strip mines or workings, except in emergencies. 8 hours in 24 hours for hoisting engineers, under certain conditions. *Motor Transportation:* 8-hour day followed by 12 hours rest in every 24 hours for drivers and attendants, except in emergencies. *Governments and First-class School Districts:* 8-hour day, unless collective bargaining agreement says otherwise, except for courthouse employees who work in sixth and seventh grade counties, engineers, firefighters, caretakers, custodians, and laborers. *Cement Plants, Quarries, and Hydroelectric Dams:* 8-hour day, except in emergencies. *Sugar Refineries:* 8-hour day, except for receiving station employees, master mechanics, and certain foremen. *Restaurants:* 8-hour day and 48-hour week, with no more than 8 hours in any 12 aggregate hours, followed by 12 hours rest. *Amusement:* 8-hour day and 48-hour week for those employed in nontraveling carnival, etc. *Retail Stores:* 8-hour day and 48-hour week for those working in retail store or leased business where lessor dictates kind of merchandise, hours, etc., in towns of 2,500 or less. *Telephone Operators:* 9 hours in 24-hour day for public switchboard operators in towns of 3,000 or more.

State Maximum Hours and Overtime Laws — Comparison Chart —Contd.

STATE	REQUIREMENTS AND PROVISIONS
Montana (Contd.)	*Railroads:* 12 consecutive hours (or 16 aggregate hours) in 24 hours, followed by 8 hours rest, for those running or operating train, except in emergencies. **Day of Rest** — No general provision. **Meal Period** — No general provision.
Nebraska	**Maximum Hours before Overtime** — No state provision. **Overtime Pay** — No provision. **Employees Covered** — No provision. **Maximum Work Hours Allowed** — *Motor Transportation:* 12 hours in 24 hours for motor carrier employees (passenger or freight), except taxicab drivers within city or village and in emergencies. *Railroads:* 16 consecutive hours followed by 10 hours of rest, or 16 hours aggregate in 24-hour period followed by 8 hours of rest. 9-hour work period for employees handling movement of trains in places operating day and night, and 13 hours in places operating during day only, except in certain emergencies allowing up to 4 more hours three times a week. **Day of Rest** — It is unlawful for any person to engage in or to employ other to engage in sale on Sunday of specified articles with listed exceptions. **Meal Period** — Employees in assembly plant, workshop, or mechanical establishments are required to have at least one-half hour lunch period between 12 noon and 1 p.m. without having to remain on premises, unless establishment operates in three 8-hour shifts each 24-hour period.
Nevada	**Maximum Hours before Overtime** — 8-hour day, 40-hour week, unless mutually agreed 10-hour day, 4-day week. **Overtime Pay** — 1½ times regular pay for hours in excess of maximum. **Employees Covered** — All employees, *except:* those paid not less than 1½ times the minimum wage; outside buyers; retail salespersons on commission if regular rate more than 1½ times the minimum rate and half of compensation comes from commissions; those in executive, administrative, or professional capacity; employees covered by collective bargaining agreement; motor carrier drivers, drivers' helpers, loaders, and mechanics subject to Motor Carrier Act; air carrier and railroad employees; drivers and helpers making local deliveries and paid on trip-rate or other delivery plan basis; taxicab and limousine drivers; agricultural workers; employees of businesses with annual gross sales less than $250,000; salespersons and mechanics primarily selling or servicing automobiles, trucks, or farm equipment; casual babysitters; live-in domestic workers; and outside salespersons on commission. **Maximum Work Hours Allowed** — *Mining:* 8-hours in 24 hour period for employees in underground and surface mines, including mechanics, engineers, blacksmiths, carpenters, and top men on surface workings of underground mines, except: in emergencies, when employee voluntarily agrees to more hours, when maintenance crew needs to complete work, or if no qualified worker available for relief. *Smelting:* 8-hour day in smelters and other places reducing or refining ore, except in emergencies or when employee voluntarily agrees to more hours. *Cement:* 8 hours, except in emergencies. *Railroads:* 16 hours followed by 10 hours off duty, or 16 hours aggregate in 24 hours followed by 8 hours off duty. 8 hours, followed by 16 hours off duty, for employees handling orders for movement of trains. *Motor Transportation:* Maximum hours upon order of public service commission. **Day of Rest** — No general provision. **Meal Period** — At least one-half hour for meal for a continuous work period of eight hours. Employer may apply for exemption.
New Hampshire	**Maximum Hours before Overtime** — 40-hour week. **Overtime Pay** — 1½ times regular pay for hours in excess of maximum. **Employees Covered** — All employees, *except:* those working in amusement, seasonal, or recreational establishment operating no more than seven months in calendar year or that received at least 75 percent of income during any six months of previous year; and employees covered by FLSA. **Maximum Work Hours Allowed** — No provision.

State Maximum Hours and Overtime Laws — Comparison Chart —Contd.

STATE	REQUIREMENTS AND PROVISIONS
New Hampshire (Contd.)	**Day of Rest** — Employers in manufacturing or mercantile establishments are required to give all employees a 24-hour rest period every 7 days. Employers in commercial, industrial, transportation, or communication establishments permitted to operate on Sunday are required to allow employees 24 hours' rest during the 6-day period thereafter, with certain specified exceptions. Employers may be exempt from Sunday provisions where mutual employer-employee agreements are reached, approval is given by the Commissioner, and it appears to be in the best interests of all concerned. **Meal Period** — Employer may not require employee to work more than five consecutive hours without granting one-half hour lunch or eating period, unless it is feasible for employee to eat during performance of work and employer permits worker to do so.
New Jersey	**Maximum Hours before Overtime** — 40-hour week. *Special rule:* 10-hour day, 48-hour week for 10 weeks, and 10-hour day, 50-hour week for 10 other weeks for employees engaged in first processing of farm products. **Overtime Pay** — 1½ times regular pay for hours in excess of maximum. **Employees Covered** — All employees, *except:* farm workers; hotel employees; those employed by passenger bus company; those raising or caring for livestock; employees in bona fide executive, administrative, or professional capacity; those working for nonprofit or religious summer camp, conference, or retreat; part-time child caretakers in employer's home; outside salespersons; motor vehicle salespersons; and volunteers working at agricultural fair for nonprofit or religious organization and receiving only incidental benefits. **Maximum Work Hours Allowed** — *Motor Transportation:* 12 hours (or 12 hours in aggregate of 16 hours) followed by 8 hours off duty. *Street and Elevated Railways:* 12 consecutive hours, except in emergencies. **Day of Rest** — It is unlawful on Sunday for any person to engage in the business of selling, either at retail, wholesale, or by auction, certain specified articles except as works of necessity and charity or as isolated transactions not in the usual course of business. These provisions shall not become operative in any county unless adopted by referendum; Bergen, Cumberland, Essex, Gloucester, Hudson, Mercer, Middlesex, Monmouth, Morris, Passaic, Somerset, and Union have voted to apply Sunday closing law. **Meal Period** — No general provision.
New Mexico	**Maximum Hours before Overtime** — 48-hour week. 54-hour week with written employer-employee agreement. **Overtime Pay** — 1½ times regular pay for hours in excess of maximum. **Employees Covered** — All employees, *except:* those in executive, administrative, professional, or supervisory capacity; domestic workers; public employees; volunteers working for educational, charitable, religious, or nonprofit organization; salespersons and employees on commission, piece-work, or flat-rate schedule; apprentices and learners; employees of ambulance services; non-college students working after school or during vacation; G.I. bill trainees; certain agricultural workers; resident employees of charitable, religious, or nonprofit group home for mentally, emotionally, or developmentally disabled; and certain seasonal employees of youth camps, with certificate from Labor Commissioner. **Maximum Work Hours Allowed** — No provision. **Day of Rest** — No general provision. **Meal Period** — Not less than one-half hour excluded from working day.
New York	**Maximum Hours before Overtime** — 40-hour week. 40-hour and 6-day week for resort hotel employees. 44-hour week for most resident employees. **Overtime Pay** — 1½ times regular pay for hours in excess of maximum. Additional hour's pay after 10 hours for restaurant employees. **Employees Covered** — Employees in beauty service; laundry, cleaning, and dyeing; restaurants; retail and wholesale trades; amusement and recreation establishments (except pin setters, ushers at sports exhibitions, and caddies); building services (except janitors); and most miscellaneous occupations. *Exceptions:* students working for nonprofit organization or college group;

State Maximum Hours and Overtime Laws — Comparison Chart —Contd.

STATE	REQUIREMENTS AND PROVISIONS
New York (Contd.)	part-time babysitters and live-in companions; volunteers for nonprofit organization; members of religious order; sextons; learners and trainees in nonprofit institution, under certain conditions; and counselors and employees in children's summer camp. **Maximum Work Hours Allowed** — Special rules for workers engaged in compressed air occupations, motor transportation, pharmacies, public works, railroad transportation, street railways, and brickyards. **Day of Rest** — At least 24 consecutive hours of rest in each calendar week must be allowed employees by factory, mercantile establishments, hotel, restaurant, freight or passenger elevator in any building or place, with certain specified exceptions. Employers operating on Sunday must post notices listing employees scheduled to work and designating day of rest for each of them. All labor on Sunday is prohibited, except works of charity and necessity. All trades, manufacturers, agricultural, or mechanical employments on Sunday are prohibited, except when the same are works of necessity. All manner of public selling or offering for sale of any property is prohibited with certain specified exceptions; provision is inapplicable to those who uniformly keep another day of the week as holy time. One day a week may be set aside for rest and relaxation by owner of business or commercial enterprise. However, retail or merchant association or organization shall not have right to determine a day of rest and relaxation for its members. No provision of law shall be construed to prohibit any owner from doing business seven days a week where any other law, rule, or regulation does not specifically prohibit such activity. **Meal Period** — Person employed in mercantile or other covered establishments and occupations shall be allowed at least 45 minutes and person employed in factories shall be allowed at least 60 minutes for a noon day meal. Employees on a shift starting before noon and continuing later than 7 p.m. allowed an additional meal period of at least 20 minutes between 5 p.m. and 7 p.m. Commissioner may grant permits for shorter meal periods.
North Carolina	**Maximum Hours before Overtime** — 45-hour week. *Special rule:* 8-hour day and 80 hours in 14-day period for hospital and nursing home employees, if employees notified in advance. **Overtime Pay** — 1½ times regular pay for hours in excess of maximum. **Employees Covered** — All employees, *except:* drivers, drivers' helpers, loaders, and mechanics, as defined by FLSA; taxicab drivers; seamen; railroad and air carrier employees; salespersons and mechanics employed by automotive, truck, or farm implement dealer; salespersons employed by trailer, boat, or aircraft dealer; child care or other live-in workers in home for dependent children; radio/TV announcers, news editors, and chief engineers; agricultural and domestic workers; babysitters; pages in state legislature and governor's office; bona fide volunteers in medical, educational, religious, or nonprofit organization where no employer-employee relationship; those confined in public penal, correctional, or mental institution; performers for TV, radio, or film; employees of outdoor drama theaters except ushers, ticket takers, and parking attendants; those working in children's summer camp or seasonal religious or nonprofit educational conference center; employees in seafood industry through first sale; employer's spouse, child, parent, or qualified dependent under state tax laws; those in bona fide executive, administrative, professional, or outside sales capacity; employee of employer with two or fewer workers in any workweek; and public employees, including those in seasonal recreation program. **Maximum Work Hours Allowed** — *Railroads:* 16 consecutive hours followed by 10 hours rest, or 16 aggregate hours in 24 hours followed by 8 hours rest. 9-hour day for employees handling movement of trains by telegraph or telephone in place operating day and night, and 13-hour day in place operating during day only, with 4 more hours a day not over three times a week in emergencies. *State Institutions:* 12 hours in any 24 hours or 84 hours in one week for employees of state correctional institution and Dorothea Dix, Broughton, and Cherry Hill Hospitals (unless emergency determined by superintendent), except

State Maximum Hours and Overtime Laws — Comparison Chart —Contd.

STATE	REQUIREMENTS AND PROVISIONS
North Carolina (Contd.)	for: state prison, institution controlled by Commissioner of Highways and Public Works, and hospital doctors and superintendents. **Day of Rest** — Board of county commissioners have power to regulate sale of merchandise on Sundays in certain designated counties. **Meal Period** — No general provision.
North Dakota	**Maximum Hours before Overtime** — 40-hour week. **Overtime Pay** — 1½ times regular pay for hours in excess of maximum. **Employees Covered** — Employees in public housekeeping, manufacturing, mercantile establishments, and in professional, technical, clerical, and similar occupations, *except* managers and management trainees who do not spend more than half their time in management duties. **Maximum Work Hours Allowed** — *Municipalities:* 8-hour day, 56-hour week for employees of cities of 5,000 or more, unless emergency, except for: elected public officials, city department heads, members of police force, and members and employees of fire department; 140 hours in any two-week period, except in emergencies, and inapplicable to fire department chief in city of 20,000 or more. *Railroads:* 12 hours, followed by 10 hours of rest. **Day of Rest** — It is forbidden on Sunday to conduct business or labor for profit as usual or to operate a business open to the public, or to cause, direct, or authorize employee or agent to do so. Provision for certain exemptions, including allowable items for sale, businesses allowed to stay open, and limitations. **Meal Period** — No general provision.
Ohio	**Maximum Hours before Overtime** — 40-hour week. **Overtime Pay** — 1½ times regular pay in excess of maximum. **Employees Covered** — All employees, *except:* agricultural workers; hand harvest laborers on piece-work basis or under 16 and working for parents, under certain conditions; federal employees; babysitters or live-in companions; those delivering newspapers to consumers; outside salespersons on commission; those in bona fide executive, administrative, or professional capacity; agricultural workers for employer using no more than 500 worker-hours during any calendar quarter of preceding calendar year; employer's parent, spouse, child, or other immediate family member; volunteers providing personal services in health institution; police and firefighters; students working part-time or seasonally for state political subdivision; employees of camp or recreational area for minors owned and operated by nonprofit organization. **Maximum Work Hours Allowed** — *Motor Transportation:* 14 hours (or 14 aggregate hours in 24 hours) followed by 8 hours off duty. *Railroads and Railways:* 15 hours, followed by 8 hours of rest (regulated so that employee has 8 consecutive hours off in each 24 hours), for conductors, engineers, firemen, brakemen, trainmen, telegraph operators, and motormen. **Day of Rest** — No general provision. **Meal Period** — No general provision.
Oklahoma	**Maximum Hours before Overtime** — No state provision. **Overtime Pay** — No provision. **Employees Covered** — No provision. **Maximum Work Hours Allowed** — No provision. **Day of Rest** — It is unlawful to do any servile work or to work at any trade, manufacturing, or mechanical employment on Sunday, except for works of charity or necessity and other specified exemptions. **Meal Period** — No general provision.
Oregon	**Maximum Hours before Overtime** — 10-hour day and 40-hour week. **Overtime Pay** — 1½ times regular pay, or 1½ times regular price for piece work, for hours in excess of maximum. **Employees Covered** — Employees in mill, factory, or manufacturing establishment, except those engaged as watch personnel, in necessary repairs, or in emergencies where life or property in imminent danger; and employees in cannery,

State Maximum Hours and Overtime Laws — Comparison Chart —Contd.

STATE	REQUIREMENTS AND PROVISIONS
Oregon (Contd.)	drier, or packing plant that primarily processes products on farm, except agricultural workers. **Maximum Work Hours Allowed** — 13-hours a day (including 3 hours overtime) for employees in mill, factory, or manufacturing establishment. *Lumber:* 8-hour day and 48-hour week for workers in saw, planing, and shingle mills and logging camps with 3 hours overtime permitted, except for: logging train crews; watch personnel; firefighters; those engaged in necessary repairs, emergencies, or transporting workers; and certain other personnel. *Mining:* 8 consecutive hours for those working in underground metal mines, excluding those in first stage of mine development. **Day of Rest** — No general provision. **Meal Period** — Employees shall receive meal period of not less than 30 minutes within first five hours and one minute of reporting for work. Where employees cannot be relieved of all duties, a period in which to eat while continuing to work is permitted, provided time is not deducted from employees' hours. Employer may apply for exemption.
Pennsylvania	**Maximum Hours before Overtime** — 40-hour week. **Overtime Pay** — 1½ times regular pay for hours in excess of maximum, except for students in seasonal work when excluded by regulation of Secretary of Labor. **Employees Covered** — All employees, *except:* seamen; salespersons, partspersons, and mechanics primarily selling or servicing automobiles, trailers, trucks, farm implements, or aircraft for retail dealer; taxicab drivers; radio/TV announcers, news editors, or chief engineers with major studio in town of 100,000 or less (except when part of standard metropolitan statistical area) or town of 25,000 or less if at least 40 airline miles from principal city; employees processing maple sap; movie theater employees; farm laborers; domestic workers; newspaper deliverers to consumers; employees of weekly, semiweekly, or daily publication with circulation under 4,000 and mostly within county where published or contiguous counties; those in bona fide executive, administrative, or professional capacity, including academic administrative personnel and elementary and secondary teachers; outside sales personnel, including certain retail and service personnel; voluntary workers for educational, charitable, religious, or nonprofit organization where no employer-employee relationship; certain seasonal workers; students working in nonprofit educational institution where enrolled; employees of public amusement or recreational establishment, organized camp, or religious or nonprofit educational conference center, under certain conditions; golf caddies; telephone company switchboard operators; and employees not subject to civil service laws (e.g., elected officials and their personal staff). **Maximum Work Hours Allowed** — *Agriculture:* 10-hour day, 48-hour, 6-day week for seasonal farm workers, including when more than one employer. *Mining:* 8 hours within 24 hours for hoisting engineers in anthracite mines. *Railway Transportation:* 12-hour day. *Bakeries:* 6-day week (between 6 p.m. Sunday and 6 p.m. Saturday) for bakery and confectionary workers. *Compressed Air:* Certain hours, as defined. **Day of Rest** — Worldly employment or business on Sunday is prohibited, except for works of necessity and charity and wholesome recreation. Special provisions for particular types of selling activity, sports, etc. Motion picture places must allow each employee one calendar day of 24 consecutive hours of rest in each calendar week. **Meal Period** — No seasonal farm worker shall be permitted to work more than five hours continuously without meal or rest period of at least 30 minutes, which shall not be considered part of labor hours. No period of less than 30 minutes shall be deemed to interrupt a continuous work period.
Puerto Rico	**Maximum Hours before Overtime** — 8-hour day, 40-hour week. **Overtime Pay** — Twice the regular pay for hours in excess of maximum. *Exceptions:* 1½ times the regular pay for: employees covered by FLSA, those whose hours are fixed by wage board or collective bargaining agreement, and tobacco and food crop workers. Twice the regular rate for ninth hour worked in one day,

State Maximum Hours and Overtime Laws — Comparison Chart —Contd.

STATE	REQUIREMENTS AND PROVISIONS
Puerto Rico (Contd.)	plus ½ times regular rate for all subsequent hours worked in same day, for transportation workers. **Employees Covered** — All employees, *except:* those in executive, administrative, or professional capacity; travelling agents and mobile salespersons; labor union officers and organizers, when acting as such; domestic workers (who are entitled to one day of rest a week); government employees, except those engaged in propri-etary endeavors; workers in continuous operation commercial establishments, if exempted by Secretary of Labor; and drivers and chauffeurs on commission. **Maximum Work Hours Allowed** — No provision. **Day of Rest** — No general provision. **Meal Period** — At least one hour must be allowed for meals unless shorter period is fixed for convenience of employee, stipulated by employee and employer and approved by Secretary of Labor. Employee who works during mealtime shall receive double-time.
Rhode Island	**Maximum Hours before Overtime** — 40-hour week. **Overtime Pay** — 1½ times regular pay for hours in excess of maximum. **Employees Covered** — All employees *except:* those working in summer camp open no more than six months a year; state employees on "non-standards" work schedule; municipal police and firefighters; those in bona fide executive, adminis-trative, or professional capacity earning at least $200 a week; salaried employees of nonprofit national voluntary health agency who elect to take time off for hours worked in excess of 40 hours; drivers, drivers' helpers, loaders, and mechanics of motor carrier under hour regulation of U.S. Department of Transportation; agri-cultural and domestic workers; volunteers for educational, charitable, religious, or nonprofit organization where no employer-employee relationship; news carri-ers for home delivery; shoe shiners; golf caddies; bowling alley pin setters; ushers in theaters; outside salespersons; employer's parent, spouse, or child under 18; and those working between May 1 and October 1 for resort establishment regu-larly serving meals to general public and open not more than six months a year. **Maximum Work Hours Allowed** — *Motor Transportation:* 12 hours followed by 8 hours off duty, or 16 aggregate hours in 24 hours followed by 10 hours off duty, except in emergencies. *Street Railways:* 12 consecutive hours followed by 10 hours off duty during 24 hours for conductors and motormen, except for emergencies or holidays when extra compensation must be paid. **Day of Rest** — No person may engage in gainful activities in any store, mill, or factory; in commercial occupations; in work of transportation or communication; or in industrial processes on Sundays, except work of necessity and charity and in licensed athletic meets and contests. Unlawful for employer to require or permit employee to work on Sunday except work of absolute necessity. "Employee" does not include individuals employed in certain specified trades. Town councils may grant licenses for certain retail sales on Sundays; certain other retail and service businesses may be carried on without a license. Retail employees who work on Sunday are compensated at no less than time and one-half and must be guaran-teed at least four hours of employment, except for retail establishments that prepare or sell bakery products and pharmacies. **Meal Period** — At least 20 minutes must be allowed for meals after 6 consecu-tive hours of work, except telephone operators who are not required to operate switchboard continuously but are able to sleep during considerable part of the night. Work period of 6½ hours allowed if employment ends no later than 1 p.m. and worker is dismissed for the day. Work period of 7½ hours allowed if employ-ment ends no later than 2 p.m. and worker has sufficient opportunity to eat on the job.
South Carolina	**Maximum Hours before Overtime** — No state provision. **Overtime Pay** — No provision. **Employees Covered** — No provision. **Maximum Work Hours Allowed** — No provision. **Day of Rest** — It is unlawful to employ others to work on Sunday except certain works of necessity or charity and in certain specified businesses and services; sale

State Maximum Hours and Overtime Laws — Comparison Chart —Contd.

STATE	REQUIREMENTS AND PROVISIONS
South Carolina (Contd.)	of certain specified items also prohibited. Not applicable to any business or service that was lawful prior to April 7, 1962. Sunday work exemptions granted to manufacture and finishing of textile products and operation of machine shops provided no person is required to work who is conscientiously opposed to Sunday work. Sunday work prohibited in manufacturing or mercantile establishments, except cafeterias and restaurants, with certain exceptions. **Meal Period** — No general provision.
South Dakota	**Maximum Hours before Overtime** — No general provision. *Special rule:* 212 hours in 28-day period, or 204 hours in 27-day period, for municipal fire department employees. **Overtime Pay** — No provision. **Employees Covered** — No general provision. **Maximum Work Hours Allowed** — 10-hour day unless express agreement to contrary. 8-hour day for employees in manufacturing or mechanical establishment unless express agreement to contrary, except those employed by week, month, or year. *Railroads:* 16 hours followed by 10 hours off duty, or 16 aggregate hours in 24 hours followed by 8 hours off duty. **Day of Rest** — No general provision. **Meal Period** — No general provision.
Tennessee	**Maximum Hours before Overtime** — No state provision. **Overtime Pay** — No provision. **Employees Covered** — No provision. **Maximum Work Hours Allowed** — No provision. **Day of Rest** — No general provision. **Meal Period** — No general provision.
Texas	**Maximum Hours before Overtime** — No general provision. **Overtime Pay** — No provision. **Employees Covered** — No provision. **Maximum Work Hours Allowed** — *Railroads:* 16 hours, followed by 10 hours of rest for railroad conductors, engineers, firemen, and brakemen. **Day of Rest** — Employer may not require employee to work seven consecutive days in retail establishment and may not deny employee at least 24 consecutive hours off for rest or worship in seven-day period. Employer must accommodate employee's religious practices unless it can be shown that to do so would constitute undue business hardship, and may not require employee to work during period employee requests to be off to attend one regular worship service a week of employee's religion. **Meal Period** — No general provision.
Utah	**Maximum Hours before Overtime** — 8-hour day and 40-hour week. *Special rule:* 40-hour week for employees on public works projects. **Overtime Pay** — 1½ times regular pay for hours in excess of maximum. **Employees Covered** — Employees in retail, restaurant, public housekeeping, laundry, cleaning, and pressing occupations. **Maximum Work Hours Allowed** — *Mining:* 8-hour day for underground miners and those reducing or refining ores or metals, except in emergencies or with written certificate from industrial commission. 8 and 1/2-hour day for hoisters and pumpers on underground pumps in continuous operation. **Day of Rest** — No general provision. **Meal Period** — No general provision.
Vermont	**Maximum Hours before Overtime** — 40-hour week. *Special rule:* 8-hour day and 80-day biweekly period for employees of hospital, public health center, nursing or maternity home, therapeutic community residence, and community care home, if employer files an election with Commissioner of Industrial Relations and pays on biweekly basis. **Overtime Pay** — 1½ times regular pay for hours in excess of maximum.

State Maximum Hours and Overtime Laws — Comparison Chart —Contd.

STATE	REQUIREMENTS AND PROVISIONS
Vermont (Contd.)	**Employees Covered** — All employees of employers with two or more workers, *except:* workers in retail or service establishment, as defined; those in amusement or recreation industry not operating more than seven months in calendar year, or whose average receipts for any six months in preceding year not more than 1/3 of average receipts for other six months; hotel, motel, or restaurant employees; transportation employees covered by FLSA; agricultural and domestic workers; federal, state, or local employees; those in public-supported nonprofit organization, except laundry workers, nurses aides or practical nurses; those in bona fide executive, administrative, or professional capacity; home deliverers of newspapers or advertising; outside salespersons; and students working during school year or vacation. **Maximum Work Hours Allowed** — No provision. **Day of Rest** — No general provision. **Meal Period** — No general provision.
Virginia	**Maximum Hours before Overtime** — No state provision. **Overtime Pay** — No provision. **Employees Covered** — No provision. **Maximum Work Hours Allowed** — No provision. **Day of Rest** — No person shall engage in work, labor, or business or employ others to engage in same on Sunday, with certain exceptions; inapplicable to works of charity conducted solely for charitable purposes by any person or nonprofit organization. Except in emergency, employer shall allow employee at least 24 consecutive hours of rest in each calendar week in addition to regular rest periods normally allowed or legally required in each work day. Nonmanagerial employee upon written notice is entitled to choose Sunday as a day of rest; however, nonmanagerial employee who conscientiously believes that the seventh day of the week ought to be observed as a Sabbath and actually refrains from all secular business and labor on that day shall be entitled to choose the seventh day of the week as a day of rest. Provision not applicable to persons engaged in certain specified industries or businesses. **Meal Period** — No general provision.
Washington	**Maximum Hours before Overtime** — 40-hour week. *Special rule:* 240 hours in 28-day period (or equivalent hour/day ratio for periods from seven to 27 days) for employees in fire protection or law enforcement, including security personnel in correctional institution. **Overtime Pay** — 1½ times regular pay, or 1½ times regular piece work rate (unless specifically exempted), for hours in excess of maximum. **Employees Covered** — All employees, *except:* those requesting time off in lieu of overtime pay; seamen, whether or not employed on U.S. vessel; seasonal workers at concessions and recreational establishments at agricultural fair employed not more than 14 days; farm employees in any aspect of an agricultural or horticultural commodity, including its packing, storing, delivering, and processing; those covered by FLSA; students in higher education employed by their schools; those in agricultural or horticultural work, including management, maintenance, or conservation, up through packing and delivering to market; domestic workers; those in bona fide executive, administrative, or professional capacity; outside salespersons, as defined by Director of Labor and Industries; volunteers in educational, charitable, religious, state or local government body or agency, or nonprofit organization where not employer-employee relationship; newspaper carriers and vendors; employees of carrier subject to Interstate Commerce Commission regulations; those in forest fire prevention activities; employees of charitable organization providing child care services or recreational services for young persons or members of U.S. armed forces; those required to live and sleep at place of employment while on call but not necessarily on active duty; residents, inmates, or patients of state, county, or municipal correctional, detention, treatment, or rehabilitation institution; elected and appointed public officeholders; employees of state legislature; and crews of ferries operated by state highway commission;

State Maximum Hours and Overtime Laws — Comparison Chart —Contd.

STATE	REQUIREMENTS AND PROVISIONS
Washington (Contd.)	**Maximum Work Hours Allowed** — *Mining:* 8-hour day for coal miners working underground; 10-hour day for mining engineers, rope-riders, motormen, cagers, and others transporting miners in and out of mines, except in emergencies or weekly change of shift. *Public Works:* 8-hour day, except in extraordinary emergencies when employees to receive overtime rate. *Street Railways:* 10-hour day for gripmen, motormen, drivers, and conductors. *Railroads:* 12-hour day followed by 10 hours of rest, or 12 aggregate hours in 24 hours followed by 8 hours of rest, for those connected with movement of trains, except in emergencies. *Domestic and Household Employees:* 60-hour week, including hours on call, except in emergencies. **Day of Rest** — No general provision. **Meal Period** — No general provision.
West Virginia	**Maximum Hours before Overtime** — 40-hour week. **Overtime Pay** — 11/2 times regular pay for hours in excess of maximum, or 11/2 times regular rate for piece work under certain conditions. **Employees Covered** — All employees of employers with six or more workers in one location or establishment, unless 80 percent of workers covered by FLSA, *except:* those covered by contract or collective bargaining agreement; salespersons, partspersons, or mechanics primarily selling or servicing automobiles, trailers, trucks, farm implements, or aircraft for retail dealer; employees under hours regulation by U.S. Department of Transportation; federal employees; volunteers in educational, charitable, religious, fraternal, or nonprofit organization with no employer-employee relationship; newsboys; shoe shiners; golf caddies; bowling alley pin setters and chasers; outside salespersons; employer's spouse, parent, or child; those in bona fide professional, executive, or administrative capacity; on-the-job trainees; severely physically and mentally handicapped employed in nonprofit sheltered workshop; employees of children's camp; agricultural workers, as defined by FLSA; state firefighters; theater ushers; students working part-time; employees of motorbus carriers; and certain employees of state legislature. **Maximum Work Hours Allowed** — *Railroads:* 8-hour day (or 12-hour day if employee agrees) in 24 hours for: railroad telephone or telegraph operators spacing and blocking trains or handling train orders or interlocking switches, where three or more passenger trains or 10 or more freight trains pass each way in 24 hours or where operators are employed 20 or more hours in 24 hours, except in emergencies when may work 12-hour days for two days or three times in calendar month. **Day of Rest** — Sunday work prohibited except in household or other work of necessity or charity; work of necessity or charity does not include selling at retail, wholesale, or auction but lengthy list of permitted Sunday activities exists. Exception also made for those who conscientiously observe Saturday as Sabbath as long as they do not compel others, not of their belief, to work on Sunday. Local option elections permitted in any county to determine if Sunday Work Law shall be continued for that county. **Meal Period** — Where employee is required to be on duty 24 hours or more, employer and employee may agree on bona fide meal and sleeping periods; if no expressed or implied agreement is made, eight hours' sleeping time and lunch periods shall constitute hours worked.
Wisconsin	**Maximum Hours before Overtime** — 40-hour week. *Special rule:* 46-hour week for restaurant employees. **Overtime Pay** — 1½ times regular pay for hours in excess of maximum. **Employees Covered** — Employees in manufacturing, mechanical, or mercantile establishment; beauty parlor; laundry; restaurant; confectionary store; telegraph or telephone office or exchange, or express or transportation company; and hotel. *Exceptions:* persons employed in farming, as defined; those primarily in administrative, executive, or professional capacity; outside salespersons spending 80 percent of time away; retail and service employees paid commission if 50 percent of earnings from commissions and 1½ times minimum wage paid for all hours

State Maximum Hours and Overtime Laws — Comparison Chart —Contd.

STATE	REQUIREMENTS AND PROVISIONS
Wisconsin (Contd.)	worked; drivers, drivers' helpers, loaders, and mechanics of motor carrier or private or contract carrier under Sec. 204 of Motor Carrier Act; rail or common carrier employees of employer subject to Part I of Interstate Commerce Act; air carrier employees subject to Railway Labor Act; taxicab drivers; salespersons, partspersons, or mechanics selling or servicing automobiles, trucks, farm implements, trailers, boats, motorcycles, recreational vehicles, or aircraft for retail dealer (except apprentice partspersons and mechanics during classroom instruction); employees of recreational or amusement establishment operating seven months or less a year; those employed by independent contractor to erect silos and farm buildings, build terraces, dig wells or build pond dam, inspect and cull poultry, or as pilots and flagpersons to dust and spray crops; movie theater employees; resident employees of hospital and institution having employer-employee overtime agreement; drivers and helpers making local deliveries and paid on trip-rate or other delivery plan basis; and funeral establishment employees. **Maximum Work Hours Allowed —** *Railroads:* 16 hours followed by 10 hours of rest, or 16 aggregate hours in 24 hours followed by 8 hours of rest, except in specified emergencies. *Motor Transportation:* Motor Vehicle Department prescribes rules. **Day of Rest —** Employees in factory or mercantile establishments are entitled to at least 24 consecutive hours of rest every seven consecutive days, with certain specified exceptions. Work on seventh day permitted in case of breakdown of machinery or equipment requiring immediate services of experienced and competent labor to prevent serious injury to person, damage to property, or suspension of essential operation. **Meal Period —** Employees must receive at least 30 minutes for each meal period reasonably close to usual meal period time or near middle of a shift. Shifts of more than six consecutive hours without a meal period should be avoided; requirements mandatory for minors under 18.
Wyoming	**Maximum Hours before Overtime —** No state provision. **Overtime Pay —** *Public Works:* 1½ times regular rate for laborers and mechanics for work in excess of 10 hours a day or 40 hours a week, except in emergency. **Employees Covered —** No provision. **Maximum Work Hours Allowed —** *Mining:* 8-hour day in all underground mines and workings, except when employer-employee agreement for longer period not to exceed 16 hours in 24 hours. **Day of Rest —** No general provision. **Meal Period —** No general provision.

APPENDIX H

CHART OF OVERTIME COMPENSATION RULES FOR STATE AND LOCAL GOVERNMENT EMPLOYEES*

* Source: 52 Fed. Reg. 2012, at 2045 (1987) (to be codified at 29 C.F.R. §§553.230–553.233).

Following is the text of Overtime Compensation Rules for police personnel and firefighters of state and local governments.

Overtime Compensation Rules

§ 553.230　Maximum hours standards for work periods of 7 to 28 days—section 7(k).

(a) For those employees engaged in fire protection activities who have a work period of at least 7 but less than 28 consecutive days, no overtime compensation is required under section 7(k) until the number of hours worked exceeds the number of hours which bears the same relationship to 212 as the number of days in the work period bears to 28.

(b) For those employees engaged in law enforcement activities (including security personnel in correctional institutions) who have a work period of at least 7 but less than 28 consecutive days, no overtime compensation is required under section 7(k) until the number of hours worked exceeds the number of hours which bears the same relationship to 171 as the number of days in the work period bears to 28.

(c) The ratio of 212 hours to 28 days for employees engaged in fire protection activities is 7.57 hours per day (rounded) and the ratio of 171 hours to 28 days for employees engaged in law enforcement activities is 6.11 hours per day (rounded). Accordingly, overtime compensation (in premium pay or compensatory time) is required for all hours worked in excess of the following maximum hours standards (rounded to the nearest whole hour):

Work period (days)	Maximum hours standards	
	Fire Protection	Law enforcement
28	212	171
27	204	165
26	197	159
25	189	153
24	182	147
23	174	141
22	167	134
21	159	128
20	151	122
19	144	116
18	136	110
17	129	104
16	121	98
15	114	92
14	106	86
13	98	79
12	91	73
11	83	67
10	76	61
9	68	55
8	61	49
7	53	43

§ 553.231 Compensatory time off.

(a) Law enforcement and fire protection employees who are subject to the section 7(k) exemption may receive compensatory time off in lieu of overtime pay for hours worked in excess of the maximum for their work period as set forth in §553.230. The rules for compensatory time off are set forth in §§553.20 through 553.28.

(b) Section 7(k) permits public agencies to balance the hours of work over an entire work period for law enforcement and fire protection employees. For example, if a firefighter's work period is 28 consecutive days and he or she works 80 hours in each of the first two weeks, but only 52 hours in the third week, and does not work in the fourth week, no overtime compensation (in cash wages or compensatory time) would be required since the total hours worked do not exceed 212 for the work period. If the same firefighter had a work period of only 14 days, overtime compensation or compensatory time off would be due for 54 hours (160 minus 106 hours) in the first 14-day work period.

§ 553.232 Overtime pay requirements.

If a public agency pays employees subject to section 7(k) for overtime hours worked in cash wages rather than compensatory time off, such wages must be paid at one and one-half times the employees' regular rates of pay. In addition, employees who have accrued the maximum 480 hours of compensatory time must be paid cash wages of time and one-half their regular rates of pay for overtime hours in excess of the maximum for the work period set forth in § 553.230.

§ 553.233 "Regular rate" defined.

The rules for computing an employee's "regular rate," for purposes of the Act's overtime pay requirements, are set forth in 29 CFR Part 778. These rules are applicable to employees for whom the section 7(k) exemption is claimed when overtime compensation is provided in cash wages. However, whenever the word "workweek" is used in Part 778, the words "work period" should be substituted.

APPENDIX I

DIRECTORY OF U.S. EQUAL EMPLOYMENT OPPORTUNITY COMMISSION ADMINISTRATIVE AND DISTRICT AREA OFFICES

Equal Employment Opportunity Commission
Administrative Offices

Address: 2401 E Street, N.W., Washington, D.C. 20507
Telephone: (202) 634-6922
Toll-free: 800-USA-EEOC

(Created by Section 705 of Title VII of the 1964 Civil Rights Act)

Commissioners

Clarence Thomas, Chairman
William A. Webb, Commissioner
Tony E. Gallegos, Commissioner
Fred W. Alvarez, Commissioner
Rosalie Gaull Silberman,
Commissioner

Office of Program Research

Paul Royston, Director

Office of Review & Appeals

Dolores L. Rozzi, Director

Office of Legal Counsel

Richard Komer, Director *(Acting)*

Office of Audit

Joseph J. Schutt, Acting Director

Office of Program Operations

James Troy, Director

Office of Congressional Affairs

Phyllis Berry, Director

Office of Management

John Seal, Director

Office of General Counsel

Johnny Butler, General Counsel *(Acting)*
William Ng, Deputy General Counsel
Gwendolyn Reams, Associate General
Counsel, Appellate Services
Phillip Sklover, Associate General
Counsel, Trial Services
James Finney, Associate General
Counsel, Systemic Litigation Services

Office of Communications

Deborah Graham, Director

EEOC District, Area, and Local Offices

*Following is an alphabetical directory of EEOC's 23 "full-service" district offices
and the area and local offices serving those districts.*

**ALBUQUERQUE AREA OFFICE
(Phoenix District)**

Western Bank Building, Suite 1105
505 Marquette, N. W.
Albuquerque, New Mexico 87101
(Hours — 7:30 a.m. — 4:30 p.m. MST)
(505) 766-2061

ATLANTA DISTRICT OFFICE

Citizens Trust Building,
75 Piedmont Avenue, N. E., Suite 1100
Atlanta, Georgia 30335
(Hours — 8:30 a.m. — 5:00 p.m. EST)
(404) 331-6091

BALTIMORE DISTRICT OFFICE

109 Market Place, Suite 4000

Baltimore, Maryland 21202
(Hours — 9:00 a.m. — 5:30 p.m. EST)
(301) 962-3932

BIRMINGHAM DISTRICT OFFICE

2121 Eighth Avenue, North, Suite 824
Birmingham, Alabama 35203
(Hours — 8:00 a.m. — 4:30 p.m. CST)
(205) 254-0082

**BOSTON AREA OFFICE (New York
District)**

JFK Building, Room 409-B
Boston, Massachusetts 02203
(Hours — 8:30 a.m. — 5:00 p.m. EST)
(617) 223-4535

BUFFALO LOCAL OFFICE (New York District)
Guaranty Building, 28 Church Street
Buffalo, New York 14202
(Hours — 8:45 a.m. — 5:15 p.m. EST)
(716) 846-4441

CHARLOTTE DISTRICT OFFICE
5500 Central Avenue
Charlotte, North Carolina 28212
(Hours — 8:30 a.m. — 5:00 p.m. EST)
(704) 567-7100

CHICAGO DISTRICT OFFICE
Federal Building, Room 930-A
536 South Clark Street
Chicago, Illinois 60605
(Hours — 8:30 a.m. — 5:00 p.m. CST)
(312) 353-2713

CINCINNATI AREA OFFICE (Cleveland District)
Federal Building, Room 7015
550 Main Street
Cincinnati, Ohio 45202
(Hours — 8:15 a.m. — 5:00 p.m. EST)
(513) 684-2851

CLEVELAND DISTRICT OFFICE
1375 Euclid Avenue, Room 600
Cleveland, Ohio 44115
(Hours — 8:15 a.m. — 5:00 p.m. EST)
(216) 522-7425

DALLAS DISTRICT OFFICE
8303 Elmbrook Drive
Dallas, Texas 75247
(Hours — 9:30 a.m. — 6:00 p.m. CST)
(214) 767-7015

DAYTON AREA OFFICE (Cleveland District)
Federal Building
200 West 2nd Street, Room 608
Dayton, Ohio 45402
(Hours — 8:15 a.m. — 5:00 p.m. EST)
(513) 225-2753

DENVER DISTRICT OFFICE
1845 Sherman Street, 2nd Floor
Denver, Colorado 80203
(Hours — 8:00 a.m. — 5:00 p.m. MST)
(303) 837-2771

DETROIT DISTRICT OFFICE
Patrick V. MacNamara Federal Building
477 Michigan Avenue, Room 1540
Detroit, Michigan 48226

(Hours — 8:30 a.m. — 5:00 p.m. EST)
(313) 226-7636

EL PASO LOCAL OFFICE (Dallas District)
First National Building, Suite 1112
109 North Oregon Street
El Paso, Texas 79901
(Hours — 7:30 a.m. — 4:30 p.m. CST)
(915) 541-7596

FRESNO AREA OFFICE (San Francisco District)
1313 P Street, Suite 103
Fresno, California 93721
(Hours — 8:30 a.m. — 5:00 p.m. PST)
(209) 487-5793

GREENSBORO LOCAL OFFICE (Charlotte District)
324 West Market Street, Room B-27
Post Office Box 3363
Greensboro, North Carolina 27402
(Hours — 8:30 a.m. — 5:00 p.m. EST)
(919) 333-5174

GREENVILLE LOCAL OFFICE (Atlanta District)
Century Plaza, Suite 109-B
211 Century Drive
Greenville, South Carolina 29607
(Hours — 8:30 a.m. — 5:00 p.m. EST)
(803) 233-1791

HOUSTON DISTRICT OFFICE
405 Main Street, Sixth Floor
Houston, Texas 77002
(Hours — 8:00 a.m. — 5:00 p.m. CST)
(713) 226-2601

INDIANAPOLIS DISTRICT OFFICE
Federal Building, U.S. Courthouse
46 East Ohio Street, Room 456
Indianapolis, Indiana 46204
(Hours — 8:00 a.m. — 4:30 p.m. EST)
(317) 269-7212

JACKSON AREA OFFICE (Birmingham District)
McCoy Federal Office Building
100 West Capitol Street, Suite 721
Jackson, Mississippi 39269
(Hours — 8:00 a.m. — 4:30 p.m. CST)
(601) 965-4537

KANSAS CITY AREA OFFICE (St. Louis District)
911 Walnut, 10th Floor
Kansas City, Missouri 94106

(Hours — 8:00 a.m. — 4:30 p.m. CST)
(816) 374-5773

LITTLE ROCK AREA OFFICE (New Orleans District)
Savers Building, Suite 621
320 West Capitol Avenue
Little Rock, Arkansas 72201
(Hours — 8:00 a.m. — 4:30 p.m. CST)
(501) 378-5060

LOS ANGELES DISTRICT OFFICE
3660 Wilshire Boulevard, 5th Floor
Los Angeles, California 90010
(Hours— 8:30 a.m. — 5:00 p.m. PST)
(213) 251-7278

LOUISVILLE AREA OFFICE (Memphis District)
601 West Broadway, Room 104
Louisville, Kentucky 40202
(Hours — 8:00 a.m. — 4:30 p.m. EST)
(502) 582-6082

MEMPHIS DISTRICT OFFICE
1407 Union Avenue, Suite 502
Memphis, Tennessee 38104
(Hours — 8:00 a.m. — 4:30 p.m. CST)
(901) 521-2617

MIAMI DISTRICT OFFICE
Metro Mall
1 Northeast First Street, 6th Floor
Miami, Florida 33132
(Hours — 8:00 a.m. — 4:30 p.m. EST)
(305) 536-4491

MILWAUKEE DISTRICT OFFICE
310 West Wisconsin Avenue, Suite 800
Milwaukee, Wisconsin 53203
(Hours — 8:00 a.m. — 4:30 p.m. CST)
(414) 291-1111

MINNEAPOLIS LOCAL OFFICE (Milwaukee District)
110 South Fourth Street, Room 178
Minneapolis, Minnesota 55401
(Hours — 8:00 a.m. — 4:30 p.m. CST)
(612) 349-3495

NASHVILLE AREA OFFICE (Memphis District)
Parkway Towers, Suite 1100
Nashville, Tennessee 37219
(Hours — 8:00 a.m. — 4:30 p.m. CST)
(615) 251-5820

NEWARK AREA OFFICE (New York District)
60 Park Place, Room 301

Newark, New Jersey 07102
(Hours — 8:45 a.m. — 5:15 p.m. CST)
(201) 645-6383

NEW ORLEANS DISTRICT OFFICE
F. Edward Hebert Federal Building
600 South Maestri Place, Room 528
New Orleans, Louisiana 70130
(Hours — 8:00 a.m. — 4:30 p.m. CST)
(504) 589-2329

NEW YORK DISTRICT OFFICE
90 Church Street, Room 1505
New York, New York 10007
(Hours — 8:45 a.m. — 5:15 p.m. EST)
(212) 264-7161

NORFOLK AREA OFFICE (Baltimore District)
Federal Building, Room 412
200 Granby Mall
Norfolk, Virginia 23510
(Hours — 8:30 a.m. — 5:00 p.m. CST)
(804) 441-3470

OAKLAND LOCAL OFFICE (San Francisco District)
Wells Fargo Bank Building
1333 Broadway, Room 430
Oakland, California 94612
(Hours — 8:00 a.m. — 4:30 p.m. CST)
(415) 273-7588

OKLAHOMA AREA OFFICE (Dallas District)
Alfred P. Marrah Federal Building
200 N.W. Fifth Street, Room 703
Oklahoma City, Oklahoma 73102
(Hours — 8:00 a.m. — 5:00 p.m. CST)
(405) 231-4911

PHILADELPHIA DISTRICT OFFICE
127 North 4th Street, Suite 300
Philadelphia, Pennsylvania 19106
(Hours — 8:00 a.m. — 5:30 p.m. EST)
(215) 597-7784

PHOENIX DISTRICT OFFICE
135 North Second Avenue, Fifth Floor
Phoenix, Arizona 85003
(Hours — 8:00 a.m. — 5:00 p.m. MST)
(602) 261-3882

PITTSBURGH AREA OFFICE (Philadelphia District)
Federal Building, Room 2038A
1000 Liberty Avenue
Pittsburgh, Pennsylvania 15222

(Hours — 8:00 a.m. — 4:30 p.m. EST)
(412) 644-3444

RALEIGH AREA OFFICE (Charlotte District)

178 West Hargett Street, Suite 500
Raleigh, North Carolina 27601
(Hours — 8:30 a.m. — 5:00 p.m. EST)
(919) 856-4064

RICHMOND AREA OFFICE (Baltimore District)

400 North 8th Street, Room 6206
Richmond, Virginia 23240
(Hours — 8:30 a.m. — 5:00 p.m. EST)
(804) 771-2692

SAN ANTONIO AREA OFFICE (Houston District)

727 East Durango, Suite 601-B
San Antonio, Texas 78206
(Hours — 8:30 a.m. — 5:00 p.m. CST)
(512) 229-6051

SAN DIEGO LOCAL OFFICE (Los Angeles District)

San Diego Federal Building
880 Front Street
San Diego, California 92188
(Hours — 8:30 a.m. — 5:00 p.m. PST)
(619) 293-6288

SAN FRANCISCO DISTRICT OFFICE

10 United Nations Plaza, Fourth Floor
San Francisco, California 94102
(Hours — 8:30 a.m. — 5:00 p.m. PST)

(415) 556-0260

SAN JOSE LOCAL OFFICE (San Francisco District)

U. S. Courthouse & Federal Building
280 South First Street, Room 4150
San Jose, California 95113
(Hours — 8:30 a.m. — 5:00 p.m. PST)
(408) 291-7352

SEATTLE DISTRICT OFFICE

Arcade Plaza Building
1321 Second Avenue, 7th Floor
Seattle, Washington 98101
(Hours — 8:30 a.m. — 5:00 p.m. PST)
(206) 442-0968

ST. LOUIS DISTRICT OFFICE

625 N. Euclid Street
St. Louis, Missouri 63108
(Hours — 8:00 a.m. — 4:30 p.m. CST)
(314) 425-6585

TAMPA AREA OFFICE (Miami District)

700 Twiggs Street, Room 302
Tampa, Florida 33602
(Hours — 8:00 a.m. — 4:30 p.m. EST)
(813) 228-2310

WASHINGTON AREA OFFICE (Baltimore District)

1717 H Street, N.W., Suite 400
Washington, D.C. 20006
(Hours — 9:00 a.m. — 5:30 p.m. EST)
(202) 653-6197

APPENDIX J

DIRECTORY OF U.S. DEPARTMENT OF DEFENSE, DEFENSE CONTRACT ADMINISTRATION SERVICES, REGIONAL OFFICES

Defense Contract Administration Services

Headquarters,
Defense Supply Agency

Address: Cameron Station, Alexandria, Va. 22314
Telephone: (703) 274-6241

(Listed below are the regional offices under the Defense Contract Administration Services. The regional offices conduct compliance reviews, follow-up reviews, pre-award reviews, and complaint investigations. About 7,000 contractors doing business in approximately 40,000 facilities are covered by the regional offices' functions.)

Regional Offices

Atlanta
805 Walker Street
Marietta, Georgia 30060
Phone: (404) 429-6000
Area covered: Alabama, Caribbean, Central America, Florida, Georgia, Mississippi, North Carolina, South America, South Carolina, and Tennessee.

Boston
495 Summer Street
Boston, Massachusetts 02210
Phone: (617) 451-4298
Area covered: Connecticut, Maine, Massachusetts, New Hampshire, New York (excluding New York City, Long Island; Orange, Putnam, Rockland, and Westchester Counties), Rhode Island, and Vermont

Chicago
O'Hare International Airport
P.O. Box 66475
Chicago, Illinois 60666
Phone: (312) 694-3031
Area covered: Indiana, Northern Illinois, and Wisconsin

Cleveland
Federal Office Building
1240 East 9th Street
Cleveland, Ohio 44199
Phone: (216) 522-6701
Area covered: Commonwealth of Canada, Kentucky, Michigan, Northwestern Pennsylvania (Erie, Crawford, and Mercer Counties), and Ohio

Dallas
500 South Ervay Street
Dallas, Texas 75201
Phone: (214) 744-4581
Area covered: Arkansas, Louisiana, Mexico (except states of Baja California and Sonora), New Mexico, Oklahoma, and Texas

Los Angeles
11099 S. La Cienega Boulevard
Los Angeles, California 90045
Phone: (213) 643-1110
Area covered: Alaska, Arizona, California, Hawaii, Idaho, Montana, Nevada, Oregon, Washington, and the Marianas and Marshall Islands

New York
60 Hudson Street
New York, New York 10013
Phone: (212) 374-9000
Area covered: New Jersey (all counties North of Burlington, Mercer, and Ocean Counties), and New York (New York City and Long Island; Orange, Putnam, Rockland, and Westchester Counties)

Philadelphia
2800 South 20th Street
Philadelphia, Pennsylvania 19101
Phone: (215) 952-1110

Area covered: Delaware, District of Columbia, Maryland, New Jersey, (Burlington, Mercer, and Ocean Counties), Pennsylvania (except Crawford, Erie, and Mercer Counties), Virginia, and West Virginia

St. Louis

1136 Washington Avenue
St. Louis, Missouri 63101
Phone: (314) 263-6510

Area covered: Colorado, Illinois (Adams, Brown, Cass, Douglas, Edgar, Macon, Menard, and Sangamon Counties and all counties to the South), Iowa, Kansas, Minnesota, Missouri, Nebraska, North Dakota, South Dakota, Utah, and Wyoming

TABLE OF CASES

INDEX

ABOUT THE AUTHOR

Joseph E. Kalet is an attorney and a Senior Legal Editor with The Bureau of National Affairs, Inc., *Labor Relations Reporter*, Washington, D.C. He received his Juris Doctor from the George Washington University-National Law Center, Washington, D.C.

Mr. Kalet is a frequent speaker on labor law before such organizations as the National Association of Attorneys General and the National Labor Relations Board. In addition to writing numerous articles for the *American Bar Association Journal*, the *Arbitration Journal, Trial Magazine*, and others, Mr. Kalet has authored *Age Discrimination in Employment Law* (BNA Books, 1986).

Mr. Kalet is admitted to practice in Pennsylvania and the District of Columbia, where he maintains a private practice and teaches labor law. In addition, Mr. Kalet provides pro bono assistance to the Washington Lawyers Committee for Civil Rights Under Law, the Bar Association of the District of Columbia, and the District of Columbia Bar.